KNOCKING DOWN BARRIERS

KNOCKING DOWN BARRIERS

MY FIGHT FOR BLACK AMERICA

Truman K. Gibson Jr.

with Steve Huntley

Northwestern University Press
Evanston, Illinois

Northwestern University Press
Evanston, Illinois 60208-4170

Printed in the United States of America

10 9 8 7 6 5 4 3 2 1

ISBN 0-8101-2292-8

Library of Congress Cataloging-in-Publication Data

Gibson, Truman K. (Truman Kella), 1912–
Knocking down barriers : my fight for Black America / Truman K. Gibson Jr., with Steve Huntley.
p. cm.
Includes bibliographical references and index.
ISBN 0-8101-2292-8 (cloth : alk. paper)
1. Gibson, Truman K. (Truman Kella), 1912– 2. Cabinet officers—United States—Biography. 3. African Americans—Biography. 4. African American lawyers—Biography. 5. African American businesspeople—Biography. 6. African Americans—Civil rights—History—20th century. 7. African American soldiers—History—20th century. 8. World War, 1939–1945—African Americans. 9. United States—Armed Forces—African Americans. I. Huntley, Steve. II. Title.
E748.G46G53 2005
305.896'073'0092—dc22

2004029460

∞ The paper used in this publication meets the minimum requirements of the American National Standard for Information Sciences—Permanence of Paper for Printed Library Materials, ANSI Z39.48-1992.

Northwestern University Press thanks The Chicago Community Trust for its support of this book and related efforts to promote Chicago's future by telling the stories of Chicago's past.

Contents

Preface

The U.S. military's greatest pride lies, after its battlefield prowess, in its phenomenal success in race relations. Nowhere else in American society have the lofty goals of integration been realized as they have in the armed forces. That success culminated years of struggle against a hidebound, obstinate, narrow-minded, and too often outright bigoted mind-set in the military's command structure that frustrated the hopes and aspirations of black servicemen at every turn. During World War II and immediately after, I was at the center of this struggle. For five years I served in the office of the civilian aide to the secretary of war, a post created in the army to represent the interests of African American soldiers.

My role in those turbulent years has been documented in *Integration of the Armed Forces, 1940–1965* by Morris J. MacGregor Jr. and *The Employment of Negro Troops* by Major Ulysses Lee, which are two comprehensive accounts of the military's handling of black servicemen. MacGregor especially was generous to me. "Dedicated to abolition of racial segregation," he wrote, "Gibson eschewed the grand gesture and emphasized those practical changes that could be effected one step at a time. . . . He also knew that his fairness made him an effective advocate in the War Department." MacGregor wrote that as a result of my close cooperation with the War Department's Advisory Committee on Negro Troop Policies, "the Army for the first time began to agree on practical if not policy changes."[1]

Still, over the years, friends have suggested I tell my own story about the long, often bitter struggle over military segregation during and after World War II and the part that others played, including men of great stature but sometimes limited vision. They noted that I am the last surviving member of the Roosevelt-Truman administrations' "black cabinet" and should set down my recollections as an insider in the government—or as much of an insider as an African American could be in Washington in those days. So after nine decades on this earth, I began a journey back in time, recalling happy successes and dredging up painful memories of being caught in the middle of controversies over racial issues in the military.

While an account of the struggle over segregation in the army is at the heart of my story, it is far from the only chapter. I also recall my involvement in a key legal fight against restrictive racial real estate covenants in Chicago, my role in the virtually forgotten black world's fair of 1940, my friendship and collaborations with the great Joe Louis, and my unexpected career as a boxing promoter in the 1950s.

Acknowledgments

This book might not exist were it not for the late Steve Neal, to whom it is dedicated. The *Chicago Sun-Times* political columnist and author of many books of history brought Steve Huntley and me together, read our proposal, offered advice, and introduced us to Northwestern University Press. In researching, writing, and editing this book, we tried to follow the example of the tireless energy, commitment to the truth, and dedication to excellence that was so evident in Steve Neal's work as a journalist and historian.

Many others also are owed our gratitude. My daughter, Karen Kelley, and her husband, William Kelley, author of the outstanding *A Different Drummer* and other novels, for years urged me to write a memoir. Two old friends, Donald Stewart, past president and CEO of the Chicago Community Trust, and Kenneth Smith, a senior fellow there, were instrumental in persuading the trust to underwrite the research and production of this book. We are deeply grateful to the trust for its financial support. Kiko Morgan, a friend of many years knowledgeable about popular culture, helped in researching the chapters of the book touching on jazz and the Errol Flynn inheritance case. Carlo Binosi, a friend from Italy, first discovered and brought to my attention an Italian account of the World War II heroics of the all-black Ninety-second Division, launching us on a voyage of discovery that I hope will contribute to righting the record of those brave fighting men. Angelo Commito, a good friend and business partner in years past, helped refresh my memory on important episodes for the chapters on my career in boxing. Waymon Smith, my law partner for the last decade, has been an indispensable friend whose support and encouragement were critical to producing this book. Dr. Edward Gibson of the Princeton University Hospital, my nephew, and Kathy Gibson, his daughter, were generous in their encouragement of this project. We are deeply grateful to Dr. Donald Hopkins of Chicago for reading the manuscript and forwarding it to former president Jimmy Carter, who read it and offered the kind words on the book jacket.

Steve's wife, Linda, and his daughters, Kristine and Katie, helped gather research materials, read the manuscript, and supported the writing of this book in every way possible.

We are thankful for the editing work, professional guidance, and commitment to this project from the staff at Northwestern University Press. We also owe thanks to the staff at the Library of Congress, Washington, D.C., and the National Archives, College Park, Maryland, for aid in finding research materials and to the Harry S. Truman Library in Independence, Missouri, for making so much of its archival material about the desegregation of the army available through Internet access.

Our thanks also go to John Cruickshank, publisher, and Michael Cooke, former editor in chief, of the *Chicago Sun-Times* for their support.

Note on Language

This book quotes documents from an era when race relations were far different than today. "Negro" and "colored people" were the proper terms for African Americans. Sometimes in documents, memos, and correspondence they were capitalized; sometimes not. To represent historical accuracy and to provide a flavor of the times, the documents are quoted with the usage of the writers. Offensive racial epithets also are part of the story of those days.

KNOCKING DOWN BARRIERS

1

The Way We Were

Little did I know what lay in store for me when I reported for duty in the War Department in Washington as an advocate for African American soldiers that late-autumn day in 1940. Oh, I was under no illusions about the realities of race in America when I accepted the job of assistant to the civilian aide to the secretary of war. Still, the things I came face-to-face with in the Munitions Building, the home of the War Department before the days of the Pentagon, and at army posts around the country disturbed and angered me. The armed forces' top commanders, whether in three-piece suits or khaki uniforms, were determined to resist all efforts to move away from policies that kept African American servicemen in segregated units on and off the battlefield. Even more alarming to me was the army's abandonment of black men who had been called to the service of their country but were ruled, abused, assaulted, and even murdered by white civilians in the South of the Jim Crow era.

Six decades ago Washington was a southern city in its unbending segregation as well as its steamy summers. When confronted with the realities of life in the nation's capital—like being told that she and a friend could not try on shoes at Garfinkel's department store—my wife broke into tears, crying to go home to Chicago. The capital was, pure and simple, a closed society, and its social and legal barriers did not trouble the thinking of people in power. None of the men in the most prominent positions of the armed forces demonstrated any interest in challenging the social inequities of the day despite the awakening of black power and its potential for the Democratic Party that President Franklin D. Roosevelt detected in the 1940 election campaign that had given him a third term in the White House.

Many times over my years in Washington I was to run into the brick wall of resistance to change in the military's segregationist policies. I never considered the office of civilian aide, where I was then serving as an assistant to Bill Hastie, to be one devoted to public relations. However, I wanted the military's position disseminated; I wanted influential black Americans to get the army's view straight from the horse's mouth.

After about a year on the job, I organized a conference of black editors and publishers at the Munitions Building. Among the fourteen notables of the Negro press who turned out were Bill Nunn of the *Pittsburgh Courier,* John Sengstacke of the *Chicago Defender,* and Carl Murphy of the *Baltimore Afro-American*. As it happened, this meeting in Washington came on December 8, 1941. It was a momentous day in our nation's history. The day before, the country was staggered by the shock of the Japanese attack on Pearl Harbor. On December 8, a Monday, President Roosevelt had delivered his famous "day of infamy" speech, and Congress had declared war. The Conference of Negro Editors and Publishers convened with anxieties and emotions running high. The newspapermen, like all Americans, knew their country faced years of war, sacrifice, and unknown danger in the struggle against fascism. Yet their anxieties were compounded because this fight in the name of liberty would be a war steeped in hypocrisy if African American servicemen were condemned to segregated units and to slinging hash and hauling supplies in support assignments behind the battlefronts. How could the country present the war as a struggle for democracy if it chained millions of its citizens to the injustices of racism? The army brass had shown up that day to explain the thinking of those in the Munitions Building, and the publishers and editors were eager to hear what the officers had to say. I was there, too. Although I was all too aware of the military's attitude, I wanted to listen to what the army commanders would tell these powerful representatives of black America and to gauge the newspapermen's reaction.

It should be remembered that back then the black press was a much more potent voice of African American aspirations and a more central spokesman for black complaints than it is today. That was a reflection of the times. The huge black migration from the tenant farms and cotton fields of the South to the bustling cities and factories of the North had yet to reach critical mass to yield the voting power that would earn African Americans ever increasing clout in politics in postwar America. In the South, Jim Crow laws continued to deny blacks access to the polls and, therefore, to influence in political affairs. The street demonstrations, sit-ins, and marches—which through television would dramatize in living rooms across America the civil rights movement—were still years away. And what we would today call the mainstream press meant essentially white newspapers, with virtually all-white staffs of writers and editors for whom the desperate struggle for racial justice was hardly a front-page story. In the South, civil rights news was never reported in the newspapers, but that did not mean southern blacks were starved of all news. Porters on Pullman cars would grab stacks of *Couriers* and *Defenders,* haul them south, and surreptitiously distribute them to African Americans hungry for news they could trust. These papers registered an impact far beyond their normal circulation numbers and zones.

The army's position was articulated that day in a speech by Colonel Eugene R. Householder, representing the adjutant general's office. He espoused what was throughout the war to be the army's bottom-line position—that the military was incapable of getting out in front of civilian society in altering the accepted social structure and mores of America:

> The Army then cannot be made the means of engendering conflict among the mass of people because of a stand with respect to Negroes which is not compatible with the position attained by the Negro in civil life. The Army is not a sociological laboratory; to be effective it must be organized and trained according to the principles which will insure success. Experiments to meet the wishes and demands of the champions of every race and creed for the solution of their problems are a danger to efficiency, discipline and morale, and would result in ultimate defeat.[1]

"The Army is not a sociological laboratory." That was the sorry rationale for segregation that I was to hear General George C. Marshall, the army's chief of staff, and other commanders repeat ad nauseam. Marshall remains an honored figure in mid-twentieth-century history for his leadership during the war and in the Marshall Plan afterward that rescued Europe from the threat of communist domination. But I saw another side of him, one that stonewalled black aspirations for full participation in the war. The office of the civilian aide was situated next door to Marshall's suite, so I got to hear directly from him or through official directives and office gossip about his opinions. His often expressed view that the army actively worked against discrimination—while maintaining segregation—involved mental gymnastics and abandonment of the laws of logic that I couldn't countenance then or now. And it wasn't only on race issues that Marshall could be hugely wrong. After the Nazis invaded the Soviet Union in 1941, I recall Marshall declaring confidently that the war now would be over in two weeks.

Naturally, the editors and publishers were, to say the least, disappointed in what they heard at the Munitions Building. It only confirmed the stories of segregation and exclusion at army posts that they had published in their own newspapers.

Another dramatic demonstration of the army intransigence on segregation came in 1942. The year before, Walter White of the National Association for the Advancement of Colored People (NAACP), A. Philip Randolph of the Brotherhood of Sleeping Car Porters, and other civil rights groups had planned a mass march on Washington to pressure the Roosevelt administration on race issues. The demonstration was called off after the Roosevelt administration assured the black leaders that their complaints would be answered. Robert Lovett, the assistant secretary of war for air, had promised my boss, Bill Hastie, that African Americans would be included in the Army Air Corps. At Hastie's direction, I went to Lovett's office, also in the Munitions Building, to discuss this promise. With him was Major General Henry "Hap" Arnold, commanding general of the air corps.

It became immediately clear that Arnold was running the show—and digging in his heels. He declared that there would never be "Negras" in the air force for two reasons. The air corps was a club where "Negras" would be out of place, he arrogantly said. "Negras" should stay where they belong, he decreed in an insufferable manner. But more compelling, he asserted in unashamed bigotry, was that white enlisted personnel would never service an aircraft flown by a "Negra" officer.

"General, it would be a waste of time talking," I replied and stormed out. Arnold and I never spoke again.

I returned to my office and got on the phone to Mary McLeod Bethune. Although largely forgotten by the general public today, Bethune deserves to be remembered as a trailblazer in the civil rights movement, a prominent educator, a founder of what today is Bethune-Cookman College in Florida, and the first black woman to head a federal agency. At the time she worked as the director of the Division of Negro Affairs of the National Youth Administration, a New Deal organization. More important, she had the ear of First Lady Eleanor Roosevelt, who was a tireless advocate for the rights of black Americans. Bethune listened to my recitation of Arnold's remarks.

"Let Mother handle this!" she reassured me.

I assume she took our case to the First Lady. Soon the air corps was receiving cadets at newly opened facilities at the Tuskegee Institute in Alabama, which would graduate what six decades later is among the best-remembered combat fighter squadrons from the war. Among the first cadets was Captain B. O. Davis Jr., a West Point graduate, a Gibson family friend, and the son of America's first black general, Benjamin O. Davis Sr. In a tribute to the first class to complete training at Tuskegee, Mrs. Roosevelt flew in a plane piloted by the chief instructor.

Formation of the Tuskegee Airmen certainly marked a triumph for advocates of black servicemen, but it was a qualified victory—for the squadron was a segregated unit. The military clung to the misguided notion that efficiency and prowess could not be achieved in an integrated fighting force. Subsequent events were to prove quite the opposite, that segregation and second-class military duty constituted obstacles to military efficiency, discipline, and morale, but that turned out to be years away.

The Tuskegee Airmen compiled a record of bravery and accomplishment that proved black fighting men were as good as the best this country had to offer. They were fortunate in that once assigned to Italy, they got the benefit of training in aerial combat from legendary pilot Philip Cochran. Then they found themselves thrown into the war. The Tuskegee unit, constituted as the Ninety-ninth Pursuit Squadron, incorporated into the air corps' 332nd Fighter Group, and headed by Davis, by then promoted to colonel, escorted bombers from Italy to raids over Germany and *never* lost a plane to enemy fire, although the attrition rate for Allied bombing runs over German targets throughout the war often was horrifically high. Yet, despite that record of achievement, the Tuskegee Airmen were slandered by innuendo and rumor back in the United States. So loudly were the unit's detractors bellowing that I finally had had enough and arranged for Colonel Davis to report on the actual record to a special War Department committee formed to deal with the unique issues facing black servicemen in segregated America. He set the record straight to everyone's satisfaction. Still, the success of the Tuskegee Airmen did nothing to persuade the generals that segregation was a waste of valuable human resources.

Marshall, Arnold, and Householder were only telling it like their bosses saw it. Secretary of War Henry Stimson, a crusty New Yorker of the old school and a Republican who had been Herbert Hoover's secretary of state, stoutly defended segregation. He told President Roosevelt that he was "sensitive to the individual tragedy which went with it to the colored man himself," but beyond that he was closed to any suggestion of change and critical of those advocating it, including the First Lady and "foolish leaders of the colored race" whose goal was "at bottom social equality."[2] Though I eventually inherited the job of civilian aide to the secretary of war after Hastie left, it was to be several years before I actually met Stimson. Ironically, when that time came, he would pin a medal on me. He had left the War Department, but he insisted on personally giving me the award, the Presidential Medal of Merit. By then, his views, enlightened by seeing the performance of black soldiers in Europe, had moderated.

However, in the opening years of the war, Stimson proved to be a captive of the racist views that permeated America. The president was, to put it mildly, not himself the ardent champion of civil rights for black Americans that his wife was. And to Stimson and others in positions of influence in Washington, her agenda was race mixing and therefore unacceptable.

That kind of thinking prevailed as well in the Congress, then dominated by politicians from the South whose years of seniority made them powerful figures in American government. In fact, civil rights leaders who wanted to make sure that African Americans were included in the selective service call-up found unwitting allies, albeit for profoundly different reasons, in southern political figures. Politicians from South Carolina, Mississippi, and Alabama, breaking with other white leaders who wanted to minimize black participation in the war effort, lobbied hard to guarantee that black men got drafted. Scared witless by their own racist mythology, these representatives of bigotry voiced the fear that with the cream of southern manhood called to arms, white women would be defenseless against rape by black men. Yes, public policy was formed by such nonsense. The irony, of course, is that in the end the service of eight hundred thousand black men in the military during World War II and the thousands more who served in the postwar years and on through the Korean conflict swelled into the irresistible force that ultimately desegregated the army.

But that was to come later. The more immediate consequences of the enlistment of black men into the war effort were tragic. Virtually all the basic training camps were in the South. The army, bowing as its policy dictated to the norms of civilian life, directed that its military bases would have to follow the mores, social code, and laws of the communities in which they existed. Therefore, Jim Crow ruled as the law of the land for army posts large and small. Segregated units meant separate barracks and mess halls. Black soldiers rode at the back of buses. Black servicemen spent off-duty hours at inferior theaters and post exchanges, or PXs as the army stores were called. Davis, before he became a Tuskegee air cadet, was assigned as a second lieutenant fresh out of West Point to the Twenty-fourth Infantry Regiment at Fort Benning, Georgia, where he was told his wife would not be permitted to use the officers' club. Nor could his mother, the wife of the first black general, use the officers' club at Fort Riley, Kansas, at a time when General

Davis was the commanding officer for the First Cavalry Brigade! That was crushing to General Davis.

Black troops lived and trained amid hostile white civilian populations in the Deep South. It was not unusual to hear of black inductees who never left their army posts out of fear of violence in the surrounding white communities. One Mississippi-based Negro unit that unfairly acquired a reputation for trouble was written about in alarmist articles in newspapers in Mississippi and Louisiana, resulting in white civilians living near the post going on a gun-buying binge. These conditions humiliated and enraged young black men from the cities of the North, where life, while far from acceptable by today's standards, carried on in a far less segregated environment. Still, most black servicemen hailed from the South for the simple reason that most African Americans lived there. For them, service to their country offered no escape from the social code that devalued and degraded their lives. Furthermore, southern African Americans got little in the way of schooling, which meant that black units were heavily weighed with poorly educated servicemen. That in turn virtually guaranteed that black companies would not perform as well as white units with much smaller proportions of unschooled troops.

Moreover, the army, relying on the worst stereotypes of the day, concluded that white officers from the South were, because of their "experience" in living with blacks, the best equipped to command African American GIs. This folly condemned thousands of black servicemen to the mercy of white officers reared on notions of white supremacy, schooled in the practices of racial oppression, and determined to keep the Negro "in his place." Naturally, commanding a black unit was not viewed by white officers as a choice assignment. Poorly educated and incompetent officers often ended up in these positions. The stage was set at army posts across the South for ugly confrontations that all too often erupted into fights and even riots and ended with African Americans facing court-martial, being beaten up, and being killed. One of the worst explosions of violence, involving three thousand black soldiers at Alexandria, Louisiana, in 1942, is known as the Lee Street Riot, and while official accounts list two dead, no one knows to this day how many blacks were killed. During the 1940s, so many black soldiers were bludgeoned or shot to death by white police, deputies, and civilians in the South that it might be only a slight exaggeration to say more black Americans were murdered by white Americans during the course of World War II than were killed by Germans.

These injustices consumed all the hours of my workday and beyond. Enraged and dispirited young men wrote of their plight to their families, their churches, civil rights organizations, politicians, and newspapers. They, in turn, wrote to the War Department. The complaints eventually landed on my desk. I investigated on my own and arranged inspection tours of bases across the South for General Davis, the NAACP and other civil rights groups, and black newspapermen. Each day meant sending inquiries and memos to captains, colonels, and generals seeking explanations of and solutions to shoddy facilities, second-class training, and racist policies. Letters poured out of my office to families of servicemen, Negro newspapers, and pastors of African American churches as well as to the NAACP, the National Urban League, and other civil rights organizations.

Typical was a letter passed on to me from a black soldier at Camp Lee, Virginia: "The prisoner of war gets much better treatment than we do even when they go to the dispensary or hospital and it is really a bearing down to our morale as we are supposed to be fighting for democracy. Yet we are treated worse than our enemies are. . . . If something isn't done quick, I am afraid a great disaster will surely come."

Bill Nunn of the *Pittsburgh Courier* wrote me complaining that white civilians "respect neither the uniform nor the man in it." He declared, "It becomes increasingly clear that the South is no place to train Negro soldiers."

No black serviceman was secure from bigotry. Perhaps the most famous recruit who rebelled against this blatant racism was Jackie Robinson, who after the war would break the color barrier to become the first black player in major league baseball. He already was a famous athlete when the war began; he had excelled in four sports and won an all-American rating in football at the University of California at Los Angeles. However, to the racist officers of the army, he was just "another one of them."

After induction into the army, Robinson was assigned to Fort Riley, Kansas, the basic training post for cavalry soldiers. He had almost completed his cavalry officer candidate school training when one day he heard a white captain call an African American soldier "a stupid black nigger son of a bitch."

"That man is a soldier in the U.S. Army," Robinson told the captain.

"That goes for you, too, nigger," the captain shot back.

Never a man to suffer an insult, Robinson had an explosive temper, and he packed a powerful punch. He slugged the officer, knocking out his front teeth. Robinson faced court-martial, prison, and who knows, given the lawless nature of race relations in those days, possibly even death.

Also at Fort Riley completing enlisted man's basic training was my friend Joe Louis, the world heavyweight boxing champion. Louis, who was a keen observer of racial issues in the military, kept in regular contact with me and immediately called about Robinson's predicament. I flew down to the post, and we met the officer in charge. I laid out Robinson's case. Then Louis began talking. He said that he was finishing his basic training and wanted to give the general a memento. The champ pulled out an expensive Piaget watch and presented it to the officer. Louis followed up by saying, "General, you have to do a lot of entertaining and I took the liberty of delivering a case of wine to your quarters. This is not any bribe or whatever, but I would like for my friend, Jackie Robinson, to finish his course." Robinson did. Louis bought uniforms for him and the other African Americans who graduated with Robinson from the officer candidate school.

However, as it turned out, Robinson was not long for the army. He was soon to confront another manifestation of the army's reprehensible caving in to southern racists. Troops were transported in buses driven by white civilians, who had orders to enforce the conventions of the strict segregation that ruled the South then. That meant blacks sat in the back of the bus or even at times rode in blacks-only buses. The drivers were sworn in as deputy sheriffs and given firearms. These pistol-packing bus drivers regularly shot black servicemen and not infrequently killed them.

Robinson found himself facing one such driver at Camp Swift, Texas. "Nigger, get to the back of the bus," commanded the driver.

"I'm getting to the back of the bus," Robinson said. "Take it easy."

"You can't talk to me like that," the driver said.

"I can talk to anybody any way I want," Robinson responded.

The bus driver drew a revolver, but his draw wasn't as fast as Robinson, who wrestled the pistol away and massaged the driver's mouth with it, depriving him of many teeth.

Louis called me again, and I flew to Texas. But, as matters turned out, I didn't have to make any arguments on Robinson's behalf. The brass at Camp Swift knew who Robinson was, apparently understood the injustice of the situation, in all likelihood reached the logical conclusion that Robinson would not put up with this kind of raw bigotry, and realized only more trouble lay ahead. Robinson was honorably discharged for the good of the service, with no court-martial.

Robinson was only the most well known soldier whose rage boiled over under bigoted treatment, negligent leadership, and inferior services and facilities. Thousands of Negro soldiers faced court-martial for insubordination and mutiny. Rage over discrimination erupted into drunken brawls, rock and bottle throwing, vandalism, gunplay, and rioting. The unhappy result was that inadequately trained, poorly disciplined Negro units got unfairly branded as troublemakers and unfit for serious duty. It was a criminal squandering of manpower and talent in a time of war.

I heard far too many stories of wasted units and wasted lives and wrote hundreds of memos and traveled thousands of miles defending black servicemen and exposing the conditions that worked against them. Many examples offer themselves. However, one that consumed my efforts for months was the saga of the 364th Infantry Regiment, a story that resurfaced half a century later in a tale of massacre that prompted the army in 1999 to conduct another investigation into the unit's history.

The 364th was created in 1942 out of the breakup of another regiment based at Camp Claiborne, Louisiana, a reassignment that had sent the best troops overseas, eventually to North Africa and the Mediterranean.[3] Right from the start, the regiment was ill starred. I followed its development closely. Its chaplain, Captain Elmer Gibson (no relation), corresponded with me regularly, and I visited Camp Claiborne after parents of soldiers wrote the War Department complaining of poor equipment, an inadequate enlisted men's club, and the hostile attitude of the surrounding community and the civilian law enforcement officers. The regiment had only six black officers, all second lieutenants, and these were smeared by the post's commanding officer as troublemakers.

The regiment, swelled by draftee replacements but neglected when it came to training, was transferred to Papago Park, a post outside Phoenix, Arizona, that was in charge of security along southwestern borders. What the troops saw no doubt dismayed them. The only permanent structures, a headquarters building and a mess hall, were tar-paper shacks that must have been sweltering furnaces in the Southwest's broiling sun. The soldiers lived in tents with desert sand for floors. A subsequent army investigation determined they were given "inadequate clothing and footgear." Worst of all were racist officers who were supposed to train the unit. Complaints about the conditions and commanders caused the army to order a shake-up, but the changes didn't come soon enough to prevent trouble.

In a misguided but well-intentioned gesture, the 364th's commanding officer gave the GIs all the beer they could drink for dinner on Thanksgiving Day 1942 and handed out plenty of passes. Some of the soldiers naturally went into town. A drunken GI and his girlfriend got involved in some kind of trouble outside a Phoenix café. Military police (MPs), black officers as it turned out, were summoned. By some accounts bad blood already existed between MPs and 364th soldiers competing for the affections of some women, although no one ever claimed that this was the root cause of the rioting to come. One soldier was arrested, a crowd gathered, and an MP fired a couple of warning shots, one of which ricocheted and wounded a soldier. Rumors spread back at Papago Park that MPs were shooting 364th soldiers in the streets. Angry soldiers took up arms and sped into town. Soldiers and Phoenix police traded gunfire throughout the night. Fourteen people were shot, and the three dead included a civilian.

This episode became known as the Phoenix Massacre. Fourteen 364th infantrymen were sentenced to prison terms of up to fifty years, and one was condemned to death. The trials were steady grist for the black newspapers' mill. Thurgood Marshall, the future U.S. Supreme Court justice, and other officers of the NAACP wrote me about the injustices inflicted on the 364th. All the convictions eventually were commuted after an army investigation determined that poor training, poor facilities, poor clothing, poor discipline, and poor leadership—all the fault of the army and not the men themselves—were the cause of the melee.

The mistreatment by civilian police of the 364th Regiment and other black soldiers got the attention of Robert P. Patterson, the undersecretary of war who became worried about the morale of black troops. Patterson summoned me to his office for a meeting with Colonel Frank Capra, the director of such famous movies as *Mr. Smith Goes to Washington* and, after the war, *It's a Wonderful Life.* Capra was producing for the War Department a series of motion pictures called *Why We Fight* that were shown as training films for troops and in civilian theaters for the general public. It was my job to enlighten him about the plight of black servicemen. In his autobiography, Capra wrote, "Gibson opened up a thick dossier of sickening acts of discrimination against Negro troops in the South."[4] Chief among the examples I related to Capra was the Phoenix Massacre.

The result was *The Negro Soldier,* a first-class motion picture produced by Capra; directed by Stuart Heisler; written by Carlton Moss, a black writer who also voiced narration for the film; and musically scored by the great Hollywood composer Dimitri Tiomkin. It recounted black history with a heavy emphasis on military accomplishments, highlighting episodes such as the killing of a black man named Crispus Attucks by British troops in the Boston Massacre of 1770, often called the first casualty of the Revolutionary War. The reviews resounded with raves. *Time* magazine hailed it as marking "just about the first time in screen history their race was presented with honest respect."[5] This motion picture had, I believe, ultimately a profound impact on the evolution of the racial views of white servicemen and officers.

After the Phoenix Massacre, the 364th Regiment got permanent barracks, new clothing and equipment, competent training, and experienced commanders, all improvements that started to make things better for the soldiers. But, unfortunately, the 364th's unhappy story didn't end there. Destined for an overseas assignment, the unit was put aboard a train and sent to Camp Van Dorn, Mississippi, for further training. Many of its latest draftees were from the North, and they were more than a little apprehensive about an assignment in the heart of Jim Crow America. Trouble began with their very arrival at Camp Van Dorn on May 26 and 27, 1943. The first two nights brought boisterous drunkenness at a service club and bottle throwing and looting at a PX by Negro troops, with elements of the 364th accused of being among the troublemakers.

On the third day, a Saturday, as many as seventy-five soldiers from the regiment marched into the neighboring town, Centreville. Their behavior was described as obscene and obnoxious by the town's citizens. Perhaps it was a show of bravado by the northern Negroes. Several accounts said some in the 364th arrived in Mississippi believing that their reputation from the Phoenix trouble preceded them and declaring they were going to "clean up" Centreville. Whatever the cause of the foray into town, it ended harmlessly with the soldiers returning to Camp Van Dorn.

Sunday brought more trouble—and death. A confrontation in the town between an MP and Private William Walker over whether his sleeve was buttoned escalated with Walker hitting the MP. Walker saw the local sheriff and two other civilian law enforcement officers approach and bolted. The sheriff shot him dead. As in Phoenix, rumors quickly spread back to the camp, and black servicemen seized some guns. The 364th's commanding officer, Colonel John Goodman, and Chaplain Gibson managed to talk them down and the four days of trouble were over.

The army's inspector general, Major General Virgil L. Peterson, was determined to punish the 364th's soldiers for what he deemed to be a mutiny. I was incensed, especially as I knew his view blaming the black soldiers represented the opinion of most of the army's high command.

I responded to the inspector general's memorandum recommending tough and speedy disciplinary action with a four-page memo declaring that "the use of harsh and repressive measures against Negroes is no solution to the problem." I noted that "northern agitators" were blamed for "inciting southern Negroes" and added, "It is a serious mistake to assume that southern Negro troops accept any more than anyone else inequitable or discriminatory treatment." Then I summarized the problem: "Negro troops on the one hand are being trained as combat soldiers. On the other hand, they are generally told to 'remain in their places' in the South. This warning has a meaning bitterly clear to most Negroes. It means not walking on sidewalks, not being able to board buses if there are any white people to ride, not possessing any rights to freedom from physical violence, to mention but a few of the types of situations that recur daily."[6]

Several investigations ensued, and the results were depressingly familiar. The two post exchanges for African American troops were run down and crowded, with slow service and a small stock of goods for the long lines that invariably snaked around one of the PXs. The movie theater was inferior to the one for white GIs. Failure to salute and sloppy dress bespoke of poor training and discipline. Gambling went on day and night. There were too many incompetent officers, white and black. All that of course confirmed my position that the army's failure to live up to its responsibility to these servicemen was the root cause of the trouble.

Camp Van Dorn wasn't the only post plagued by trouble. General Marshall, to his credit, responded to outbreaks of trouble across the South with a July 13, 1943, memo telling commanding officers it was their responsibility to tackle the causes of racial unrest, head off trouble, and prevent the spread of rumor. This memo was run by me for approval, which I gave. But I cannot help but point out the Orwellian nature of some of the language: Marshall commanded his officers "to prevent incidents of discrimination"—this in an army built on the rotten foundation of segregation!

Still, its reputation as troublemakers stuck to the 364th. It did get better training but because of its unsavory image was shunted off to the Aleutian Islands off Alaska, an assignment far from the World War II battlefields. Its task was to defend several important installations. There, once given a job to do, the 364th showed to everyone's satisfaction that it could perform its duties commendably.

That, however, was not to be the end of the saga of this regiment. In 1998, author Carroll Case published a book entitled *The Slaughter: An American Atrocity* in which he claimed the army killed as many as twelve hundred black soldiers at Camp Van Dorn in 1943 and covered it up. A major part of the book was devoted to what Case called a "fact-based novel" laying out the case against the army. The allegations stirred up so much comment and so many inquiries to the army, civil rights organizations, and African American politicians that the army launched an extensive investigation. It's worth remembering that what made this tale seem plausible was actual history. African Americans were murdered with impunity at posts across the South in the 1940s. The distrust engendered by that history combined with modern-day African American suspicions that America's power structure is aligned against them made Case's charges ring true to many blacks.

But not to me. Because of my involvement, I had gained intimate knowledge of the history of this troubled unit. After Case's book was published and news accounts repeated the charges with allegations of an even higher death toll, I wrote my friend Irv Kupcinet of the *Chicago Sun-Times,* and he published, in his widely read column on July 18, 1999, my comments. I wrote that the allegations were "totally untrue. At the time of the alleged incident, I was acting civilian aide to the secretary of war. In that capacity, I had numerous exchanges of correspondence with the men of the 364th Infantry Regiment. There are no references to the 'slaughter' of 1,500 men or any lesser number and no references to the Case charges." Kweisi Mfume of the NAACP accused me of collaborating in a cover-up of an atrocity against black soldiers.

Subsequent investigation backed my position. Army personnel scrutinized the records about the 364th and Camp Van Dorn. They documented the enlistment and separation of each of the more than 3,850 men who served in the regiment. The investigation found that four soldiers had died at Camp Van Dorn, one of them Walker. Specialists examined aerial photographs of the post taken over the years, looking for the mass grave described in the novel and, of course, found no sign of anything like that. Investigators interviewed 364th soldiers still alive more than sixty years after the war. In the end, not an iota of evidence was found to suggest there had been an actual event that could form the basis for the novel's fictional massacre. Another rumor about the 364th had been laid to rest.

The problem with *The Slaughter* was that this fiction cast a shadow over the actual, wretched conditions of the day. The truth was bad enough and needed no embellishment. Case's book focused attention on something that did not happen. That was an injustice to the black soldiers of World War II who bore the brunt of official segregation and its attendant curses—inadequate training, second-class facilities, racist officers, poor discipline, abuse by civilians, kangaroo courts-martial, and murder. Those were the real-life problems and challenges I had to grapple with from the moment I reported for duty at the Munitions Building that autumn day in 1940. And looking back years later, I can now see how the early years of my life prepared me to tackle these challenges.

2

Atlanta, Columbus, and W. E. B. DuBois

The knock at the door announced the arrival of a great man, but my mother was decidedly unimpressed. In fact, my mother didn't much like W. E. B. DuBois. As a teacher, she acknowledged the splendid achievements of his mind. But as a woman who adhered to a strict code of manners and proper behavior, she found the personality of the imperious DuBois to be, well, barely tolerable.

In my mother's eyes, DuBois, with his homburg hat, his gold-topped cane, and his pince-nez glasses, displayed the air of a German nobleman who carried himself as if he were superior to everyone else. She was a fiercely independent woman who bowed her head to no one and had little patience with anyone looking down his nose at others. One of the vivid memories from my teenage years was being a witness to a clash of these two powerful personalities when DuBois stopped by our Columbus, Ohio, home toward the end of the 1920s.

"Mistress Gibson," declared DuBois, "I have my own coffee," offering it up for her to brew for him.

"Well, I have my coffee, and you're going to drink my coffee," she replied matter-of-factly.

I gulped. I knew who DuBois was. He was revered as the founder of the NAACP. I had hawked his publication, *The Crisis,* in the streets of Columbus. And he had been a visitor in our home before, but this was the first time I had seen my mother bristle over something he wanted.

DuBois, perhaps because he was a guest in her home, gave a little ground but not much. He said, "I'll prefer to have my coffee served by the half cup."

My mother retired to the kitchen and returned shortly with a cup—filled to the brim. "I thought I told you a half cup," a startled DuBois protested.

"Well, I'm telling you that you drink a half cup and I won't have to get up to get another half cup."

DuBois was speechless, and he visited not too frequently after that.

As this story illustrates, my mother, Alberta Dickerson Gibson, left her mark as a very determined woman. She grew up in Jersey City, finished teachers' college there, and went south to teach school at Lawrenceville, Virginia, where she met my father when he came to town on a speaking engagement and subsequently found employment as a teacher. She was proud, well read, fond of quoting Shakespeare, and ever ready with an aphorism such as "How sharper than a serpent's tooth it is to have a thankless child."

Stern admonition, clear rules, strict parental love, and the example of her own life constituted the tools she used to rear me, my brother, and my sister. Only once did she ever raise her hand to me and administer a whipping. I was a teenager, that combustible mixture of adolescent defiance and yearning for independence. Some friends had come to the house to suggest that we drive over to Chillicothe, Ohio, where the girls were pretty and welcoming to boys from the big city of Columbus. I asked her permission. No, came the immediate answer. I, of course, went anyway. When I returned home at about two or three o'clock, she was still up, angry, and with a chain-link dog leash in her hand. It took only a couple of lashes for me to realize the error of my ways. I could have told DuBois that she was not to be messed with.

As much as she disliked DuBois, my father worshiped him. But as much as they differed about DuBois, my father, like my mother, was a rugged individual, smart, industrious, entrepreneurial, quick to anger, and given to keeping his own counsel, sometimes to the point of being secretive. His strong sense of himself flowed in his blood. His grandmother, my great-grandmother—her full name is lost to me, I remember her only as "Granny" Cox—was a slave, part black, part Seminole

Indian. Such mixing was far from uncommon in the antebellum South, with runaway slaves frequently finding refuge among Indians who shared an antipathy for the white man. I recall a photograph of her with my brother sitting on her lap; she looked like an old Indian woman.

Granny lived the life of a slave in Macon. She was not a field hand, we believe, but probably a house slave to a family named Cox. Born or bred with her own firebrand of rebellious independence, she ran away at least four times. The slave master's son was enamored of her. So when she ran away, they would know where she went—to hide out among Indians in Florida. They would go there and pick her up and bring her back.

The daughter (my grandmother) she had with the slave master's son was named Annie Cox. She was a beautiful woman, a stunning blending of black, Indian, and white blood. She inherited her mother's intensely proud and independent spirit. As a young girl, she decided she wanted to attend Fisk University in Tennessee. Her father, a white man who was living with Annie's mother as husband and wife, was willing to put up the money. But her mother would have none of that. Over and over she lectured her daughter, "No nigger woman can be educated. She belongs in the kitchen to cook and clean clothes." It poisoned my grandmother's relationship with her mother. For fifty years, my grandmother didn't speak to Granny even though they were living in the same house. We kids got pulled into the feud. Granny and my grandmother would use my brother Harry and me to relay messages and requests between the two of them. It was all that Harry and I ever knew regarding them, so to us their mutual silence and use of us children as messengers seemed as normal as dew on grass on a Georgia summer night.

The first Truman Gibson in the family was Truman Kella Gibson, a painter-handyman originally from the Anacostia area of the District of Columbia. For some reason, he pulled up stakes and moved to Georgia. Why a freedman would relocate to a slave state in the Deep South boggles my mind to this day. Macon in those days did have a notable population of freedmen who mingled with the slaves—as much as one-third of Macon's black population consisted of freedmen. His son, John Arthur Gibson, married Annie Cox. Decades later, when my father was a successful businessman, he wrote about his life in a children's book, *The Lord Is My Shepherd,* but he could recall little about John Arthur Gibson, other than that he worked hard in the draying business, hiring himself and his horse and wagon out to haul whatever needed to be hauled. He died when my father was five.[1]

Things were tough after my grandfather's death, and my father wrote about his hard life doing odd jobs—sweeping, stacking firewood, waiting tables, repairing umbrellas, and hauling sand in a steel mill—first to help out his mother and then to put himself through Atlanta University and then Harvard University.

It was at Atlanta University that my father met DuBois, a professor of economics and history, the first black to earn a doctorate from Harvard and a towering intellect universally recognized today as the twentieth century's most original thinker about race in America. My father came under his spell, and DuBois saw in my father the talent, ambition, and drive that would eventually make him one of the most successful African American businessmen in the country. I have a copy of the letter DuBois wrote recommending my father to Harvard. "He is one of the best students we have had here and ought easily to get into the Harvard rank lists," DuBois wrote. "He is a boy of sound body, attractive personality and good moral character."[2]

The two kept up a long relationship through letters and visits to our home until frustration, anger, and revulsion at American racism drove DuBois to immigrate to Ghana. Curiously, my father made no mention of DuBois in his book. Not one word. Why, I don't know. It was a relationship of which he was intensely proud. I have a photograph of the two of them together, and my father is literally beaming. Perhaps he didn't include DuBois in his book because his autobiography was a children's book and my father wanted to keep it simple without too many characters. Maybe because that at the time it was written, DuBois, due to his self-imposed exile to Africa, was considered a suspect figure to serve as an example for young Americans. Or maybe it was just something as simple as my father's tendency to keep parts of himself to himself.

Annie Cox Gibson, ever mindful of how she had been deprived of schooling, was proud that all her children attended college, especially that her son had graduated from Harvard with honors. During the Harvard graduation processional, she rose in the middle of the ceremony to announce to all assembled: "That's my boy." After graduation, my father tried his hand at a number of jobs—working for a newspaper, launching a speaker's bureau on Negro history, and teaching at Lawrenceville, Virginia, where he met my mother—before Atlanta called him back to Georgia in 1910.

While at Atlanta University, my father had been a student and participant in dramas put on by Adrienne McNeil Herndon, wife of the phenomenally successful and rich African American businessman Alonzo Herndon. Born into slavery, Herndon had prospered in one of the few businesses open to blacks in the white world, running a barbershop catering to white men. He eventually had several such businesses, including one on Peachtree Street with twenty-five chairs billed as "the largest and finest barbershop in the world." The mansion his wealth brought him is a museum and National Historic Landmark in modern Atlanta. Every winter this wealthy black businessman drove his Apperson Touring Car, the luxury automobile of the day, to Florida; our family benefited from the grapefruit and oranges that he had loaded into the car before returning.

Herndon also invested in real estate and in 1910 found himself in the insurance business, owning Atlanta Mutual. Adrienne Herndon was dying of Addison's disease, and she summoned my father from Lawrenceville to Atlanta to take over the insurance business. She told him, "My husband has recently acquired a small insurance company and I have persuaded him that you are able, ambitious and capable of making it a success—helping him to preserve his own investment and creating a name for yourself in a new field of human endeavor."[3] My father became vice president and secretary of Atlanta Mutual, got rid of the man who had been looting it for ten years, and helped Herndon launch it into what would eventually become a major black business in America.

It was in Atlanta on January 22, 1912, that I was born. Except for rare visits to Herndon's barbershop in downtown Atlanta with my father, who kept the books for Herndon, I lived the early years of my life within a few blocks of our three-bedroom home at 54 Walnut Street, which no longer exists, and within the physical confines and social life of the Atlanta University community. Our home was an old house, and the bathroom with running water was an add-on. The plumbing didn't always work, and we had to resort to the old pump at back, which would occasionally freeze even in the relatively mild Georgia winter.

Our home was a short stroll from Atlanta University. We attended Oglethorpe grammar and secondary school on the Atlanta University campus. We lived in a cocoon, a black enclave in which the wider white world of Atlanta rarely intruded. The university provided a robust intellectual environment, entertainment with musicals and plays, recreational facilities with tennis courts, and even barns with cows—I remember many mornings that my brother and I walked to those barns to get fresh milk. We really had a life separate and apart from Atlanta, from the racial prejudice of the day. *That* I got introduced to in Macon when we visited my grandmother. (Somehow street addresses impress themselves on me; my grandmother lived at 230 Jones Street.)

I can remember that moment of awakening to racial awareness. It was summer. I must have been around four or five years old. My grandmother had taken me to a local drugstore to get some refreshment. I can't remember whether it was a scoop of ice cream or a bottle of Coke or a glass of lemonade. But I do recall this: Such was the oppressive cloak of segregation, its overpowering and pervasive lock on life, that at an existential level I intuitively sensed that I didn't belong on a stool at the soda fountain. That was my first taste of segregation and race consciousness, my first realization of a world that rejected me because of the color of my skin, and my first confrontation with the fundamental injustice of American society.

Georgia and Atlanta were hostile places for blacks in those days. The state's long history of lynching prompted one northern investigator of the practice to observe, "A Negro's life is a very cheap thing in Georgia."[4] During the 1960s civil rights era Atlanta prided itself as a city too busy to hate, but earlier in the century it was a city busy at hating. An awful race riot in 1906, sparked and fanned by irresponsible and false newspaper stories claiming blacks were raping white women, haunted black Atlanta for years. Walter White, then a thirteen-year-old boy and later to be an executive secretary of the NAACP, was making the rounds with his postal collector father amid the trouble. White, with white skin, blue eyes, and blond hair, was so visibly and superficially white that he could escape the wrath of white mobs; he witnessed a bootblack from Herndon's elite barbershop being chased down by a mob and murdered in a frenzy of blows from fists and clubs.[5] Two dozen blacks or more were killed over several days of rioting. Black businesses were devastated. More than one thousand African Americans left the city for good. One historian of Atlanta wrote that the rioting and its aftermath set "the tone of race relations" in the city for half a century and that "the unspeakable horror of the 1906 race riot lurked in the recesses of black families in Atlanta for generations."[6] My father grew increasingly worried about the South's racial animosity. He decided to move north to Ohio.

But why leave Atlanta Mutual, a firm he spent six years working to build and which was prospering thanks in large part to his efforts? The Herndon family chronicler says there was a falling out over the distribution of some stock.[7] No mention of such a dispute is in my father's book. Instead, he said he was hitching his fortunes to the vanguard of what would swell to become the historic migration of southern blacks to the industrial North. "I felt I should follow my policyholders north, as ministers were following their parishioners and doctors were following their patients."[8] True to his reticent nature, he gave not a hint to his family that he was selling stock in West Virginia and Ohio for a new insurance company.

So we left Atlanta. I was only in the fifth grade and have few memories of the city. But I do recollect that marching bands were all the vogue in Atlanta then, and for several years after our departure I entertained daydreams of returning as part of a marching band.

In Columbus, Ohio, where my father began the work that culminated only a decade later in the Supreme Life and Casualty Company, one of the nation's most prominent black-owned and -run businesses, life was marginally better for blacks. We lived at 1221 East Long Street, just a block from the governor's mansion. I attended a racially integrated high school, East High School, where the governor's daughter was a student. The big downtown department stores, Lazarus and Union, had clubs

(High Tower was, I recall, the name of the Lazarus club) with a low bar for membership—just buy a suit. The clubs would treat their members to shows at the ornate downtown movie palaces and to football games.

In truth that was about the extent of racial interaction. Ohio, along with Indiana and Illinois, constituted the nation's "butternut" region, states with populations that had migrated from the South and brought with them their prejudices and even the Ku Klux Klan.[9] I recall Klan marches through Columbus. Right from the start, my brother Harry and I were thrust into a strange world we never knew in the cocoon of the neighborhood of Atlanta University. Whether your skin was as black as a Nubian in Africa or as light as that of the Walter White family, all of whom could pass for white, you were part of the community. That didn't turn out to be true in Columbus. At Eastwood Grammar School in Columbus, the black kids called me Mr. Yellow. If you lay a plank on grass for a few days and then pick it up, what was once green will be yellow. That was the metaphor applied to Harry and me, black kids with—thanks to our mixture of Negro, Indian, and white ancestry—a light copper-tone skin.

Harry and I also got a rude introduction into the morals of Columbus. We'd never seen snow. When the first winter brought a bountiful snowfall, we persuaded our parents to buy us sleds, both of which we inscribed with our names. Our Atlanta University neighborhood was as crime free as the richest white suburb of today, so we never thought to lock up the sleds; we just put them on the back porch. The next day they were gone. A few days later we saw black kids frolicking in the snow with sleds that bore the inscriptions of our names. The leader of the pack declared: "Look, you're a Buckeye now. When you want something, you take it."

We attended integrated schools, but by high school most black kids wound up in Central High in the black section of town derisively called Flytown. I was among the very fortunate handful of blacks at East, but it was a schizophrenic existence. We were distant from the other kids; I had no white friends at school. If there were parties, I never heard of them. No invitation to graduation festivities came to me, although I had the grades to qualify for the honor society. When I was seventeen, a group of my friends and I organized a club, called the Merry Makers, and we had taffy pulls and dances on Friday nights. (The club continued long after I left Columbus, and it recently celebrated the seventy-fifth anniversary of its founding. I attended a commemorative party, but I didn't know anyone.)

I was a guard on the football team, but when we visited Cincinnati, the other black player on the team, a guy named Huckabee, and I were sent away to find a hamburger while the white kids dined at the YMCA. In Columbus there was a separate Y for Negroes, the Spring Street YMCA. Outside of the exemption of department store club membership, movie theaters sold no tickets to African Americans. Restaurants didn't serve us. No hotels catered to blacks, which is why my parents' five-bedroom home was a stopping place for DuBois and many other traveling black people. My father once took me to a ball game in Cincinnati. At one point, he jumped up in excitement and someone shouted, "Sit down you black Mussolini." If we wanted to see picture and vaudeville shows, we had to go on excursions to Cleveland, a more tolerant city.

I worked every summer. In junior high, I had a job first working in a sign maker's shop and later as a helper on an ice truck and in an icehouse. A three-hundred-pound block of ice fell, smashing my foot and putting me out of work for months. In the summer before my junior year in high school, I was employed by the Godman Guild Association, a settlement house in the middle of Flytown. It operated a summer camp for black kids at Chesterfield, about fifty miles outside of Columbus, and I served as a lifeguard and an assistant director. The settlement house had an REO Speedwagon truck, and I learned to drive at the wheel of it. Eventually I saved enough money to buy an old Model T Ford for the princely sum of fifteen dollars. Back in the days before antifreeze, on freezing winter nights people would drain the radiators of their cars. One morning I came out to find that my brother, intending to get the car ready to take us to school, had poured hot water into the radiator and cracked the block. It cost me ten dollars, again a lot of money in those days, to find an engine to replace it.

On the whole, my teen years in Columbus were happy ones. But in truth, Columbus turned out to be not too much different from Atlanta in race relations. The beginnings of racial consciousness awakened at Macon ripened in "butternut" Columbus into a realization of the plight of blacks in America. After high school my ambitions turned to a bigger place, Chicago, and I wondered what promise, hope, or disappointment it held for a young black man fired with ambition.

3

Black Metropolis

Chicago, as it turned out, rose to the challenge of my ambition in ways I could not have foreseen, and it opened opportunities to make my mark in the world in ways unimaginable for black Americans before that time. Most important, Chicago led me to the law, the arena best suited to my personality and my intellect for tackling the great injustices of segregation.

However, that was to come later. To be honest, my immediate ambition in focusing on Chicago had to do with football. My crowning moment at East High in Columbus came during my last year in the big game of the year against our archrival, South High. Late in the game the opposing team's kick was blocked. The ball was lying there on the ground. I didn't know what to do with it, and I said to the other guard, "You pick it up!" "No," he shot back, "you pick it up!" So I did, and I ran twenty yards for the touchdown and victory, the first for East over South High in many years. Oh, what a sweet moment it was! I savored the moment in the instant replay of my mind a thousand times, and on occasion the twenty yards got stretched a bit. At any rate, that moment left me with a powerful desire to play Big Ten football.

I don't recall how I settled on Northwestern University, but I did. I hadn't even visited the campus. My sole contact transpired through correspondence. Still, my academic record at East combined with my football prowess were good enough to earn admittance and some scholarship money to boot.

In the meantime, unbeknownst to his family, my father also had set his sights on Chicago, the bustling, ever expanding, rough-and-tumble industrial giant by Lake Michigan. The Supreme Life and Casualty Company he had founded in Columbus had prospered. However, according to his book, my father sensed that "a national financial crisis was near"[1] and that to survive his company must move and grow through merger with other institutions, become a bigger fish in a bigger pond. He merged his business with two others, one owned by his good friend and Atlanta University classmate Harry H. Pace, to form the Supreme Liberty Life Insurance Company in Chicago. That's what led the family to pull up stakes and move to the South Side of Chicago in 1929. That meant I didn't have to go far to visit Evanston, the North Shore suburb that was home to Northwestern.

In Evanston I renewed my acquaintance with Bill Pyant, who had headed the Spring Street YMCA in Columbus and was then secretary at the Emerson Street YMCA in Evanston. He immediately disabused me of any notions about life for an African American in the tony community just north of Chicago. "If you think segregation in Columbus was bad, wait till you get a load of life in Evanston," he warned me.

That was all I needed to know. But what to do about college? Well, what I did will sound strange and bizarre in twenty-first-century America, where the selection of a college is the product of much study through the evaluation of college rankings found in books and magazines and often through personal visits to numerous campuses by prospective students. All I did was consult the phone book and find the University of Chicago. In a matter of days I was enrolled to start college at its Hyde Park campus.

Now, Chicago in 1930 was a definite improvement over Evanston at that time, but it did not qualify as any kind of paradise for blacks. Only eleven years earlier, several days of race riots had left twenty-three blacks and fifteen whites dead; more than five hundred people injured; and a thousand people, mostly blacks, homeless. African Americans attempting to move into white neighborhoods saw their homes bombed. As if the violence weren't enough—and it wasn't enough to discourage blacks seeking to break the chains of segregation—white Chicagoans had discovered the effectiveness of restrictive real estate covenants to bar blacks from purchasing homes in white communities.

Still, Chicago in the early years of the Great Depression afforded African Americans opportunity unmatched by any other place in America. The migration to industrial jobs in the North and Midwest spawned by the demands on manufacturing by World War I had swelled the city's black population to 233,903, and one out of every twelve adults was African American, turning the midwestern metropolis into the city with the second-largest black population in the world. Furthermore, its black population was concentrated on the South Side, forming the nucleus of what St. Clair Drake and Horace R. Cayton popularized in their book as the "Black Metropolis."[2] This concentration enabled the city's African Americans to achieve political power unrivaled by blacks anywhere else in America at that time. Two of Chicago's fifty aldermen were black, and the first African American elected to Congress since Reconstruction, in 1928, hailed from the South Side of the Windy City—Oscar DePriest, who also had the distinction of having been elected the city's first Negro alderman in 1915. Chicago's flamboyant Republican mayor, William Hale "Big Bill" Thompson, like all survivors in the boisterous world of Second City politics, knew whose backs to slap and on whom to shower political spoils. He appointed African Americans to city hall jobs, and when the First Congressional District seat came open after the death of its longtime white occupant, Thompson flouted the appeals of national Republican leaders to find another white and threw in his lot with the notion that the district's representative on Capitol Hill should be of the race of the majority of its constituents.[3]

Until the 1930s, the black vote remained solidly Republican because the GOP lived in the hearts of African Americans as the party of emancipation while the Democrats constituted the party of Jim Crow and the "solid South." Chicago Democrats were pretty much clueless to the rising black power on the South Side. During his successful 1931 campaign for mayor, Anton Cermak had a flatbed truck roaming around town with a band aboard playing "Bye Bye Blackbird"—a far from subtle campaign promise to rid city hall of blacks. Cermak was killed in an assassination attempt against President Roosevelt in 1933, but other Democrats already were looking beyond his myopic viewpoint. Democratic landslides during the early Depression years and New Deal relief programs began attracting black votes, and in 1934 DePriest was ousted from Congress by a black Democrat, Arthur W. Mitchell, thanks in part to white support generated by the infamous Chicago ward heeler Michael "Hinky Dink" Kenna. Mitchell's victory heralded the beginning of the long allegiance of Chicago blacks to the Democratic Party.

Chicago's South Side "black belt" meant more than political clout. Within the Second and Third Wards developed a vibrant black economy. Banks, law firms, doctors and dentists, insurance companies like the one my father ran, real estate agencies, and the whole gamut of the businesses of everyday life from drugstores to restaurants to barbershops to funeral parlors were black owned or black run. Of course, there was no escaping the Depression. My father's insurance company, of which I became a board member after graduation, limped insolvent through most of the 1930s. Unskilled minorities faced harder sledding than white workers, themselves flung into the worst economic times in the country's history.

In their desperation, many blacks grasped at hope through gambling on the ubiquitous policy games common throughout the South Side. In effect an illegal lottery, policy operations mushroomed into a major pillar of the South Side economic infrastructure, accounting by one estimate for at least six thousand jobs for "policy writers,"[4] as the bet takers were called. By another calculation, in 1938 a South Side policy "syndicate" employed more than five thousand people on a weekly payroll of twenty-five thousand dollars, generated annual gross proceeds of at least eighteen million dollars, and kicked back up to half a million dollars to the downtown politicians in protection money.[5] That was a big business that to some degree ameliorated the pounding the Depression inflicted on the black community.

The readily visible economic contribution of policy to the community and the hope—or false promise—of monetary profit it held out for South Siders in the Depression helped turn this lottery into what Drake and Cayton labeled a cult: "It has a hold on its devotees which is stronger than the concrete gains from an occasional winning would warrant. It has an element of mystery and anticipation. It has developed an esoteric language. It organizes, to some extent, the daily lives of the participants. And, as in all cults, it has developed a group of functionaries and subsidiary businesses dealing in supplies."[6]

Being such a huge enterprise, policy naturally accounted for some of my business as a young lawyer. Leon Motts, Charlie Ferrell, and Henry Young, partners in one of the policy wheels, came to be my clients. Young bought a tract of land and created the Peaceful Valley Country Club. It had a swimming pool but not much else. Having policy guys for clients didn't mean representing them only in criminal proceedings. I had a close friend in law school, Bernie Sang, whose brother was president and chief executive officer of the Goldenrod Ice Cream Company. Sang needed retail outlets for the firm's fine ice cream. Ferrell and Young opened four drugstores to sell it. That's just an indication of how policy gambling integrated into the economic life of the community.

While it's true that the Great Depression rained misery, destitution, and despair on countless individuals and families, that's not the whole story of the 1930s. It's also true that Chicago thrived as a vibrant, pulsating city—on the South Side as well as in the Loop, where we occasionally journeyed to take in a big band at the Chicago Theater or a vaudeville show at a theater in the Bismarck Hotel on Randolph Street. Restaurants, fraternal clubs, bars—wide open and illegal during Prohibition and just plain wide open after repeal—and nightclubs enlivened and animated life south of Thirty-first Street after the sun went down.

As a young lawyer I became a habitué of the Midnight Club in the basement of Alderman William L. Dawson's ward office at 3140 South Indiana Avenue, as did world-famous bandleader Benny Goodman. He frequently was there to visit his musical mentor, the man who had taught him how to transmute a clarinet from a mere horn into a wellspring of music artistry—Jimmy Noone, the greatest clarinet virtuoso of his day and a regular on the Midnight Club's stage. Another favorite was the Grand Terrace at Thirty-ninth Street and South Parkway Avenue, owned by the mob-connected Joe Glazer, who went on to become the major booker for black bands. Louis Armstrong and Earl Hines frequently headlined that club. I was swept up in the torrent of beautiful, sensuous, jazzy, exciting black culture that seemed light-years and worlds away from Columbus.

Life in Chicago turned out to be all that any young man could pray for and an exciting distraction that led plenty of young people astray, but the University of Chicago first and my law career later anchored me firmly to the earth. In my freshman year at the Hyde Park campus, I made the dean's list and found a niche on the freshman football team. My second year was to see change for the worse—and for the better.

The worse came when my football aspirations collided with the realities of race in America. When I showed up for practice for the fall season, I heard varsity football coach Alonzo Stagg ask one of his assistants, "Which is the one?" That, of course, meant which one was the black player. I knew I was out. Stagg may be a football legend, but he failed as a human being in his inability to overcome the racial prejudice of the day. Not that he was much out of step with the university. Blacks were not allowed to reside in the dorms; I lived at home at 4524 South Park Avenue (now named Dr. Martin Luther King Jr. Drive). I had no white friends at the University of Chicago until I advanced to its Law School, where I enjoyed the camaraderie of several white students, most notably Ed Levi, who later became president of the university and a United States attorney general.

I also dropped off the dean's list my sophomore year, but it had nothing to do with my disappointment over football dragging down my studies. I was simply too busy to do the work needed for an A average. I had met Cayton, the black sociologist, on campus, and he introduced me to Harold Gosnell, who employed me as a research assistant on what turned out to be a groundbreaking project and eye-opening learning experience for me.

I never actually knew what, if any, academic position at the University of Chicago Cayton held. The grandson of a Reconstruction senator from the South and the son of a newspaper editor in Washington State, Cayton profited from a varied and colorful background that included a job as a deputy sheriff in Washington. He regaled people in the Political Science Department with stories of his life and exploits. I met him at the Reynolds Club, where students ate, mingled, and got to know one another.

Gosnell's project was the study of the rise of Negro politics in Chicago with the surging of the city's black population through the African American migration from the South after the collapse of Reconstruction and the expansion of job opportunities in northern industry during World War I. A woman student by the name of Frances McClemore had been his research assistant in 1929 and 1930, but she had returned home to St. Louis, and I succeeded her as his legman.

I interviewed politicians and lawyers, researched the history of black Chicago, and attended South Side political meetings. A few of the politicians I already knew. DePriest, a tall man at six-foot-six with white hair and a blustery way of talking, had turned up in Columbus at the Supreme Life office. Irvin C. Mollison was a Phi Beta Kappa law graduate of the University of Chicago and active in the Legal Defense Fund for the NAACP. His wife had family in Atlanta, was a relative of Walter White, and was acquainted with my parents. Of course, most of the people I interviewed were new to me. I got to meet and talk to the black trailblazers of Chicago politics such as Robert Jackson and Louis Anderson, aldermen of the Second and Third Wards, respectively; men now largely forgotten such as William E. King, the leading Republican mover and shaker in the black community who shared law offices at 35 South Dearborn Street with Earl Dickerson; Congressman Arthur W. Mitchell, the symbol of the Democratic black emergence; future judges such as Sidney Jones, a graduate of Northwestern Law School; and the most successful black lawyers of the day, such as Ed Morris. Morris represented interests who succeeded in floating a gambling boat in the Chicago River for a year during the Depression, the precursor to the riverboats that dominate gambling today in the Midwest.

The precinct and ward meetings were always theatrical, usually raucous, and even occasionally elevating. They often provided a stage for one of the South Side's great political orators, Roscoe Conklin Simmons. His eloquence perhaps did pour out of a bottle, since he was always three-quarters drunk. He never missed a chance to pay his sarcastic respects to the Negro-hating Anton Cermak. "When Cermak's family was laboring in the poppy fields of Bohemia, I was attending a great American university!" he bellowed to an appreciative hand-clapping, laughing audience.

I tried to blend into the background at these meetings, to be the fly on the wall to observe the nuts and bolts mechanics of black politics in Chicago. I wasn't always successful. Once I got called out at the Eighth Regiment Armory during a meeting of Dawson's organization. Dawson, who in the 1950s would swing the black votes instrumental in the election of the first Mayor Richard Daley, was another notable orator with the range and passion of a Baptist preacher. He took center stage to shout to the assembled, "Let the spy come down to a suitable seat in front of the lectern!" The people around me commenced to mumble and gesture in, well, a not very friendly way. I knew I had the choice of an embarrassing march down to the front row or standing my ground and getting my tail whipped. No fool, I elected for embarrassment.

I'm proud of my part in Gosnell's research. His analysis, synthesis, and writing of *Negro Politicians: The Rise of Negro Politics in Chicago* constituted a most impressive achievement. To this day, his work hasn't lost its sense of immediacy. It remains an informative, rich, authoritative, and very readable account of the impact of the Great War black migration on Chicago's politics and social life.

All that interviewing of politicians, getting to know some of the top black lawyers in the country, and learning how the legal system could be a weapon against racial injustice confirmed in me a growing ambition to be an attorney, and I enrolled in the University of Chicago Law School. Today graduates of that renowned institution enjoy the honor of being recruited by the best firms around. That was true too in the 1930s—for white students. It was another story for black graduates. No white firm would hire African Americans, not even those attaining the high academic honors of an Irvin Mollison. The Chicago Bar Association admitted no black lawyers. I had a degree from one of the best law schools in the country but no job. Fate intervened at a social function at Mollison's home in 1935.

"What are you doing?" Mollison asked me.

"I'm not doing," I replied.

"Well, why don't you come down to our firm; you can work out of Dawson's office."

Starting pay was the princely sum of three dollars a week, of which two and a half went for an El pass to get back and forth from my parents' home to the law offices at 180 West Washington. Even if the pay wasn't much, it was a job. Actually it was much more than a job, it was a school in the practical world of law and courts. It afforded me the opportunity to learn from some of the top black lawyers and politicians of the day, including Dawson, Herman Moore, William Haynes, and above all Mollison. He was a brilliant student of the law, a master of the technical aspects of American jurisprudence, and a teacher par excellence. What's more, he would eventually introduce me to the world of boxing, which was to play such an important part in my life later, and recruit me for a legal crusade against the restrictive real estate covenants that were the curse of black aspirations.

All that was to come later. First, I had to experience all the travails of young lawyers, including having my immodest assessment of my own abilities subjected to the ridicule of the courthouse veterans. Emblazoned in my memory is one of my first visits to the Forty-eighth Street branch of the Circuit Court of Cook County. My client was a low-level policy functionary. The prosecuting attorney was Roy Washington, the father of Harold Washington, who was later Chicago's first black mayor. Literally bursting to demonstrate my legal prowess with insightful and persuasive motions and pleadings, I was brought to a full stop by Washington.

"In this court, we rule on a motion for a writ of slapadarus," declared Washington.

"What's that?" I innocently asked.

"Ten dollars," he replied.

"I don't have ten dollars."

Washington turned and addressed the bench, "Judge, this young man wants to file a writ of slapadarus, but he doesn't have the right credentials!"

They all had a good laugh at my expense, chuckling over my inexperience and innocence. The apprehension of my client numbered among the token arrests Chicago police made for the benefit of the newspapers. Policy workers were routinely rounded up to meet quotas, but each was soon released on payment of ten dollars.

That wasn't the only humbling experience I had. On another occasion I showed up at municipal court to defend a Dawson precinct worker accused of assault. I was out to demonstrate that I could interpose the most learned objections. The judge quickly grew tired of me. "Young man," he intoned, "you speak up one more time and I'm going to throw you out of court." I learned then that it was not wise to advertise erudition in the law.

Fortunately, the law had more to offer a young man than embarrassment. Right from the start I found myself where I wanted to be—fighting segregation. Ironically, one of my early cases originated in Evanston, the North Shore suburb whose rigid segregation had sent me reeling from Northwestern to the Hyde Park home of the rival University of Chicago. Evanston had a significant black population—one large enough in 1931 to elect a black alderman, former college track star Ed Jourdain. The city council tried in 1936 to deprive him of his seat. The council held a hearing on his election where I argued the law and the principles of democracy, and Jourdain kept his seat.

A number of the South Side's policy kings became my clients. Not only did I work to spring their policy writers from jail, I also advised them on legal matters as they increasingly invested their fortunes in legal businesses and real estate ventures. But even the most successful gambler can miss out on a good bet. I remember being introduced to a not very well dressed young man down from Canada. I was told that he had an assistant working to extract oil from the sands in the Athabasca River in Alberta. I took him to Ed Jones, who owned big pieces of real estate, hotels, and other businesses, including the "Jones Boys' Store" that opened in 1937 to the acclaim of thousands of Chicago blacks overjoyed to see a black-owned general department store to compete with the big department stores operated by whites.[7] Jones listened to the Canadian for about fifteen minutes and then dismissed him with an "I've got to go." To me, he sneered, "What the hell are you doing bringing this tramp to me?" Of course, the process turned out to be a success, and they're still extracting oil from the sands of the Athabasca River, producing a fortune that Jones and I turned our backs on.

A pleasant surprise awaited me one day in 1937 at our offices at 180 West Washington. I showed up for work to find a striking young woman with lovely legs seated in our waiting room reading the book *Anthony Adverse.* I immediately marched into Mollison's office and announced, "I'll take care of this one."

Her name was Isabelle Carson, an alumna of Northwestern University who was a graduate student in social work at the University of Chicago. She had gone out one day with some white friends for lunch at a Greek restaurant and been denied service. Illinois, the land of Lincoln and a state where racial history was a jumble mixing the horrors of the 1919 race riots with the honor of seating the first black from the North in Congress, had in 1885 enacted a Civil Rights Act forbidding discrimination in restaurants, hotels, theaters, railroads, streetcars, and other places of public accommodation and amusement.[8] I won for my client the handsome damages of twenty-five dollars. More important, I won my client—Isabelle Carson became my wife on February 12, 1939. Our marriage lasted sixty years.

As the 1930s closed, I found my career increasingly centering around issues of race, which W. E. B. DuBois had so brilliantly identified as the twentieth century's fundamental challenge to the idea and ideals of America. Mollison drafted me to help him in what would be one of the key battlefronts of the civil rights struggle, the fight against restrictive covenants, namely, *Lee v. Hansberry.* It was a legal battle that was fought all the way to the United States Supreme Court, shook the South Side to its foundation, and inspired a transcending work of art.

4

A Raisin in the Sun

It's a moment pregnant with possibilities. For the black family in Lorraine Hansberry's play *A Raisin in the Sun,*[1] a yearning for a better life inspires a hope of a warm welcome, a gesture of acceptance, and an expression of neighborly feeling from their soon-to-be neighbors who are white. For us in the audience, foreboding makes us almost want to avert our eyes as we know that something quite different from the family's aspirations is about to befall them. Still, thanks to the power of Hansberry's words and the depth of the performances by the actors (Sidney Poitier, Ruby Dee, Claudia McNeil, and the others in the movie adapted from the 1959 play), we too are stunned when the bland young man from the Clybourne Park Improvement Association reveals that the white neighborhood wants to buy back from the black family the house on which they've just made a down payment. "You people" is the phrase he uses over and over, working himself up to his point: "I want you to believe me when I tell you that race prejudice simply doesn't enter into it. It's a matter of the people of Clybourne Park believing, rightly or wrongly, as I say, that for the happiness of all concerned that our Negro families are happier when they live in their own communities."

The family is crushed. We in the audience are repulsed by the soulless ugliness of the moment. Yet, the reality that served as the inspiration for this play was much harsher. Whereas the black family in the play confronted a 1950s white neighborhood that wanted to buy them out, that was in effect trying to talk them out of coming into the area by offering a quick profit on the home, Carl Hansberry, Lorraine's father, faced the full weight of a legal system out to deny him by force of law the right to move his family into a white neighborhood during the Depression.

Chicago in the first third of the twentieth century was of two minds about its burgeoning black population. While its industries, straining to meet the production demands of World War I, had thrown open their arms to the African Americans migrating from the South, white Chicagoans did not turn out the welcome mat for blacks seeking to put down roots in their neighborhoods. The city's political power structure struggled to contain African Americans within the already established black belt on the South Side. A bomb, not a welcome wagon, all too often announced the arrival of a black family to a previously all-white block. Still, racial violence was not an attribute by which any city wanted to be known. Chicago's city fathers and business community had recoiled in horror from the bloody 1919 race riot, and law-abiding Chicagoans were not happy with the brand of lawlessness burned on the city's good name by Al Capone and other gangsters during Prohibition.

So a nonviolent way had to be found to keep blacks out of white neighborhoods. Indeed, the bombings abated as the city adopted a more effective and legalistic approach—the restrictive real estate covenant. Now, restrictive covenants were not, and are not, unusual in real estate contracts to protect property values. They lay down parameters on, for instance, right of way, utilities, or the number of people who can occupy a structure. Applying the covenants to race—in effect declaring that blacks had to be kept out of communities to preserve home values—became widespread in the 1920s.[2]

A typical example was the racial covenant for the Washington Park subdivision on Chicago's South Side, written in 1927. This was the covenant that Hansberry challenged in the mid-1930s. This document[3] prohibited the sale, rental, and leasing to Negroes of residential property in a defined area. The crude language of the covenant defined a Negro as "every person having one-eighth part or more of negro blood, or having any appreciable mixture of negro blood, and every person who is what is commonly known as a 'Colored person.' " The only exceptions to the ban on black occupation of living quarters in a covenant-restricted neighborhood were African Americans employed as janitors, chauffeurs, or house servants, who could live "in the basement or in a barn or garage in the rear, or . . . servants' quarters."

Hansberry was an astute businessman who had found prosperity in buying three-flat apartment buildings and converting them to ten-flat kitchenette structures. The sturdy homes and apartment buildings in the Washington Park subdivision appealed to his business instincts. He set his sights on a three-flat brick building at 6140 South Rhodes Avenue, put down earnest money, got a mortgage, and proceeded to move his wife, Nannie, and their four children into the first-floor unit.

Knowing that he was in for a hard legal fight, Hansberry and his attorney, C. Francis Stradford, approached the NAACP. The star legal counsel for the NAACP was Earl Dickerson, also general counsel for my father's firm, Supreme Liberty Life Insurance. Dickerson already had made a name for himself as an activist in the NAACP and the liberal Chicago Lawyers Guild, put his stamp on the black business community through his work as vice president and general counsel for the Supreme Life firm, earned a reputation as an effective litigator, and, from his service as an assistant Illinois attorney general, gained a keen insight into the workings of the courts and the power structure of Chicago. He was a natural selection for anyone wishing to challenge the restrictive racial covenant.

Dickerson presented Hansberry's case to the insurance company, and it readily agreed to put up the money for the forty-four-hundred-dollar note on the property and to fund the legal challenge to these bigoted contracts. Supreme made that mortgage with eyes wide open to the risks and expense of a long legal fight. My father chaired the executive committee that approved the mortgage for Hansberry to buy the property. Although the decision was made with little discussion, my father, Dickerson, and the others knew that they faced an uphill fight. Only a few years earlier, the U.S. Supreme Court had ruled in favor of racial covenants. Still, the overwhelming sentiment was in favor of another challenge. Irvin C. Mollison and I were recruited for the struggle as pro bono attorneys.

Hansberry's property wasn't the only stab at black ownership within the Washington Park subdivision. My father's business associate, Harry Pace, also bought a building nearby, and that became part of the *Hansberry* case.

Independent of our action, a black physician named James Lowell Hall bought a dwelling west of the building at Sixtieth Street and Vernon Avenue in which my parents rented an apartment. Such was the arbitrary and capricious nature of the covenant that while our building was not covered by it, the one Hall bought was.

Hansberry and Hall both moved their families into the buildings and were promptly evicted on the basis of the covenant. As evidenced by *Raisin,* that made a powerful impression on Lorraine, who couldn't have been more than seven or eight years of age at that time. The upheaval must have been traumatic. Hansberry lived well. He already owned a very pleasant home on Forestville Avenue, a short street of houses for the affluent between Forty-fifth and Forty-seventh Streets. Almost overnight, she was uprooted from that familiar home, moved into the ground-floor apartment of the three-flat building on Rhodes, and then hustled back to Forestville Avenue after eviction. No man puts his family through that lightly. The compelling factor for Hansberry that made that bruising turmoil necessary was the goal of busting the covenant.

After forcibly getting Hansberry's family out of the building, the Woodlawn Property Owners Association, as the covenant's governing body was known, filed papers in circuit court to force the real estate broker to relinquish ownership of the building. The legal battle had been joined. At the center of it, plotting strategy and articulating the case against the covenant, was Dickerson.

The chance for Hansberry, Hall, and Pace to buy property arose unexpectedly out of bickering and betrayal inside the Woodlawn Property Owners Association. Its executive secretary and prime conspirator in buttressing the covenant had been an individual named James Joseph Burke. He quit the association on March 1, 1937, in a dispute over—what else?—money. It was a bitter parting. According to the complaint[4] the association filed against the Hansberry purchase, Burke resigned after, on various occasions, hurling threats at his erstwhile comrades.

"I'm going to put niggers into twenty or thirty buildings in the Washington Park subdivision," he was quoted as saying within four to six weeks before he left. "I will get even with the Woodlawn Property Owners Association by putting niggers in every block," he declared on another occasion. "You property owners in the subdivision will soon have headaches." And, he added, "I will get even with the Association and with certain directors of said Association if that is the last thing I do."

He then "conspired," according to the complaint, to sell the Rhodes Avenue property to Hansberry and the nearby building on Sixtieth Street to Pace. Indeed, a conspiracy existed, but it was a necessary conspiracy, intrigue aimed at righting a wrong.

As the youngest attorney, I was the junior partner on the legal team and got the most tedious job. For the covenant to be in force, it had to be signed by 95 percent of the home owners in the covered area. I spent much of the next year and a half working in the law library at City Hall in the Loop and at the nearby office of the Cook County Recorder of Deeds. Poring over legal descriptions of the property in the stacks at the law library, I transcribed, in my bad handwriting, the characteristics and boundaries of the plots in the subdivision. Then at the recorder's office, I hunted up the deeds to the properties and compared the signatures on them to those on the covenant. It was a laborious, tiresome, boring task. Squinting to make out the signatures was hard on my eyes; days hunched over property records left my back aching, and copying reams of legal papers cramped my hand. But I wasn't married at the time, so my time was my own, and although I wasn't paid, expenses back then weren't what they are today.

More important, the payoff was big. My long hours revealed that only 54 percent of the property owners actually had signed the covenant. We thought we had the stake to drive through the heart of this racial covenant. During the trial in circuit court, I spent almost ten days on the witness stand explaining my research, going over individual pieces of property to show that I had the goods on them.

But the white home owners' association anted up what turned out to be an ace in the hole. Back in 1928, Burke had cooked up a fraudulent suit, a friendly legal action which maneuvered a circuit court judge into accepting the covenant as valid and binding. This was precedent, the judge in our case declared—despite the evidence I had presented, despite the fact that barely more than half of the required 95 percent of home owners had signed the covenant, and despite testimony from Burke that the 1928 action was the work of collusion. The legal term employed by the court was res judicata, meaning the issue had been decided, had been settled. We, of course, appealed.

Litigation is expensive. My best estimate is that Supreme Life pumped more than a hundred thousand dollars—a huge sum during the Depression—into fighting this case. But where did the money come from to pay the phalanx of attorneys representing the white home owners of this middle-class neighborhood?

The University of Chicago!

Dickerson, Mollison, and I—all graduates of the University of Chicago Law School—sought and got a meeting with university president Robert Maynard Hutchins, considered then and remembered today as a great liberal. We urged him to cut off university financing of the defense of the racist real estate contracts. He steadfastly refused.

"It's a matter of economics," he lectured us. "The university has a huge investment in the South Side, and I've got to protect it."

As we pressed our case, he became increasingly irritated and finally blurted out, "Why don't you people stay where you belong!"

"You people." Hutchins would never say the word "nigger," but the phrase "you people" carried the same message.

That was the end of the hope that the University of Chicago would step up to do the right thing. Yet, those words from this icon of progressive politics grated on me long after. In fact, some years later after I had gone to work for the War Department, I ran into my old Chicago Law School friend Ed Levi in Washington, where he was employed by the attorney general. I hadn't seen him for several years, and as we exchanged pleasantries, the resentment over that insult bubbled up and I said, "Ed, why don't you let Hutchins know we belong everywhere?" I think the vehemence of my feelings left him nonplussed. He muttered something about that's how things are and isn't that awful, and went on his way. Ed was a good man, but he didn't know how to answer my anger.

As our case worked its way to the Illinois Supreme Court and then finally to the U.S. Supreme Court, I would occasionally see Hansberry, and I even had him as a client in a business matter—a deal that inspired another plotline in *A Raisin in the Sun*. In the play, the family matriarch comes into ten thousand dollars from an insurance policy paid on the death of her husband. There are competing interests within the family for the money. Her daughter wants part of it to attend medical school. The Sidney Poitier character is consumed with ambition to invest it in a liquor store with a couple of other men so he can become his own boss instead of serving out his life as a chauffeur to a white man. The mother says no, invests part of the money in a down payment on the house in the white neighborhood, and entrusts the rest to her son to deposit in the bank. He promptly takes the money to the acquaintance who is putting together the liquor store deal, and, of course, that man disappears with the money.

Hansberry, as I've noted, made a good living because he was an astute businessman. But like too many people, then and now, and like the Sidney Poitier character, he yearned for the surefire chance to make a killing. He socialized with the policy guys, which served only to feed his appetite for the fast buck. At the time oil exploration was recognized as a lucrative business, thanks to the ever growing popularity of the automobile and the ever increasing incorporation of the internal combustion engine into American industry. Speculation in petroleum wells was rampant. Today, we think of oil as an asset of the American Southwest and the Middle East. However, oil drilling first made fortunes in Pennsylvania, and oil had been struck in downstate Illinois.

Now, a couple of businessmen named Horne and Faulkner (I've forgotten their first names) persuaded Hansberry and several other men to invest in the mineral rights to land in Centralia, Illinois, that they touted as oil fields likely to produce a bonanza for those bold enough to cough up the money for exploratory drilling. Hansberry and the others bought it hook, line, and sinker. One weekend we drove down to Centralia, and they spent hours gazing at the property, walking around it, and imagining oil derricks pumping black gold out of the ground, their heads filled with visions of oil dollars gushing out of the rich agricultural dirt of central Illinois. Naturally, the upshot was that Hansberry's property produced about two teaspoons of oil, and Horne and Faulkner skipped town with his money and that of the other investors. Like the Poitier character, they had been cheated by a couple of sharp guys preying on others' hunger for quick riches. Fortunately, no one had invested his life savings in this scheme.

It's an ill wind that blows no good; my law partner Mollison also put some money in this scheme. His property turned out to be a drainage ditch running by the so-called oil field, so it looked like he had got the worst deal of all. However, his drilling operation actually struck oil, and, while its production didn't make him an oil baron, the well produced enough petroleum for him to earn a good return on his investment. His success prolonged the hope of the other investors but to no avail.

Horne and Faulkner had had offices next to mine in the Supreme Life building at Thirty-fifth Street. They had fooled me, too, but fortunately, I had not invested in their oil scheme.

Not too long after the oil scheme fizzled, on October 15, 1939, the Illinois Supreme Court rendered its decision on our appeal. The ruling began with a lot of flowery praise for the briefs presented by both sides. They were "very studiously prepared," were read by the justices "with the greatest interest and enjoyment," were appreciated for the quality of the "language employed," and some of their arguments were regarded as "almost classical." For us, the justices no doubt intended that fulsome and condescending praise to soften the blow to come. They rejected our appeal, declaring that res judicata indeed applied. Incredibly, the court found that the stipulation resulting from the contrived lawsuit was untrue but ruled that the sweetheart deal was not fraudulent or collusive.

We took our case to the United States Supreme Court. The high court heard arguments October 25, 1940. We traveled to Washington several days ahead of that to prepare. As I said, I wasn't being paid, so I stayed with Robert Ming, a law professor at Howard University and a close friend who had managed to graduate at the top of his class from the University of Chicago Law School even though he spent his last year presiding over a blackjack game rather than in class.

Two nights before the arguments to the high court, we laid out our case to sixty students and faculty members at Howard in an auditorium on campus. Listening and questioning us were some of the best minds in America's black intelligentsia. William Hastie, a man who was to play such an important role in my life and who had become the first black federal judge, was dean of Howard's Law School. Others from the faculty included Jim Nabrit Sr., a top graduate of the Northwestern University Law School and later president of Howard; Bernard Jefferson, a recent graduate of Harvard who would become a distinguished judge in California, and my old friend Bob Ming. Bill Hastie was an intense questioner. His time in Chicago enabled Nabrit to pose especially detailed and relevant questions.

The rehearsal went on for three or four hours. Dickerson recited his oral argument. Back in Chicago, we had gone over it countless times, looking for weak logic, revising and refining our legal reasoning, and polishing the phrasing and structure of our argument. The audience was clearly impressed.

I took the stage to explain the research on the covenant's signers that I had done and fielded all manner of probing questions.

Before we could present our case to the U.S. Supreme Court, we had to be admitted to its bar. The morning before our case was to be heard, Mollison, Moore, Dickerson, and I showed up for the swearing-in ceremony. Of course, I had never visited the court before. We were among a troop of attorneys who marched into the courtroom in late morning to be formally sworn in. Our hearts were fluttering. I was awed by the majesty of the courtroom, the bench, and the justices themselves. We were in quite a daze and didn't say anything but yes when called upon by the presiding justice.

Finally, with the next day came the main event. Mollison, Moore, and I took our seats while Dickerson assumed the lectern. He was the supreme egotist who didn't suffer fools gladly. But that day he proved beyond a shadow of a doubt that his own high opinion of himself was richly deserved. To say that Dickerson did extremely well is an understatement.

He made his presentation with aplomb, forcefully advancing our arguments and agilely responding to the challenging questions from several of the justices.

Ours was a three-pronged attack: the concept of the covenant denied equal protection of the law guaranteed by the Fourteenth Amendment, the Washington Park subdivision covenant was invalid because of the inadequacy of the signatures, and res judicata did not apply because the suit on which it was based was a trumped-up affair.

The pattern of questioning, led by Justice James McReynolds from Tennessee, avoided the conceptual argument and focused on the technical questions of res judicata, signatures, and the sanctity of contracts. The high-priced Loop attorneys representing the Woodlawn Association and funded by the University of Chicago, led by McKenzie Shannon, also came under sharp questioning.

The questions were precise, addressing specific legal issues of contract, but the experience was not intense. The justices listened attentively. After our hour-long presentation, we walked away convinced that Dickerson had done a fine job in articulating our case, though of course we had no way of knowing how it had played with the court. We retired to Ming's apartment to replay over and over the day's events and to unwind by playing a little poker.

As it turned out, we had to wait only three weeks for a decision. A quick ruling from the U.S. Supreme Court was very unusual. Normally the justices considered an issue for months, typically hearing a case in the fall and rendering opinion in late May. A decision after only three weeks was surprising. The results, however, showed that the court wasn't ready to tackle the constitutional issues we presented regarding Fourteenth Amendment protections and wanted only to concentrate on the technical issues.

Still, the result was a vindication of my research, the big payoff for those hours, days, weeks, and months spent stooped over deeds and property descriptions. Knocking down the case for res judicata, the justices declared that no one was bound by the contrived lawsuit and that because my research showed that only 54 percent—not 95 percent—of the home owners had signed the covenant, no restriction was in force.[5]

The ruling—while short of a landmark decision outlawing all such contractual language, which had to wait for cases from Michigan and Missouri in 1948—was a resounding victory. It meant that each challenge to the covenant, that each contested sale of a home, had to be litigated individually—a stipulation that made it economically impossible to defend the Washington Park subdivision contracts.

Hansberry and his family at long last could move into their new home. The decision had an immediate and profound impact, igniting one of the first waves of the white flight phenomenon that was to plague Chicago and other urban centers for decades to come. White families panicked and pushed their homes onto a crowded market and sold them cheaply. Black real estate speculators made a killing. I represented Claude Barnett, director of the Associated Negro Press. He bought three buildings and confided to me that they were the best investments he had ever made because they came at so little cost.

Ironically, Hansberry didn't live very long at the house he had waged such a long legal battle to acquire. After his wife died, he moved to Mexico in the 1940s. But even before that I had lost touch with him. Word of the Supreme Court's decision reached me while I was fighting a lawsuit in Cook County Circuit Court. If there was a celebration dinner or party for Hansberry, Dickerson, and the others, I am unaware of it.

I did write to the University of Chicago president Hutchins declaring, "We belong in the Washington Park subdivision. The Supreme Court says so." He didn't respond. However, by then my life had branched out to other endeavors. I was headed for Washington and the War Department after pulling off a feat that had nothing to do with the law or rumors of war—successfully staging the American Negro Exposition of 1940, a black world's fair.

5

The Black World's Fair

The American Negro Exposition of 1940 is a forgotten chapter in African American history. For a brief span it blazed like the noontime sun in the black press—"the greatest show of educational advancement ever exhibited by any race of people," proclaimed the *Chicago Defender*[1]—and in the consciousness of black Americans. It even gained notice in white newspapers at a time when they mostly ignored African Americans. Unfortunately, the fair never quite lived up to ambitious attendance projections, and it suffered from being, perhaps inevitably, eclipsed by news of the spreading war in Europe that was sinking the world into catastrophe.

The idea behind the two-month-long fair, running from July 4 to Labor Day, was to commemorate the seventy-fifth anniversary of emancipation. For years the notion of an exposition to showcase black achievement and the African American contributions to the making of America had consumed a real estate agent and former farm extension agent by the name of James W. Washington. He had tried for five years to persuade leaders in America's black community of the merits of the idea but "most of them laughed at him."[2] Slowly, the concept caught on. Some folks recalled that a quarter of a century earlier, a fourteen-day celebration of the fiftieth anniversary of emancipation had drawn 247,000 people to Chicago.[3] The intervening years, of course, had witnessed the Great Migration of African Americans from the South to the North and Midwest. Leading black political figures in Chicago, exulting in the dramatic improvement in the lives of Negroes accompanying the migration, latched on to Washington's idea as a way of celebrating the new vigor and swelling hopes of the African American community. The clout blacks had amassed in Chicago and Illinois politics made the metropolis on the prairie a natural location for the diamond jubilee of emancipation.

Washington, who knew many of the prominent Republican politicians of the day, had lobbied for the exposition with the legislature in the Illinois capital of Springfield. He apparently proved to be an effective lobbyist, and, as momentum for the idea gained among black opinion leaders, others added their voices to the drive to win government backing for the project. Among them was Wendell E. Green, the city's civil service commissioner, the chairman of the get-out-the-Negro-vote committee for President Franklin D. Roosevelt's campaign, and a veteran criminal trial lawyer with, as luck would have it, offices across the street from my own law firm. As we came to know each other better, he got me involved in the Roosevelt committee, and I made speeches on behalf of the president.

As a result of the lobbying in Springfield, the legislature created the Afra-Merican Emancipation Exposition Commission. Governor Henry Horner was named chairman, but the work was done by the vice chairman—Green. I confess that I was only dimly aware of the exposition when Green approached me in late 1939 to become its executive director, to be in charge of the day-to-day organization and running of the black world's fair. I came on board in January of 1940.

The job paid two hundred dollars or two hundred fifty dollars a month, a nice sum for a young lawyer still trying to establish himself during the Great Depression. More significant, the job introduced me to some of the most prominent politicians, businessmen, and journalists of the day. A. W. Williams, who as secretary-treasurer controlled under Green's direction the purse strings of the exposition, was an insurance executive whose family hailed from Louisiana. He was president of the Unity Mutual Insurance Company and owned the Unity Funeral Parlors in Chicago. Another prominent member of the expo board of directors was Claude A. Barnett, director of the Associated Negro Press news service, who oversaw the fair's publicity campaign. He was married to

Etta Moten Barnett, the female lead in the 1940s Broadway production of *Porgy and Bess* (who, by the way, had sung at my wedding). Also on the board were journalists A. N. Fields and Lucius C. Harper of the *Chicago Defender.* Alderman Earl B. Dickerson, with whom I worked on the *Hansberry* case, served on the city commission for the fair. Among the state commissioners were Dr. M. O. Bousfield, president of Liberty Life Insurance when my father merged it into his company, a Rosenwald Fund expert on African American health, and later a frequent reporter for me on conditions for black soldiers during World War II, and Charles J. Jenkins, a leading black member of the Illinois House of Representatives, whose name appeared first on the list of forty legislators sponsoring the bill establishing the exposition.[4]

The job also brought me into contact with major white politicians. Mayor Edward J. Kelly served as chairman of the city commission. Its members included Barnet Hodes, the city's corporation counsel who as such was, with Jake Arvey, the chief of Kelly's patronage operations in Cook County. Robert Bishop, a major player in the expo's administration, was a chain-smoking downstate political sage with a deep voice who was Governor Horner's handpicked representative. Prominent among the state commissioners and a leading backer of efforts in Springfield to get state funding for the project was a man who became a beloved figure in Chicago: Abraham Lincoln Marovitz, then a state senator, a marine during World War II, and later a federal judge.

Already a successful lawyer, Marovitz knew how to live in style. He had a chauffeur in those days when the hard life of the Great Depression remained a reality to millions of Americans. He came to all the expo meetings, and once when he showed up in his chauffeur-driven Cadillac, I remarked, "Abe, when I get big I'm going to have what you have." He laughed and wished me well. He became a good friend, and during the war wrote me several cards while he was stationed in the Pacific with the marines.

Years later I showed up one night at Toots Shor's, the famous restaurant in New York, and Abe, who was dining with the comedian Joe E. Lewis, called me over. Shor was a bumptious, arrogant guy, but I knew him well. Obviously drunk as he shambled over to our table, Shor motioned to me and said to Abe and Joe, "This nigger, he can come in here anytime."

Abe's face darkened in anger, and he shot up out of his chair. Now, he was in the neighborhood of five-foot-two and maybe 140 pounds dripping wet, but this ex-marine was a pugnacious guy who could fight—and would fight. "Come here, Toots," he snapped. They walked out into the entryway and Abe, a Jew, sneered at Shor, "You big fat Jew, I'm going to kill you." Shor was immediately contrite. That little episode tells you a lot about Abe; he always stood up for his friends.

Thanks to the chorus of both white and black politicians voicing support for the expo, the Illinois legislature appropriated $75,160 for the fair, Congress approved $75,000 to support it, and Chicago chipped in $2,000. The Julius Rosenwald Fund, established by a multimillionaire Sears executive and remembered today throughout the South for the African American schools it helped build, contributed $15,000. The General Education Board provided $15,000 to produce short films about African American progress in education.[5] Black colleges, schools, state boards of education, fraternities and sororities, national organizations, and business institutions provided input and cooperation in the staging of the exposition.[6]

As we began meeting to plan and organize the event, one thing became apparent: However effective he had been in churning up support for the expo when no one else cared, Washington was a loose cannon when the time came to stage the event. His ideas and thoughts were all over the map and knew no financial bounds. He talked the talk about the expo but nobody, including people in government he had successfully lobbied, would approve his handling of a dime of the fair's funds. Slowly but surely he was edged out from the effective operations of the expo, and he, perhaps understandably, became somewhat embittered and disenchanted with the rest of us. Unfortunately, he stirred up some discontent in the community toward those of us who were entrusted with running the black world's fair.

The agenda of the expo would be divided among three venues: an exhibition of three hundred works of art by African American painters and sculptors; a display of African American contributions to history encompassing 120 exhibits, including murals and dioramas; and musical and stage performances showcasing the genius of black entertainment from spirituals to operetta to that most American of musical art forms, jazz.

Three buildings of the Chicago Coliseum complex—the North Hall, the South Hall, and the Coliseum itself, with its more than fifty-two thousand square feet of floor space—would be required to house the expo's ambitious program. The *Pittsburgh Courier* saw important symbolism in the setting for the exposition. The facade of the Coliseum had been constructed with stones that originally constituted the walls of the infamous Confederate Libby Prison for Union prisoners of war in Richmond, Virginia.[7]

The official agenda for the black world's fair was as follows:

> To promote racial understanding and good will, enlighten the world on the contributions of the Negro to civilization, and make the Negro conscious of his dramatic progress since emancipation.
>
> Produce amazing facts with complete proof to substantiate the black man's claim that he has made large and valuable contributions to both American and world history and civilization.
>
> Portray, in graphic fashion, through diorama, mural and exhibit, the spectacular achievements of America's Tenth Citizen from his voyage to the New World with Columbus to his status in the nation in 1940. ["Tenth Citizen" referred to the statistic that African Americans made up 10 percent of the U.S. population.][8]

Alonzo J. Aden, the renowned art authority from Howard University, assembled what was billed as "the most comprehensive and representative collection of the Negro's art that has ever been presented to public view."[9] It was an astounding collection of black art and was the first national exposition of black artists.

The juries responsible for selecting work for the exhibition included such notables as Daniel Catton Rich, director of the Art Institute of Chicago; Edward Bruce, director of the Section of Fine Arts of the U.S. Treasury; Holger Cahill, director of the Federal Art Projects; and George Thorpe, director of the Illinois Art Project. The works included landscapes, portraits, still lifes, pastoral scenes, biblical subjects, historical images, and depictions of everyday Negro life.

Headlining the show were twelve works by the greatest of black painters, Henry Ossawa Tanner, who had died only three years before. Also on display were paintings by Robert S. Duncanson (billed as "the first Negro painter to receive recognition in Europe"),[10] Edwin A. Harleston (a close friend of my father's from their Boston days), William Harper, Edward M. Bannister ("the first to gain fame in this country"),[11] Marvin Gray Johnson, and Albert Alexander Smith. The show also exhibited sculpture such as *The Mother,* a powerful study by New York artist Richmond Barthe of a woman holding a son who had been lynched.

Contemporary artists were recognized, with prizes going to Charles White of Illinois, Frederic Flemister of Georgia, Eldzier Cortor of Illinois, and Marvin Smith of New York. White's black-and-white *There Were No Crops This Year* adorned the cover of the show's program. (White was the husband of the accomplished sculptor Elizabeth Catlett, who was my wife's first cousin.) Cartoons by Elmer Simms Campbell and ceramics as well as other decorative arts were on display as well.

"One of those unexpected great little shows" is how the *Chicago Defender* characterized the exhibition.[12]

Perhaps the most attention was focused on the historical exhibits. Directing a staff of more than 120 artists, craftsmen, and skilled workers in erecting the dioramas and exhibits was Erik Lindgren, a Swedish-born and German-educated designer who had been responsible for the Illinois exhibits at the world's fairs in New York and San Francisco. He was an incredible artist, and we all got to know him quite well. Lindgren liked his drink, and for all his accomplishments, some of us will remember him for a concoction he produced at Christmastime called glogg. I can testify from personal experience that glogg was guaranteed to knock you dead.

Lindgren had been dispatched to work on the black expo by Governor Horner.[13] His top aide was Joseph W. Evans, director of drafting and construction. Lindgren was full of praise for Evans's work:

> Evans is one of the most capable men I have ever encountered in the field. He is unselfish, unaffected by the petty jealousies which plague so many artists, and a tireless and brilliant worker. He is a natural leader, and has the ability to work painstakingly so that a job will be done right. I was impressed by him when I first saw some of his designs and was insistent that he work with us.[14]

Lindgren lauded all involved in the exposition: "When I started supervising this project a few months ago I was amazed at the quality of work these persons were turning out. Some of them, of course, were experienced Negro artists, but there also was a number of young and old persons who had to be trained in the minor aspects of fashioning the exhibits. The latter work is excellent."[15]

To our twenty-first-century ears, Lindgren's words about Evans and the other black craftsmen and artists sound perhaps a little fulsome and a bit tainted by condescension. But we must take his comments in the context of his times, prewar America when the white and black worlds were mostly isolated from each other, when most depictions of Negroes in radio and movies were comedic or servant roles, usually far from flattering and too often demeaning. It was a time when Joe Louis was just beginning to break the color line by rising from being regarded as a black athlete to being acknowledged as an American hero. In that vein, Lindgren comes through as a man who is learning something about his fellow human beings. And that, after all, was the point of the expo. As Charles R. Hall, manager of the Chicago Coliseum, put it, "There is so much that the Negro has done in this country that the rest of the population doesn't know about that it will be good to put it on display."[16] As the *Pittsburgh Courier* noted, the exposition afforded Evans and other young blacks "their first opportunity for real work in their chosen field."[17] In my experience with Lindgren, I never saw anything but an artist working with other artists to put on the best show they could.

In all, Lindgren supervised construction of thirty-one dioramas encompassing black involvement in the history of mankind: the building of the sphinx in ancient Egypt; African tribes smelting iron; Alonzo Pietro, a black man, piloting the Christopher Columbus flagship the *Santa Maria;* Negroes working American cotton fields; the Tenth Cavalry charging on San Juan Hill in the Spanish-American War; and Matt Henson accompanying Admiral Peary to the North Pole, to name just a few. While Lindgren was responsible for construction of the dioramas, the ideas for the themes came from Barnett, Horace Cayton, and myself but principally from Barnett. He had an intense interest in Africa and made sure the ancestral homeland was not forgotten in documenting the history of the black Americans. Cayton, who had the title of assistant to the director and who also was running the Good Shepherd Community Center at Fiftieth Street and South Park Avenue, plumbed his deep knowledge of African American history to help us fill in the details for the content of the dioramas.

Accompanying the three-dimensional dioramas were twenty-four large murals illustrating other chapters in the African American's role in American history. The murals, such as ten-foot paintings depicting black soldiers fighting in France during World War I, African American troops in the Union army during the Civil War, and a black French regiment that laid siege to the British at Savannah, Georgia, in the Revolutionary War, were the work of the noted black artist William Edouard Scott. Other murals illustrated Haitian peasants making tortillas and Marian Anderson performing at the Lincoln Memorial in Washington, D.C. Hanging between the murals were two dozen portraits of prominent blacks and mixed blood individuals, including Russian poet Aleksandr Pushkin and French novelist Alexandre Dumas. The dioramas, murals, and other exhibits were arrayed around a twelve-foot wooden replica of the Lincoln Tomb in Springfield, created by black sculptor Robert Jones, in tribute to the Great Emancipator.

A sports hall of fame paid tribute to sporting greats such as Joe Louis, Jesse Owens, and Ralph Metcalfe. On display were a number of Louis's trophies, as well as a plaster cast of Joe's powerful punching right hand and the boxing gloves he wore when he knocked out German fighter Max Schmeling in a bout in 1938 that had assumed patriotic dimensions because of the threat of war in Europe.

Complementing the art and historical exhibits were performances by leading black entertainers of prewar America. Noted author Arna Bontemps served as research and cultural director for the expo and principal writer of *Cavalcade of the American Negro,* a book surveying black American life throughout the history of the republic and produced by the Illinois Writers Project in conjunction with the expo. Bontemps and Edward Embree, head of the Rosenwald Fund, were instrumental in attracting poet Langston Hughes to become our director of performing arts. His biographer recalls that Hughes was hired to prepare an original revue titled *The Tropics after Dark* and to write a book for *Jubilee: A Cavalcade of the Negro Theater,* described as a "compendium of scenes from celebrated musicals such as 'Shuffle Along.' "[18]

The most impressive production in the Coliseum's North Hall Theater was *The Chimes of Normandy*. The Chicago Operetta Company put on a "Negro version" of Robert Planquette's famous opéra comique. The performances by the eighty-member cast, staged by Harry Minturn and choreographed by Sammy Dyer, were a big hit with all the audiences. "Uncle Sam's singers and dancers have done it again . . . and on a greater scale than ever before!" proclaimed the *Pittsburgh Courier,* which called it "a sensational Grade A musical show, with flashy, modern dances."[19]

All this makes the expo sound very high toned, and it mostly was. But even Shakespeare knew you had to play to the cheap seats as well. I was aware that world's fairs had their risqué elements, the most famous example being Little Egypt at the 1893 World's Columbian Exposition and Sally Rand at the 1933 world's fair in Chicago. So I proposed we have a nude ranch, combining the naughty with a play on the words "dude ranch." Under a photograph of "one of the pretties" appearing in the nude ranch, the caption in the *Chicago Defender* declared the show "is expected to outdo Sally Rand's best." The girls in the floor show, a *Defender* article said, "danced about the place with a religious fervor that is hotter than that."[20] Well, I was put right on this issue immediately by Green. Very prim and proper, as befitting a man who would later become the first black superior court judge in Illinois, Green took me aside and told me in no uncertain terms that nudity would not be part of the American Negro Exposition! So the nude ranch promptly closed. We did, in the end, have a room where the men could go to order a drink while ogling a few scantily clad girls.

Like any big event, the expo had to have a beauty queen. A newspaper article declared that we were conducting a "nationwide contest to select the most beautiful and shapely Negro girl in the country" to be our Miss Bronze America. In a good-natured acknowledgment of an issue that bedeviled black America then as it does now, I declared, "Entrants may range from nut brown, ebony, tan, high brown, to high yellow and blue veined. Winners will not be chosen on the basis of color."[21] The winner, Miriam Ali of Chicago, was described by her sponsor, the *Defender*, as "a beautiful café-au-lait colored nineteen-year-old girl with lustrous black hair and shining eyes."[22]

Another contest was held to select an official poster. It drew more than a hundred entries. Robert S. Pious, a Harlem artist born in Mississippi and educated at the School of the Art Institute of Chicago, won first place with a poster of a man and woman partly surrounded with a laurel wreath and icons of black achievement, with the visage of Abraham Lincoln looming in the background.[23]

As spring gave way to summer and July 4 neared, the pace of preparations quickened. The pounding of hammers and singing of saws reverberated through the Coliseum as the exhibit booths were erected. Evans's staff more than doubled in the final weeks leading up to the start of the exposition.[24] The dioramas were being completed, some of the figures carved out of wood but most made of baked clay and painted in watercolors.[25] Scott was working sixteen hours a day putting the finishing touches to the mural displays so they would be ready on time.[26] I seemed to be constantly in motion, making sure everyone was on schedule; gathering the ticket sellers, guides, and other support staff needed for the opening; and occasionally smoothing over the ruffled feathers that are inevitable anytime a large number of people come together in a major artistic endeavor.

Expectations were running high. There were even press reports that President Roosevelt might show up to launch the expo himself.[27] Virtually every news account of the impending fair mentioned my name prominently. "Truman K. Gibson's dynamic influence" read a headline in the *Chicago Defender* for a story about exposition preparations. "Gibson, youthful director, organizing genius of fair" trumpeted another headline, this one in the *Pittsburgh Courier.* That story was accompanied by three photographs of me with the caption proclaiming that "he smiles at the thought of the bright prospects of the coming celebration." And I was only twenty-nine! I couldn't help but be flattered by that kind of stuff. But when I took on the tough task of representing black interests in the War Department, I was to learn just how fleeting fame and newspaper gratitude can be.

Finally the big day arrived, and the American Negro Exposition opened with great fanfare. Roosevelt didn't make it in person, but he did kick off the event. At one-thirty P.M. on Thursday, July 4, the president of the United States, sitting in his home in Hyde Park, New York, pressed a button, flooding the Coliseum hall in light and formally opening the expo. I introduced the main speaker, Mayor Kelly, as "a man who went down into his own pocket to aid the exposition." Kelly's speech set just the right tone: "The nation pays a debt of gratitude to the Negroes today. Not alone for their contributions to the arts and sciences, not alone to the good and great names that stand out in the book of American achievements, but to the great mass of 14 million Negroes who help to form the backbone of American democracy."[28]

Attendance was brisk at the start, and it was not only African Americans who plunked down the quarter admission fee. The exposition enjoyed significant white attendance. The event, of course, had earned a ton of publicity in African American newspapers, thanks to the efforts of Barnett and to the fact that several black journalists were actively involved in the fair. The *Defender* ran a series of cartoons, entitled *Exposition Follies,* by Lacy Jackson heralding the forthcoming celebration of black America. One Jackson cartoon featured a couple standing before a fair poster featuring an attractive young woman with the enticing caption of "Meet me at the American Negro Exposition." Enticing because the woman was nude! I wonder if Lacy had heard about my idea for the nude ranch.

The fair also got ink in Chicago's white newspapers. Several days before the opening, the *Herald American* in its Sunday, June 30, editions previewed the fair and reproduced the expo poster. The *Tribune* covered the opening event with a story and small picture of Washington being congratulated by U.S. senator James Slattery of Illinois. The *Daily Times* on July 23 devoted a full page to photographs of dioramas and sports trophies. One of the pictures showed Mrs. Tillie Lawson, sixty-two, with the American flag she had crocheted over two years using 198 spools of cotton.

The fair got plenty of airtime on two radio stations, one on the AM and the other the FM dial, owned by Chess Records. Al Benson, one of the first black DJs, was a great help. Black music was becoming more popular with whites, so Benson's shows helped get the word out about the black world's fair to white audiences as well as African Americans.

Music, of course, was an important element of the exposition. *The Tropics after Dark,* the musical production written by Arna Bontemps and Langston Hughes with music composed by Margaret Bonds and Zilner Randolph, arranger for Woody Herman's orchestra, was staged with a nightclub ambiance by producer Ted Blackman, who had previewed the show at the Cozy Corner in Detroit before opening it at the fair.[29] Hughes wrote two songs for *Tropics* and *Cavalcade.* One was set to music by gospel composer Tommy Dorsey and the other was scored by Duke Ellington.[30] Unfortunately, the talent for *The Tropics after Dark* proved too costly, and, as the *Pittsburgh Courier* reported, the show "gave up the theatrical ghost after two weeks of much praise, fair crowds and a terrific overhead."[31]

Duke Ellington had flown into Chicago in June, and after an all-day conference with me, he signed on as musical director and consultant for the exposition.[32] Ellington had performed frequently in Chicago and agreed to have his band do a one-week gig for us. His Chicago headquarters was the Vincennes Hotel at Thirty-fourth Street and Vincennes Avenue, which was owned by me, Ted Jones, an accountant who was an associate in my law office, and Carl Nelson, a bodyguard for Joe Louis and a police sergeant who was what was termed the "bull dick" of the Forty-eighth Street police station, which meant he collected the payoffs from policy gambling for the police captain. So I got to know Ellington intimately.

Ellington brought a lot of other musicians on board, most notably Lionel Hampton. Also lending their efforts to the fair were songwriter

W. C. Handy, composer of "St. Louis Blues"; Will Marion Cook, a principal musical writer for the Ziegfeld Follies, my wife's godson, and the father of an ambassador to Niger; and musicians William Grant Still, Harry T. Burleigh, Noble Sissle, Count Basie, Erskine Hawkins, Fats Waller, and J. C. Johnson. The ever frenetic Horace Cayton used his connections to lure the great Paul Robeson to Chicago. Robeson performed for three weeks, singing "Ol' Man River" and a collection of Negro spirituals.

Crowds also thronged among the exhibitions. The historic dioramas and Scott's murals weren't the only draws. The City of Chicago provided a topographical map of the South Side black community and models of the DuSable cabin that was Chicago's first structure, the Ida B. Wells housing project, and the George Cleveland Hall Library. The Rosenwald Fund and Provident Hospital supplied health and medical exhibits. On the lighter side was a depiction of an old-fashioned medicine show. Black family life was illustrated in a series of dioramas based on the book *The Negro Family in the United States* by E. Franklin Frazier, who collaborated on the display. Paying heed to the vital role of religion in black life, muralist Aaron Douglas reproduced large versions of seven of his illustrations from the book *God's Trombones* by James Weldon Johnson. A number of federal agencies, including the Agriculture Department, the Federal Works Agency, the National Youth Administration, the Social Security Administration, the Civilian Conservation Corps, the Labor Department, and the Civil Aeronautics Authority, had booths. The U.S. Post Office displayed a recently released Booker T. Washington stamp. Liberia, described as "the only republic controlled by Negroes on the continent of Africa," erected an exhibit portraying its history as a nation founded for the settlement of freed slaves.[33]

Special speakers highlighted some days. Henry Wallace, the secretary of agriculture and soon to be vice president of the United States, spoke three times. He was a good friend of liberal America and of Paul Robeson. Wallace's service in the Agriculture Department had brought to his attention the condition of black farmers in the South, and he had appointed several Negroes to Agriculture Department posts. Robeson enthralled audiences with his recounting of his life story: his battling his way to all-American fame on the Rutgers football team, his earning a law degree from Columbia, and the problems he faced when hired by a law firm that put him in a corner with no real work to do and only trotted him out from time to time for show. Langston Hughes charmed fairgoers with his recollections of the life of an artist and readings of his poetry.

It's a fact of life that big talent is often accompanied by big egos. Paul Robeson was a terror when it came to women. One day a prominent official of the exposition arrived home to find his wife in Robeson's arms. The wife was anything but contrite. "It's your fault," she snapped at her husband. "You knew he was a dirty son of a bitch!" Their marriage survived.

One other thing I remember about Robeson was that he loved watermelon. Many blacks avoided watermelon because of the stereotype associated with the fruit and African Americans, but not Robeson. Every night he savored ice-cold watermelon at a basement watermelon stand at Thirty-seventh Street and South Park Avenue.

Langston Hughes was embittered by his experience in Chicago. He made a series of outrageous and unfounded charges, among them that a white Chicago politician had dictated a history of African Americans to cash in on the government appropriations for the fair and that Chicago labor unions inflicted unreasonable demands on expo officials. The *Tropics* show was stripped of his dialogue and given short shrift in rehearsal, Hughes also charged, while the *Cavalcade* withered on the vine and was never staged. Finally, he alleged that I told him the fair was losing money and it wouldn't be able to pay him.[34] That was a complete fantasy as far as I was involved. All money matters were handled by A. W. Williams. All government moneys were accounted for. No losses to my knowledge were incurred. Indeed, I believe the exposition took in enough money to turn some back to the state. Not even a hint of corruption was ever alleged other than by Hughes. With the exception of one minor suit by a woman worker over her pay, which we won, no litigation marred the financial record of the exposition.

Still, attendance fell far short of the two million predicted. After the fair closed, it disappeared from the public consciousness. It's not hard to understand why. The war virtually obliterated memories of the American Negro Exposition. France had fallen to the Nazi blitzkrieg. England stood alone, and the Battle of Britain was about to commence. It was increasingly apparent to any thinking individual that it was only a matter of time before the United States would be drawn into the conflict.

Yet, the expo would leave a legacy in two ways. For one thing, more than six decades later, in 2003, the Art Institute of Chicago exhibited its collection of masterpieces of African American art, an exhibition that featured the artists whose work had graced the expo. The institute gave me an award for my work during the expo in spreading the word about African American painters and sculptors.

The second legacy was splashed across the silver screen. The history of black life as depicted in the colorful but static dioramas of Eric Lindgren, Joseph Evans, and the black artists and craftsmen was brought to life in Frank Capra's *The Negro Soldier* during World War II. The expo produced the outline for this important film explaining to America the role its black citizens had played in the life of the country.

Although the expo fell short of some expectations, those of us involved in it were more than satisfied with the attention it had garnered for African Americans. However, even in *our* minds it was being supplanted by the events in Europe. Within a few short months after the closing of the black world's fair, I would be drawn into the nation's preparations for war. That change would have many profound influences on my life, not the least of which would be the blossoming of a friendship that had begun in Chicago.

6

Joe Louis: Chicago

The first time I laid eyes on Joe Louis he was perched on the corner of a desk in one of the offices at our law firm, taking a bite out of an apple. It was 1935, and my assignment was to keep this up-and-coming boxer occupied and amused. The only reason Joe had shown up at our law firm was that he had accompanied his manager, Julian Black, there. Black owned substantial real estate on the South Side of Chicago and employed Irvin Mollison as his attorney. While Black and Mollison conducted their business, Mollison asked me to entertain the future heavyweight boxing champion of the world.

Though not yet the world champion, Joe already was famous in the black community because his powerful punching portended great things. It is not too much to say that in an era when black opportunities in professional sports continued to be virtually nonexistent outside of segregated venues, Joe inspired tremendous hope for a black breakthrough into the white-dominated world. He would not be the first black heavyweight champion. Jack Johnson battled his way to that distinction in 1908 and held the crown until 1915, but his drinking, carousing, and marrying white women at a time when white America's racial attitudes were taking a turn for the worse had slammed the door shut on another African American contender for a couple of decades. Now Joe had his foot in the door, and under the right circumstances it appeared just possible that he might achieve the breakthrough. Black America sensed that something extraordinary was about to happen.

Now Julian Black was determined that Joe would not repeat Johnson's mistakes, and he knew Johnson well because they had become business partners. Joe didn't drink and didn't mess around with women, especially white women—well, at least not in any way that would attract a lot of unfavorable publicity. The truth was that Joe did have an eye for the ladies, and a few years later I would find myself enlisted in Black's strategy to keep it out of the public eye. But he didn't drink, and he didn't smoke. He did, however, have a fierce appetite for apples, and he was usually chowing down on one during our conversations.

I, like every other African American, was intrigued by Joe and the possibilities he represented. I had never seen a boxing match, had no interest in the sport, and of course had no way of knowing the huge role it was to play in my life. Still, I knew chance had placed me in the presence of someone special who might make history. After all, he had won a Golden Gloves championship, had fought a slew of amateur fights, and had twelve professional victories under his belt.

During these first meetings, Joe wasn't very talkative. He later acquired a comfort level in conversing with people he didn't know. But in 1935, he was still naturally reticent, in part because he had a slight speech impediment. That put the burden of conversing on me. Ours turned out to be a mostly one-way conversation, with me talking and Joe responding—only occasionally—in monosyllables.

We slowly warmed to each other. Athletics obviously jumped out as a natural topic. And, as luck would have it, we did have a common interest—horseback riding—probably acquired from the same source, John Roxborough, Joe's other manager. I met Roxborough through family friends in 1932 when, as a college student, I was in Detroit on a summer job of selling "industrial" insurance policies, basically burial insurance costing a quarter to seventy-five cents a week, for my father's firm in an area of town called Black Bottom. I got to know the Roxborough family very well. John Roxborough's brother, Charlie, was a lawyer, a politician who had served in the Michigan legislature, and the owner of an insurance company. John Roxborough, however, had made his wealth in the numbers game, a fortune large enough for him and his wife, named Cutie, to buy a farm outside Detroit with a barn full of polo ponies. He taught me to ride, and that summer I would spend my weekends there getting a taste of the high life before returning to the dismal trade of selling cheap insurance policies in Black Bottom.

A year later, John Roxborough, who knew Joe from amateur fights, approached the nineteen-year-old boxer while Joe was training in a Detroit gym and took him under his wing. Joe was the son of an Alabama sharecropper and had spent a couple of months working on a Ford Motor Company Lincoln assembly line before abandoning that job to devote all his energies to his dream of a life as a successful fighter. (Ford later would give Joe a brand-new Lincoln every year.) Roxborough gave the young boxer clothes, outfitted him with the bandages, rubbing alcohol, and other accoutrements of the boxing life, took him home for dinner, introduced him to a style of life he never imagined black folks lived, and, I presume, instructed him in the agreeable sport of horseback riding.

In any event, an affinity for horseback riding provided an opening that pulled me into Joe's orbit. I owned a couple of horses at a stable near Provident Hospital on the South Side. Joe rode horses from the stable over into Washington Park. A frequent riding companion was Charlie Glenn, a Cadillac salesman who served all the numbers guys and had sold Joe a car. (During the war Glenn would get Joe to invest forty thousand dollars in the Rhumboogie nightclub on Garfield Boulevard, a deal which would have fateful consequences for me.) After Joe became the famous champion and found himself doing a lot of traveling, Glenn made sure that there was a car readily available to him. When Joe went out to California, Glenn would put him on the train, meet the train in California with a Cadillac in the parking lot, and drive him around. Joe always had a driver, he never drove himself. Glenn was an excellent horseman, and they would ride through Washington Park. Several times, I rode along. You couldn't miss the girls hanging around the stable in hopes of hooking up with the most famous black athlete in America.

I wouldn't want to leave the impression that I formed a close friendship with Joe in those early days. He was in some ways a difficult person. He didn't open up to people he hadn't known for a while or to those he hadn't come to trust, as he did with Charlie Glenn. Joe's constant companion was Freddy Guinyard, a childhood friend from Detroit. As the years went on and Joe's accomplishments accumulated and his fame spread, Joe became a man on the go, frequently away from Chicago where my life was anchored. Joe was a guy for activity, not for talking. Besides horses, golf became a passion. And as champion, he sponsored a women's softball team called the Brown Bombers. I rode, but I didn't play golf. I represented Jack Blackburn, the indispensable trainer who beat the fundamentals of boxing into Joe, but that didn't make me Joe's friend. Our relationship would grow and mature during World War II and the postwar years, but that was still a while away.

In 1937, I was pushed out of the Dawson-Mollison firm by Dawson for some reason that I can no longer remember. (Years later, after World War II, Dawson got upset with me again, this time over a plum position I had landed. I had been appointed a member of Chicago's land clearance commission by Mayor Kennelly. Dawson was bitter that his view on such an appointment was not sought, and he upbraided Kennelly for not consulting him and turned cold on me. I became the secretary of the commission, which supervised land condemned and seized by the city and subsequently sold. At issue was a swatch of land near Lake Michigan on the South Side with rooming houses lining the streets. Some years later this neighborhood was razed and redeveloped into a community of townhouses, mid-rises, and high-rises called Lake Meadows, which is where I live today.)

Dawson, thankfully, was not a man to carry a grudge. Bighearted and ever ready to help out a young black man, he permitted me to put his name on the new law firm I set up in the Supreme Liberty Life Insurance Building. Joining me as a partner was Ted Jones, a certified public accountant who would later handle Joe Louis's tax problems.

Shortly after this, Mollison advanced to become a judge in the U.S. Customs Court. Julian Black, looking for another lawyer to represent his real estate interests on the South Side, had come to know me as Mollison's partner and settled on me as his lawyer. Black was a fascinating character. Born into an extremely poor family, he came to Chicago from Wisconsin and found work with Charlie Jackson, an undertaker who was the éminence grise to the South Side policy guys. Charlie and his brother Dan Jackson were favorites of Big Bill Thompson, the Republican mayor of Chicago who had angered the city's Democratic white ethnic population by putting African Americans into jobs in city hall. Dan Jackson found himself the victim in one of the more embarrassing but virtually unknown episodes of the Thompson years, a crime that was hushed up. Jackson had arrived at City Hall with seventy thousand dollars in payoff money from the policy operators for the mayor when he was accosted in the foyer of the seat of city government by a gunman. Jackson had no choice but to hand over the cash, and Thompson had no choice but to cover up the crime that had occurred under his very nose.

The Jacksons, thanks to the fortune they amassed from policy and the undertaking trade, lived the high life. They ate well and they dressed well, in sharp contrast to the gold chain–adorned hoodlums of today. They drank, but they didn't mess with dope. They entered horses in the big sulky races, and Dan Jackson drove. Hunting was a passion; they shot pheasants and owned land with a duck blind near Monee, Illinois. I was no hunter, so I never went out there, but they invited me to dinner to partake of the bounty of their shotguns. Unfortunately for me, they demonstrated what happened before the cooked duck reached the dinner table. They gleefully gathered the day's kill, placed the dead ducks in a duck press, and squeezed the blood out of them. That turned me off of ducks for all time.

Opportunity, not duck meat, was what Charlie Jackson offered Julian Black. The young Black kept busy driving Jackson's horse-drawn death wagon. As this hearse wound its way through the more affluent neighborhoods of the Black Metropolis, he would peer into the windows of the dining and drawing rooms of Chicago's black elites to have revealed for him a style of high living to which he immediately aspired. Hunkered over the reins of the horses, he swore to himself that he one day would host fancy dinners, toast important friends with expensive drinks, and throw swank parties for the black smart set. By the time I knew him, he had achieved all that and more. Besides his many real estate holdings, he partnered with former boxing champ Jack Johnson to run a black-and-tan cabaret called Elite No. 2 and was raking in cash from his policy operation.

Black had a bad hip that affected the way he walked. His reddish brown complexion and straight hair were evidence of his mix of Indian ancestry. He was very, very clever and especially clever with numbers. And, through Roxborough, he had acquired a piece of the man who would become the world's most famous black athlete.

It wasn't only real estate matters that brought Black to me. In late 1935, when I was still with Mollison, Black introduced me to a new client, Jack Blackburn. What an extraordinary character Blackburn was. A ferocious boxer himself, Blackburn, though seldom weighing more than a welterweight, fought all comers and once even bloodied the great Jack Johnson, who never forgave him for it. But Blackburn had a dark side. I've been quoted as saying that when Blackburn was drinking, he was wholly unnatural.[1] An aphorism from the South has it that when a guy's eyes get red, avoid him. When Blackburn got drunk, his eyes turned blood red, he was ungovernable, mean, and just plain bad, with his temper just a hair trigger away from violence. In 1909, he shot and killed another man and wounded two women, one of them his "white wife or paramour," after some sort of quarrel. Blackburn was sentenced to ten or fifteen years in prison but was released after four.[2]

Now, another murder charge had been lodged against him. The details of the case remain obscure, and the record is virtually nonexistent. A United Press story carried by the *New York Sun* on March 3, 1936, reported that Blackburn, with two other men, faced manslaughter charges in "the fatal shooting of Enoch Hauser, Negro, in a South Side argument last fall. . . . With Blackburn at the time of the argument were William Parnell and John Bowman. Blackburn and Parnell, it is alleged, argued with Bowman over the purchase of a garage. The shooting, in which Hauser was killed and a child wounded, followed."[3]

That's not the way it went down. The truth was that Jack liked to gamble and had been shooting craps, while of course drinking, when he caught another player cheating. That proved more than enough to ignite Jack's fiery temper, and he pulled a gun and fired. Perhaps because of his inebriated state, he missed his target and hit a little girl, killing her. She was eight years old.

Black had hired me to represent Jack at the coroner's inquest, and I showed up full of the law that I had learned at the University of Chicago and eager to expose my knowledge to the benefit of my client. But the fix already was in. Benny Grant, later an alderman, was the deputy coroner and he pretty much told me to shut up. He let Jack walk; still, an indictment followed. That was the subject of the United Press report. Then the case just disappeared. Ronald K. Fried, who wrote a book about boxing trainers, reported that neither he nor Louis biographer Chris Mead could find another word about the murder or the trial. Fried speculated that Black and Roxborough had used their influence to prevent news coverage of the case and noted that six days after the United Press report, prosecutors simply dropped the charge.[4] In fact, a civil suit had been filed by the girl's family, and Black and Roxborough paid a settlement to get the indictment quashed. Justice is not the word to characterize what happened here, but that's the way America worked in the mid-1930s.

It happened because Joe needed Blackburn. The demanding, pushy, confrontational Blackburn knew all there was to know about boxing. Some people called Joe a natural boxer. There's no such thing. Sure, some athletes have a special talent for a sport, and Joe, a brawler from his days on the mean streets of Detroit, knew how to punch. Blackburn transformed him from street fighter to professional boxer, teaching him the skills of balance and ring strategy. Joe immediately appreciated the knowledge of his mentor and listened carefully to what Blackburn said and almost always followed his advice.

It was from Blackburn that Joe developed the habit of calling people Chappie. That's what Blackburn commonly called other men, and the young boxer picked that up like any impressionable young man mimics the traits of an admirable older mentor who serves as his guide into the bewildering world of adulthood and professional life.

Though Joe had a dozen professional victories under his belt by the time I met him, I remained unfamiliar with the sport. In those early years, I saw only two Louis contests—but what fights they were! The first one was the June 22, 1937, bout when Joe won the world heavyweight championship. More than forty-five thousand people turned out to see that battle in Comiskey Park, the South Side home of the

Chicago White Sox. Joe battered the champion James J. Braddock with his powerful jab and then in the eighth round scored a technical knockout that ignited a frenzy of celebration among the twenty thousand blacks watching from the bleachers. I was lucky enough to have ringside seats along with my father, my brother Harry, and *Pittsburgh Courier* sports editor Wendel Smith. It's difficult to characterize the atmosphere of a championship boxing contest. It's a cliché, but it's entirely accurate to say that there's an electricity in the air at a big boxing match. I found myself mesmerized by the excitement. Crowd noise thundered in my ears, and a pall of cigarette and cigar smoke hovered over the ring. Perhaps because I was unfamiliar with the sport, my memories survive as a confusing mix, a kaleidoscope of images of Joe pounding away at Braddock, of us jumping from our seats to cheer, and of my heart virtually exploding with pride, joy, and relief when Joe vanquished Braddock. It was a unique experience.

After the fight, African Americans poured out into the streets to celebrate. In New York, exuberant Joe Louis fans surrounded the Cadillac of the famous vaudeville comedian Dusty Fletcher, whose trademark song was "Open the Door, Richard." The crowd rocked the auto back and forth, Fletcher later told Joe. Everywhere you went that night, folks had radios on, listening to the postgame commentary about the new black champion of the world. Those are the kinds of memories you can carry for years, and while the details may fade, the power of the emotions remain as strong as ever.

The only other fight I saw before the postwar years proved to be another stunner—Louis's rematch against the German boxer Max Schmeling, the only man who had beaten Joe in his professional career up to then. That defeat came on July 19, 1936, in New York's Yankee Stadium. Joe readily acknowledged that he had lost because he did not follow Blackburn's advice to "keep your guard up"[5] and thus allowed Schmeling's relentless counterpunching to wear him down for a twelfth-round knockout.[6]

This loss essentially hung an asterisk over Louis's championship. The man Louis had beaten for the championship, Braddock, was nobody's idea of a great fighter, and everyone believed Joe needed to beat

Schmeling to cement his hold on the world heavyweight championship. In the meantime, Hitler's Nazi Germany had cast a long shadow of aggression and oppression over Europe. Hitler had annexed Austria and was menacing Czechoslovakia. A rematch between the two fighters was arranged in 1938, and as the months leading up to it progressed, the bout became increasingly characterized as one of democratic America versus Nazi Germany.

American boxing interests feared that if Schmeling were to win, he wouldn't defend the championship anywhere but in Germany. The fight naturally took on racial overtones. How could it not with a black American facing off with a member of Hitler's Aryan race? Schmeling himself didn't see it that way, but an Associated Press story from Berlin reported that "it is tacitly understood that a Louis victory would be taken here as a disgrace from the Nazi racial viewpoint."[7] America's white newspapers, incredibly given the times, warmed to the black champion, and many sportswriters cast him simply as an American.

Like the first fight, this one took place at Yankee Stadium, within a month of being exactly two years later, on June 22, 1938. Joe destroyed him, landing crushing blows that broke two of Schmeling's vertebrae. I was seated at ringside again but on the opposite side of the ring from where Schmeling suffered those blows. Still, I was close enough to hear Schmeling scream when Joe hit him in the kidney. Joe, determined to extract revenge for the blemish on his record, landed a frenzy of punches and jabs that scored a technical knockout over Schmeling just two minutes and four seconds into the first round.[8] Like the Braddock fight, this was an exhilarating experience for me. The noise, the already high stakes further inflamed by international politics, and the swiftness of the victory added up to an unforgettable moment.

That turned out to be the last fight I was to see until after the war, but my relationship with Joe continued. I traveled frequently with Julian Black to New York City for talks with Mike Jacobs, the preeminent boxing promoter of the day, about boxing matches for Joe. I also represented Joe's legal interests while my accountant partner Ted Jones looked after his financial interests. The most notable case was a libel suit against *Look* magazine in 1939. *Look* had published a scurrilous article about Joe's womanizing. Now, the truth be told, he was guilty of a lot of that, but the article conflicted with the public image that Black and Blackburn had assiduously worked out to portray Joe to white America. So we sued. And *Look* settled. The settlement worked this way: Joe would give an interview to writer Barney Nagler for *Look,* and the champ would be paid twenty thousand dollars. Unfortunately, it went awry. For some reason, Joe told Nagler that he was hanging up his gloves. Of course, Joe had no intention of retiring, but the article was published and quickly proven to be wrong. Nagler never forgave Joe, and his ill will toward the champ colored the book he eventually wrote about Joe.

The work for Joe was just one facet of my life during that time. I was trying to build my new law practice, working on the *Hansberry* case, and running the American Negro Exposition. Still, I had achieved a professional relationship with the heavyweight boxing champion of the world, although little did I know then how our relationship would blossom during the coming war.

7

On to the War Department

President Roosevelt thought he could solve the military's race problem with a few government appointments of African Americans.

Obviously a heavy dose of sarcasm and hyperbole went into writing those words. But it's hard to avoid the conclusion that Roosevelt didn't display much commitment to tackling the injustices for blacks in the armed forces. His goal in making the appointments that would bring me to Washington envisioned shunting the race issue aside for a while as he built national consensus for the anti-Nazi crusade. He was also trying to assuage the black anger he faced in an election year.

That anger boiled in the aftermath of a White House meeting the president had with several black leaders in the fall of 1940. That session on September 27 grew out of two years of African American agitation and lobbying to overturn repressive measures against African Americans in the military, a campaign particularly targeting the army since the navy had pretty much squeezed blacks out of meaningful seagoing service. "Double V" would become the rallying cry, a call for victory over fascism abroad and victory over segregation at home, a goal that originated in the *Pittsburgh Courier* and that caught fire in the hearts and imagination of black America.

Carrying the black agenda into the White House for the September conference with Roosevelt were Walter White of the NAACP, T. Arnold Hill, an adviser in the National Youth Administration formerly with the National Urban League, and A. Philip Randolph of the Brotherhood of Sleeping Car Porters. They presented Roosevelt, Secretary of the Navy Frank Knox, and Undersecretary of War Robert P. Patterson with a memorandum listing their demands, calling above all for integration of the armed services and specifically proposing training of African American officers; incorporation of blacks into all phases of the U.S. Army Air Corps from pilots, navigators, and bombers to radiomen and mechanics; recruitment of African American doctors, dentists, and pharmacists; a black role in administration of the draft; service in the navy beyond the menial roles relegated to Negroes at the time; and participation of black women as army, navy, and Red Cross nurses.[1] Roosevelt's response to these demands was, according to White's biographer, "predictably vague," and the three black leaders exploded in anger when in October the White House released a statement saying they had acquiesced to continued segregation.[2]

Still, as reported in the first chapter of this book, the army's attitude precluded anything but continued segregation. The War Department—and remember that in the days before consolidation of military policy under the secretary of defense that "War Department" specifically meant the army—responded to the September 27 conference with its own memorandum. That document provided for a quota system to employ blacks in the army based on their representation in the population, separate African American organizations in major branches of the service, black officers assigned to Negro units, opportunity for training of African Americans in officer candidate schools, segregated aviation training for blacks, and equal opportunity for work at arsenals and army posts.

But above all, the army document declared that "the policy of the War Department is not to intermingle colored and white enlisted personnel in the same regimental organizations. This policy has been proven satisfactory over a long period of years, and to make changes now would produce situations destructive to morale and detrimental to the preparation for national defense." Roosevelt scribbled "O.K." and his initials on the document, in effect setting it in cement as army policy for World War II.[3]

The outrage over this boiled over as Republican Wendell Wilkie was contesting the 1940 presidential election with a strong civil rights platform. The president responded with what today we might call an "October surprise" only days before blacks exercising ever increasing political clout in northern and midwestern urban centers were to go to the polls. Roosevelt announced three appointments. Most prominently, he promoted Colonel Benjamin O. Davis Sr., the highest-ranking African American officer in the army, to brigadier general, making him the first black to reach that exalted rank. (He was a family friend whose son, Benjamin O. Davis Jr., the leader of the Tuskegee Airmen and later the first African American air force general, had roomed at our house while he attended the University of Chicago before going on to West Point.) Campbell C. Johnson, a reserve officer running the ROTC program at Howard University, was appointed special aide to the director of selective service. In addition, Bill Hastie, the dean of the Howard University Law School, whom I had gotten to know only weeks earlier, was named civilian aide to the secretary of war.

In one sense, these appointments represented a continuation of an admirable Roosevelt policy of naming black leaders to represent African American interests in government agencies, creating what history remembers as a "black cabinet." Prominent among its New Deal and World War II members were Mary McLeod Bethune and Arnold Hill at the National Youth Administration; Dr. Ralph J. Bunche in the State Department; Lawrence A. Oxley of the Department of Labor; Eugene K. Jones of the Department of Commerce; Joseph H. B. Evans of the Farm Security Administration; Frank Horne, Lena Horne's uncle, in the Interior Department; and, significant for me, Bill Trent and Robert C. Weaver, also at Interior. Weaver was a senior adviser in the Public Works Administration, during the war he served on the War Manpower Commission, and in 1966 President Lyndon B. Johnson made him the first African American cabinet secretary by naming him the first secretary of the Department of Housing and Urban Development.

The members of the "black cabinet" didn't have cabinet-level status or power but their presence marked the emergence of black influence in the halls of power in Washington. Hastie himself had worked for four years as a lawyer in the Interior Department and was therefore viewed with favor by Interior Secretary Harold Ickes when Roosevelt went looking for a black member for his defense ministry. Over the years, Trent and Weaver had assumed the role of chief recruiters for the black cabinet.

I don't know exactly how my name surfaced when it came to finding an assistant for Hastie, a big-picture man who needed someone to cope with the mundane day-to-day details of high office. Hastie had seemed friendly and open to me when we were at Howard preparing for the *Hansberry* arguments before the U.S. Supreme Court. Remaining in Washington several days after the court hearing, I had spent time at the home of a mutual friend, Bob Ming, and Hastie and I had talked further.

But when the offer to join the War Department came, I didn't hear from Hastie first. The initial feelers originated with Trent. He was a family friend from our Atlanta days. His father, head of a YMCA branch in Atlanta, was close to my father. In fact, stored among the boxes of my family mementos is a photograph of two naked babies, myself and Bill Trent. Years later, we renewed our friendship during the American Negro Exposition.

"Truman, would you be interested in coming to Washington?" Bill asked after the opening pleasantries of his telephone call in the fall of 1940.

"For what?" I responded.

"To work for Bill Hastie in the War Department."

To say I was surprised is an understatement; I was shocked by this bolt out of the blue summoning me to Washington. "Bill, I don't know anything about the War Department," I averred.

After running through the major arguments why African Americans had to be mobilized to protect their rights during what was obviously a mobilization for war, Bill said, "Why don't you come out and let's talk about it." I indicated that I was definitely interested.

Shortly after, I got another call, this one from Hastie. "Bill Trent tells me you two have talked about the War Department, and he told you that I'd like you to be my aide. He said you're interested, so why don't you come out to Washington, and let's talk about it some more." I was flattered to hear directly from this eminent black lawyer and immediately agreed to drive out to Washington.

In all, I spent a week in Washington. The war in Europe, the chances that America would be drawn into it, the institutional roadblocks to African Americans in the military, the hopes that war might inspire movement on black issues, and the role Hastie and I might play in Washington were examined, dissected, and analyzed over and over. Hastie and I got to know each other a little better in discussions in his office at Howard. Bob Weaver, a high school classmate and Harvard alum with Hastie, had us over to his house on California Street for dinner.

Trent and Weaver, it turned out, counted themselves among a coterie of poker players who regularly anted up at the home of Bob Ming, my friend from the University of Chicago. Hastie showed up one night as well, as did Ralph Bunche. Besides taking in lessons on the problems for blacks in the military and the culture of politics in Washington, I saw my chips disappear on the poker table. They wiped me out. Bunche taught me how not to play poker. I quickly found out that I had a lot to learn about the game. Amid the haze of cigarette smoke, the clinking of ice in the drinks, and hand after hand of five-card stud, the table talk returned time and again to exploring avenues to influence federal policy on African Americans in the military. Hastie used words sparingly but effectively. Trent and Weaver poured out all the arguments about duty, responsibility, and challenge.

All week long I listened and asked questions; then I drove back to Chicago. I had a lot to think about. The challenge of tackling segregation in the army registered strongly with me, especially coming off the celebration of black achievement in Chicago. War loomed, and the opportunities it offered for the advancement of the race intrigued me. The pleasures I found in Chicago politics provoked curiosity about seeing the great game played out at the national level. Trent, Weaver, and the others constituted a compatible circle of men, and I found myself eager to spend more time with them.

Other more personal concerns made the idea of a new start in a new endeavor attractive. The American Negro Exposition had eaten up all my time for two-thirds of the year, starving my law practice. Isabelle was pregnant. And, I have to admit, tugging at the back of my mind was the awareness of a high draft number. Isabelle even found herself the object of lobbying by her Washington friends, and she declared herself open to my taking the job, although she remained cool to the idea of moving to what was still a southern city. In the end, she said, "Make up your own mind."

In all, I wrestled with the offer for two weeks, couldn't find any good reasons not to go, and conversely saw lots of reasons to take it. So I did. My appointment as assistant to Hastie came December 9, 1940.

Ironically, after all that talk and all the mulling over of the issues in my mind, when I finally arrived at the Munitions Building, the "temporary" World War I–era stucco building on Constitution Avenue housing the warren of offices that was the War Department, I found that I had no conception of what the job of the civilian aide should be; what's more, neither did Hastie. Years later, Hastie recalled that "Secretary Stimson wanted to bring someone onto his staff with a general responsibility to assist in and recommend and criticize action or nonaction by the War Department" and added that "with some reluctance I agreed to take that rather general responsibility." Hastie said he was reluctant "not because of any lack of interest or because it was not an important area, but I was rather skeptical as to what a person with no authority of his own, whom I was sure the military did not want," could accomplish.[4]

Indeed we went into the Munitions Building over the opposition of the military establishment, but General George C. Marshall, the army's chief of staff, said all matters relating to African Americans would come through our office. All matters didn't come there but most did.

Appointed the first black federal judge in 1937, for the Virgin Island District, Hastie turned out to be aloof, distant, and hard to get to know. However, he was an intellectual with a sharp analytical mind, and he immediately seized on the idea that we had to get an overarching view of the status of African Americans in the army. He instructed me to start gathering information for a report he would write describing the state of the army regarding African Americans and what the goals for improving their status should be. The result was a twenty-four-page memo with eight further pages of recommendations submitted to Stimson on September 22, 1941.[5]

On the opening page, Hastie went to the heart of the problem: "The traditional mores of the South have been widely accepted and adopted by the Army as the basis of policy and practice in matters affecting the Negro soldier." The logical, toxic result was segregation with a racial hierarchy of white officers commanding black soldiers. In a telling anecdote destroying the myth that southerners were best suited by nature of familiarity and understanding of the black race to command African Americans, Hastie related how a black chaplain had been relegated to bedding down in enlisted men's barracks because his fellow white officers had rebelled at sharing quarters with him. They threatened to sleep in their cars.

Humiliation was a fact of life for the black soldier. Far from demanding that white communities in the South respect the black man in uniform, the federal government turned its back as African Americans asked to defend their country were expected to be "humble and subordinate in accepting the insulting and humiliating manifestations of the traditional Southern concept of the Negro's place." Resentment and poor morale undermining the fighting spirit of the black soldier were the inevitable fruits of such a policy. "It is impossible to create a dual personality which will be on the one hand a fighting man toward the foreign enemy, and on the other, a craven who will accept treatment as less than a man at home."

From that general overview, Hastie proceeded to dismantle in detail the sorry state of the army's racial policy. The army proved to be nowhere near inducting numbers of black soldiers to reflect the 10 percent of the population that was African American. Worse, only token numbers of black soldiers showed up in combat units. The overwhelming proportion of black servicemen found themselves doing kitchen duty, digging latrines, and hauling supplies to combat units. Nothing was being done to overcome the educational deficiencies of black recruits. The army had no idea what to do with the few thousand black infantrymen it indeed had trained for combat. When new combat units, such as armored forces or parachute units, were created, no thought was given to including black troops. Aversion to drafting blacks, even with high selective service numbers, meant whites with low numbers were being called up earlier, a sure formula for political trouble. Our research found that twenty-five thousand blacks at the top of the selective service lists had gone uncalled. All of which led to the inescapable conclusion that "the Negro soldier is being approached all too often as an unwelcome requirement to be handled with a view primarily to avoid embarrassment to the prejudiced sensibilities, rather than as an opportunity to exploit a valuable military asset."

Among the most depressing findings was the report that three-fourths of the black soldiers asked to defend their country were being trained at posts in the hostile South. We cited the case of the Ninety-fourth Engineer Battalion, whose black soldiers and white officers in Arkansas had to survive "violence and armed assault." How did the army handle this outrageous case? "The military authorities in the field . . . were satisfied to drop the whole matter after an apology to a white officer who was beaten and the removal of the Battalion from the immediate area of controversy."

Segregation forced extra expenses on the army to construct and maintain separate housing, theaters, and service clubs for African Americans. Elaborate housing or recreational facilities might be built to accommodate a relative handful of black soldiers, a ridiculous financial sacrifice to the altar of segregation. In a bitter anecdote, Hastie told of white soldiers reporting that junior officers warned them against fraternizing with soldiers of color.

If the quota system held down black enlisted strength, the impact of army policy on the officer corps veered toward farce. "In the Regular Army there are three Negro Line officers, one a Brigadier General recently retired, but called back to active duty; one a Captain; and one a Second Lieutenant." The army demonstrated itself intent on keeping the number of black officers low and prohibiting the mixing of African American and white officers in the same unit. At the time, fewer than 150 black line officers were available in the reserve, and quotas prevented ROTC programs at Howard and Wilberforce Universities from turning out more than 30 officers a year. "As of September 12, there were 17 Negroes among the approximately 2,000 officer candidates attending the several officer candidate schools." Assignment opportunities for the few African American officers were low and virtually nonexistent in many commands.

Hastie had a particular interest in the Army Air Corps, and obstacles there for blacks were particularly grating on him. "It is inexcusable that the Army invests in national advertising for aviation cadets, organizes units in college communities to stimulate recruiting, relaxes education requirements for flying cadets, and inaugurates plans for noncommissioned pilots, all to meet the increasing need for Army flyers, and at the same time requires a Negro to wait three years to begin pilot training." Funneling all black aviation candidates to Tuskegee had to end, as did separate training for black ground crews at Chanute Field in Illinois.

Rancor and bitterness, reflected in letters home, were rife among black men to a degree whites couldn't appreciate. Dissatisfaction with the military registered as especially remarkable given the limited opportunities in civilian life for African Americans. White MPs, notable for their bullying, abuse, and violence against blacks, further depressed morale. Throw in the hostility, abuse, and physical attacks by white civilians, and the morale of African American soldiers plumbed the depths of despair and anger.

As bad as all this was, it was even more disturbing that the army evidenced "no apparent disposition to make a beginning or a trial of any different plan" for African American soldiers. Was it any wonder that black men grumbled that they had no business fighting the American white man's battles against European white men? "Much of the difficulty being experienced in arousing the nation today is traceable to the fact that we have lost that passion for national ideals which a people must have if it is to work and sacrifice for its own survival," Hastie wrote. "So long as we condone and appease un-American attitudes and practices within our own military and civilian life, we can never arouse ourselves to the exertion which the present emergency requires."

Our report offered many recommendations: creation of military organizations, units, and commands to accommodate the increased selective service call-up numbers for African Americans; integration of black combat regiments into larger organizations; placement of qualified African Americans in artillery, combat infantry, and other specialized services rather than condemning Negroes to menial labor; formulation of plans to select and train African Americans to be officers; development of a coordinated plan to train and assign black line officers; an end to the policy against the use of black and white line officers in the same regiment; development of a declaration stating the policy of the army to be the equal treatment of all soldiers; prohibition against racial epithets; an end to separate drinking fountains and toilets; placement of morale officers who are black in African American regiments; recruitment and training of black servicemen to be MPs; issuance of a War Department communiqué to governors and municipal officials in the states, especially in the South, calling on them to respect the rights of black soldiers; and adoption of a policy to have the federal government prosecute civilian police or mobs who harm blacks. The most far-reaching recommendation was that "at some point in the Armed Service, a beginning should be made in the employment of soldiers without racial separation."

While the army would respond to some of our complaints by organizing African American divisions and a black tank battalion, it largely rejected the report. General Marshall responded, in what would become familiar language, that the army could not solve the social ills of the nation. In a December 1 memo to Stimson, Marshall wrote that confronting the issues we had raised "would be tantamount to solving a social problem which has perplexed the American people throughout the history of this nation. The Army cannot accomplish such a solution and should not be charged with the undertaking. The settlement of vexing racial problems cannot be permitted to complicate the tremendous task of the War Department and thereby jeopardize discipline and morale."[6]

These were hard words to swallow. They meant the prospects for achieving our goal looked to be, to say the least, bleak. Secretary of War Stimson would not deviate from the army's hard line. His top assistant was Assistant Secretary of War John J. McCloy. Years later I would learn that McCloy worked behind the scenes for the betterment of black soldiers, but in those days that was not obvious because of the things he was saying. He told Hastie, "I do not think that the basic issues of this war are involved in the question of whether Colored troops serve in segregated units or in mixed units and I doubt whether you can convince the people of the United States that the basic issues of freedom are involved in such a question."[7]

Someone today reading the words of Marshall or McCloy might wonder why Hastie and I didn't just resign then and there. But that would have been surrender. Frustration and denial of hope were commonplace for African Americans, and we would not be discouraged.

Besides, all doors were not closed to us. A couple of men worked in the Munitions Building who revealed a receptivity to our views and our issues.

Our direct superior was Undersecretary of War Robert Patterson. A federal judge from New York, Patterson was a small man, a bundle of nervous energy who burned it up by constantly chewing gum, and a man who wasted no time on small talk, nonsense, or extended conversations. Above all, he showed himself to be a man of conscience who bristled over the army treating African Americans as soldiers—when they were needed—but not as soldiers when the army brass buckled under to tradition. He seemed to be troubled by segregation and its costs. His frustrations led Patterson to call in Frank Capra to produce the movie *The Negro Soldier.*

One incident sticks vividly in my memory. Joe Louis had called me from Fort Bragg, North Carolina, to report that the army brass there had solved the problem of segregated seating on buses; they segregated the buses altogether. "We can't get on the buses with white boys." I passed on the complaint to Patterson.

"That can't be true," he declared. He called up a brigadier general who hailed from North Carolina, and this officer said that no, Joe's complaint was not possible.

"Judge Patterson, why don't you pick up the phone, call Fort Bragg, and see what is possible and what isn't possible," I suggested.

Well, he made the call and found out that Joe was right. Patterson hit the ceiling and ordered all segregation eliminated on post camps and stations. The army didn't do that, of course, but his outrage over separate buses demonstrated the caliber of the man. Patterson was sensitive to the injustices of the army, especially troubled by black soldiers being assaulted and killed by civilian peace officers. But the sad fact was that the army was supreme. Patterson was sensitive to the ills of segregation but powerless to do anything about it.

As it turned out, one thing he could do something about was to keep me from jumping to a better-paying job. While still an assistant to Hastie in 1942, I was approached to head the staff of the Fair Employment Practices Committee, the organization created by Roosevelt to combat discrimination in employment in defense industries. A bit of flattery from General Sarnoff softened me up for that job, but the major attraction turned out to be a big pay raise. I was earning thirty-five hundred dollars a year at the War Department. Starting salary for this job was sixty-five hundred. It was a time of war, and Patterson had a veto over my leaving the Munitions Building. I told him I wanted to leave.

"No," he immediately replied.

"But—"

"No," he cut me off.

"Judge Patterson—"

"No, no."

And that was that. It was nice to know he valued my work at the War Department, but I hated taking a pass on a three-thousand-dollar pay raise.

Another open mind in the Munitions Building belonged to Captain Otto Nelson, secretary to General Marshall and to the army's general staff. A West Point graduate with an MBA from Harvard, Nelson was not the steely ramrod-straight martinet the military academy often turned out. Our relationship was forged entirely in the office, but it transcended the social conventions of the day. Our offices were next door to one another, and the conversations between us strayed beyond business into chitchat about sports and the news of the day. While I wouldn't want to make our relationship out as something it wasn't, he was open at a time when the constraints of Washington argued against black-white interchange not predicated on the cruel boundaries of segregation.

I acknowledge being a bit crafty in how I broke the ice with Otto. Big-time sports was literally my ticket to opening the relationship. Joe Louis had agreed to box in two charity fights, one for the Navy Relief Fund and one for the Army Relief Fund. Mike Jacobs, the premier boxing promoter of the day whom I had gotten to know over the last couple of years, gave me fifty tickets to each bout. I turned them over to Nelson. Overnight, he became the most popular man in the military. Who got the tickets, I don't know, but I do know that General Marshall and Admiral Ernest King did, and they threw big parties on the nights of the fights. My experience in Chicago taught me that a fight ticket was better than money, and having a hundred boxing tickets was like owning a bank.

Through Otto Nelson I got to know all the major players in the Munitions Building. I found him to be a stand-up guy, ready to advocate on behalf of black soldiers in general and many of my positions in particular. In a crude sense, he became my rabbi.

It was a relief to have guys in the Munitions Building like Nelson and Patterson who didn't have on blinders. From my first day on the job, I was struck by the insulation of the War Department from ordinary blacks. For the most part, it thought of blacks in terms of the NAACP and the few big-name black leaders. That was true too even of Hastie.

It became apparent to me that no revolution was possible in the army. The best approach to its hierarchy was not one of confrontation but rather a slow chipping away at the attitudes. You had to bring the generals around slowly. Now, that was time consuming and certainly not appealing to the African American public, and it was not an approach that lent itself to publicity. However, it was the only one that would work with the army in those days.

The same was true with changing the attitudes of white America. For example, I lobbied the producers in Chicago of the soap opera *As the World Turns* to include a couple of black characters but to no avail. Still, out of that effort and subsequent conversations with Chuck Dollard of the Information and Education Division of the War Department about how to get blacks mentioned in the media as part of America's everyday life cycle emerged the idea of doing a radio broadcast in the summer of 1941 to explain the ambitions of black Americans to be part of the defense effort and to extol the role of African American soldiers. The Negro Actors Guild embraced the idea and recruited black actors, singers, and comedians for the project. Its executive secretary, actress

Edna Thomas, wrote me proposing cast members for the broadcast including Frank Wilson, who played Porgy in the original performance of the famous play *Porgy and Bess;* Maurice Ellis, who starred in Orson Welles's Federal Theatre production of *Macbeth;* Juano Hernandez, who adapted and performed the radio series *John Henry;* stage, screen, and radio artist Eddie Green; and Edna Thomas herself, who had portrayed Lady Macbeth in the Federal Theatre show.[8]

I solicited ideas from the rank-and-file black soldiers as well. The Forty-first Engineers at Fort Bragg proposed a quartet to sing "two engineer songs" and offered up Company D's ventriloquist. "He is really clever and good and I suggest a skit about shooting on the range," reported the Fort Bragg public relations officer. Also suggested for the program was an "unusual item of interest" segment that would note that the Forty-first might be the only regiment in the army which is regimented based on height, starting off with Company A having men six feet tall and running down to Company F manned by soldiers five-foot-two. Ideas from Fort Bragg's Thirty-fourth C. A. Brigade ranged from performances of swing band music to the recital of a poem describing the history of the Negro in America to an "old-type minstrel show," although the public relations officer added "this may be regarded as 'corny' by today's radio listeners." The Thirty-fourth also opined, "A dramatization of the transition of a Negro farm-hand, factory worker or 'loafer,' with appropriate humorous incidents for levity, from civilian into soldier should be interesting, informative and beneficial to the War Department."[9]

Tickets for a studio audience of one thousand at the NBC studio in New York were available there and at our office in Washington. An invitation went out to some prominent persons trumpeting a show featuring "music by leading Negro artists and by the NBC Symphony Orchestra," a "dramatic sketch depicting the role of the Negro soldier in the last war," interviews from Chicago with black air corps trainees from Chanute Field, and short addresses by Patterson and Hastie.[10]

Finally, after weeks of preparation and being rescheduled a couple of times, the show entitled *America's Negro Soldiers* hit the airwaves, from 10:00 to 10:45 P.M., Eastern Daylight Saving Time, Tuesday, August 12, from Studio 8-H, on the NBC–Blue Network to major metropolitan areas across the country.[11]

Bandleader Noble Sissle served as master of ceremonies, who related to the audience his own service during World War I: "I'll never forget those days—twenty-four years ago—when Jim Europe and I were playing with our orchestra at Ziegfeld's Cocoanut Grove atop the old Century Theatre in New York. Then came the call to the colors! Yes sir, with 400,000 others of our race, Jim and I joined our great United States Army for service overseas. Enough other musicians joined our outfit—the old Fifteenth New York Infantry—so that we were able to organize the 369th Infantry Band. And when we weren't using our machine guns over there, we made music. Jazz was new to Europe—and man did they love it."

Sissle recalled that "the Germans didn't realize . . . just how loyal the American Negro soldier could be." That opened a skit depicting a German *Kapitän* and his lieutenant getting an education about black loyalty when African American doughboys reject messages from the German asserting that they were fighting for "white folks and the lying English American papers" who "don't believe in humanity and Democracy." The performers included Juano Hernandez, Frank Wilson, Canada Lee, Maurice Ellis, Lionel Monages, and Percy Verwayn. Sissle closed out this segment by noting that citations and awards to black soldiers for bravery and heroism demonstrated the fighting spirit and loyalty of African Americans to the United States.

Patterson then took the microphone to sound the alarm about the war raging around the world that summer night. "This is every American's emergency. It is no more particular than a hurricane or blizzard," he declared. "There is nothing exclusive about the war that is flaming in three continents. Let me remind you that an aerial bomb draws no color line." President Roosevelt's executive order for full participation by all Americans in the war effort was cited by Patterson. Highlighting Davis's promotion to the rank of general, he said seventy thousand African Americans were serving in the army, among them more than four hundred commissioned officers, and fifty-six black nurses were being trained. He pointed to the Tuskegee Airmen and a black tank unit.

Looking back to World War I, he named several winners of the Distinguished Service Cross and then recounted the contemporary heroism of Sergeant Samuel F. Baker, who risked his life to keep oil drums from exploding during a fire at Fort Huachuca, Arizona. Patterson closed with a message of tribute to black soldiers from General "Black Jack" Pershing.

Entertainment followed. A song and dance number featured a dazzling performance by Bill "Bojangles" Robinson. Eddie Green and Edna Thomas starred in a skit about a service club with Edna playing the hostess fending off attempts by soldier Green to get her to play a kissing game. To contemporary ears, the humor harkens back to a more innocent era. For instance, Eddie tells Edna his buddy is in the guardhouse, and she wonders why. "For going on a furlong," he replied. "You mean a furlough," she said, providing the straight line. "No," he deadpanned. "A furlong. He got out, went too fur, and stayed too long." Coming after the skit was the NBC Symphony playing a version of Dvořák's *New World Symphony* based on "the Negro folk theme 'Going Home' " and an orchestral rendition of Nathaniel Dett's "Juba Dance."

The show wound down with interviews with the black air corps trainees from Chanute and a performance of the Negro spiritual "Go Down Moses" dedicated to the French, Poles, Belgians, Czechs, and, in Sissle's words, "all peoples struggling against slavery which Democracy opposes."

All in all, given the realities of 1941, we were happy with the broadcast. I told Earl Dickerson, who had done some of the interviews from Chicago, "Undoubtedly, there will be many charges that the program was a soft soap affair. I think it should be pointed out that it reached a number of persons who know nothing at all about the Negro soldier and who probably would have turned off a program of another sort, particularly since the one presented is the first of its kind."[12]

However, there's no denying the soft soap. Hard to take was the hypocrisy of the army's attitude toward black soldiers underlying these words uttered by Patterson: "General Marshall enjoys the confidence of these [black] soldiers as he does of all our soldiers, and I can assure you that he reciprocates that confidence."[13]

Still, I have to give Patterson credit for urging the whites in the audience to treat black soldiers with respect. It was only a faint echo of Hastie's and my call for the government to direct civilian officials to prevent violence against African Americans, but it was important that he said what he did: "Everyone can help to make life more pleasant for the men who constitute it [the army], particularly when they are on leave in or passing through the larger cities. The civilian population of the South and Southwest can be especially helpful in such a collaboration, since the preponderance of our military population is in that area."[14]

It quickly became apparent how that plea fell on deaf ears.

8

The War at Home

The tidal wave of patriotism, national solidarity, and camaraderie that swept across the nation in the weeks and months after Pearl Harbor never seemed to embrace black soldiers. Only weeks after the Japanese attack, the new year opened with a spasm of racial violence in Alexandria, Louisiana. Exactly what happened, how many, if any, African Americans were killed—various accounts ranged from none to eighteen—and who was responsible for the outbreak of violence remain a source of debate even today.

Nearly a year after the rioting, a U.S. Department of Justice investigator in town looking into another racial murder made a reference in his report to the earlier violence involving black soldiers, African American MPs, Alexandria police, and Louisiana state police. "During the course of the trouble someone produced a machine gun and shot at random into the crowd, wounding some 26 negro soldiers and killing 12." His report stated that no one knew what ignited the riot or who pulled the trigger on the machine gun.[1]

Machine guns and twelve dead constituted among the most sensational allegations about the January 10 rioting—and they were passed along as fact in a Justice Department document. In a report by our office to Secretary Stimson about violence to black soldiers during 1942, Hastie and I recounted that "several Negro soldiers were injured in the course of promiscuous shooting by civilian policemen in Alexandria last winter."[2] The army denied in the days after the rioting that anyone had been killed. Still, rumors swept the town that as many as eighteen had been slain.

Years later a historian at Louisiana College, William M. Simpson, conducted extensive research into the "Lee Street Riot" and could turn up no factual evidence of any deaths and makes no mention of machine guns. However, he did interviews with townspeople and others who reported seeing or hearing about fatalities.

Alexandria was a small southern town unprepared to cope with the tens of thousands of soldiers, as many as twenty thousand of them being black, concentrated at four army training camps in central Louisiana. GIs had flooded the town on weekend passes that January. The black troops hailed mostly from Pennsylvania, Illinois, and New York and were unaccustomed to the rigorous restrictions of Jim Crow, which black newspapers cited as the cause of the trouble. The violence apparently began with the arrest of a black soldier by a white MP. Several thousand black troops throwing bricks, rocks, and sticks battled MPs, city police, and state troopers, who fired tear gas and guns, along four or five blocks of Lee Street. Contemporary accounts said twenty-eight black soldiers and one black female civilian were wounded with four of the GIs seriously hurt. A War Department statement written by Hastie put the number of black soldiers injured by the police's "indiscriminate and unnecessary shooting" at twenty-nine, three of them critically wounded. An NAACP official claimed ten black soldiers had been killed and that white funeral homes had secretly shipped the bodies out of town. A year after the events in Alexandria, I reported that the army had found no fatalities.[3]

Out of this spasm of violence came the *Pittsburgh Courier*'s Double V campaign, a rallying cry for racial justice during World War II. An article by James G. Thompson proposed that "colored Americans adopt the double V for a double victory. The first V for victory over our enemies from without, the second V for victory over our enemies from within."[4]

Unfortunately, Alexandria was far from an isolated incident. Disturbances like this broke out time and again, and humiliation constituted a daily diet for African American soldiers. With the nation girding for a long war, African American troopers enjoying a little liberty on a winter Saturday night in Houston, Texas, found that—as far as they were concerned—the war had changed nothing. The soldiers, from nearby Ellington Field and Camp Wallace, were enjoying a few beers in a tavern in the heart of Houston's black section when a white cop wandered in. A black newspaperman was present, and he reported what followed to Illinois congressman Arthur W. Mitchell, who in turn complained to the commander at Fort Sam Houston.[5]

"You nigger soldiers," the policeman bellowed at the GIs as he proceeded to deliver what the newspaper reporter, not identified by Mitchell, called "a lecture on their iniquities."

"I am not a nigger soldier, we are American soldiers," shot back an African American sergeant.

"You are a nigger soldier if I say so, and if you don't like it I will kill you," the cop said. He called for help, and several other police officers and white MPs showed up.

"The white MP [told] them they were in the South and were niggers and that they would be treated as such as long as they were there," the newsman related. "To give the boys credit, they did not back up an inch."

A standoff ensued, and death threats were hurled at the blacks. A black civilian who attempted to intervene was thrown into jail on a charge of "inciting to riot." Three soldiers were also jailed on the same charge, and one of them was threatened with arrest the next time and every time he showed up in town. Still, the incident ended without violence. "But for the courageous attitude of the sergeant and his comrades, there would have been some head whipping at this time," the reporter wrote. It was a close call. White MPs, armed with pistols and billy clubs, regularly patrolled the black neighborhoods of Houston and beat black soldiers. The reporter was told by the officer commanding the MPs, "The Army policy is to permit civil authorities and police to treat Negro soldiers as they see fit. They may talk to them in any way they wish."

Again, this could not be chalked up as an isolated case. Across the South "occurred several uprisings between white civilians and uniformed Negro soldiers," Mitchell wrote. "The morale of the Negro has been tremendously lowered by the treatment of the white civilian population toward Negro soldiers in some of the camps in North Carolina, Louisiana, Arkansas and Texas." Hundreds of complaints had poured into his office. "The shedding of blood and the destruction of life" already had occurred at some places and the threat of violence was imminent in others.

Hastie and I were hearing the same thing and told Stimson so. "Violence and abusive treatment of Negro military personnel by civilian public officials in the South continues and seems to be increasing," our report concluded. "This matter has reached the stage where the Army can no longer afford to dismiss the situation by saying that these cases are beyond its jurisdiction. This continuing wave of violence may lead to rioting at any time and certainly it is raising havoc with the spirit of Negro soldiers, many of whom have reached the stage that they would much rather fight their domestic enemies than the foreign foe. The stake is nothing less than the combat efficiency of our Negro troops."[6]

Mitchell wasn't the only member of Congress writing letters about black soldiers. Unfortunately, Representative Pat Cannon of Florida had nothing good or constructive to say in his letter to Assistant Secretary of War John J. McCloy in the late spring of 1942.[7] Cannon had heard rumors that African Americans were to be assigned to air corps officer candidate training school in Miami Beach, and he was upset about it. Miami Beach was not accustomed, he wrote, to the southern practice of segregation for the simple reason that blacks were not allowed to live there. "Negro servants at Miami Beach are not permitted to sleep on the premises at which they are employed." This represented a more egregious insult than the restrictive real estate covenants I had battled in Chicago.

Cannon described Miami Beach as America's "modern gold coast" with hotels second to none. The army was housing officer candidates in some of the country's most expensive hotels. Any hotel "in which is permitted the occupancy of any member of the negro race is doomed for all time as far as future white occupancy is concerned." What's more, he wrote, sending blacks to Miami Beach would provoke "a distinct failure of civilian morale." Keep the black soldiers out of Miami

Beach altogether, he urged McCloy, but if they must be trained there, house them in neighboring Miami.

This rumor turned out to be baseless, as McCloy reported that no blacks were due to be assigned to Miami Beach.[8] As it happened, a few African Americans eventually did get training there. Somehow Miami Beach managed to survive.

If the morale of white civilians in Miami Beach was threatened by the prospect of a few black officer candidates descending on the Atlantic coast community, African Americans everywhere expressed dismay over the way America treated them as the country went to war against the enemies of democracy. This was especially true in Washington, D.C., the city were the war effort was being planned.

"Only lip service is paid to the theory of equality of all citizens in this, the capital of the world's greatest democracy," complained the District of Columbia Branch of the NAACP. "The exclusion of Negroes from places of public accommodation, both governmentally and privately operated, is shameful at all times but incomprehensible in time of war. As a result, thousands of Negro defense workers literally are without places to obtain food during work hours. Housing facilities . . . are totally insufficient to meet the needs of the war-time capital. As if the effect of these conditions on morale were not bad enough, the gratuitous insult of the white taxicab drivers who habitually refuse to carry Negroes is added."[9]

The NAACP proceeded to recount the injustices to the black race in Washington. Blacks were excluded from skilled and professional employment, with government agencies feeling free to "flaunt their 'lily-white' set-ups." Blacks suffered "abuse, maltreatment and even homicidal assault at the hands of the Metropolitan, Park and Capitol Police." The courts didn't protect the lives or rights of African Americans. Segregated schools perpetuated inequality. The Jim Crow philosophy of the army and the all-white navy and marine corps undermined black attitudes toward the war effort. Blacks had even been denied civil defense training. Black leaders were "engaged in the Herculean task of bolstering Negro morale," but, the NAACP concluded, "without tangible and material change in the underlying causes, their efforts will be unavailing."

Is it any wonder I would seize on any opportunity to get out of Washington? Most times my travels took me to camps to find oppressive segregation even worse than in the nation's capital, but every once in a while along came the rare exception.

Ten days after Pearl Harbor I found myself aboard a train chugging into Monterey, California, in what turned out to be one of the few escapes for me from the downward spiral of black hopes for a fair deal in the army. The army post there, Fort Ord, had only one black unit, the 632nd Ordnance Company. "The boys said they had exceptionally good officers and had received good treatment since their arrival," I reported to Hastie.[10]

They hadn't, however, been spared an attempt to push them aside. "Some white soldiers objected to their presence in the Post Movie theatres, but after several fights, decided not to press their objections." Still, "the boys appear to be thoroughly integrated into all camp activities and had no complaints, except that they were not given very much work to do."

Traveling on to Los Angeles, I got a darker report from several community leaders with whom I met. Leon Washington told me black soldiers had run into resentment in small towns surrounding California army posts, especially when they showed up for dances. And Bill Hopkins, industrial relations counselor for Columbia Studios, worried that the California legislature was about to enact legislation to let women work for regular pay rather than a time-and-a-half overtime rate in industry during the overnight hours, a move that would forestall new work for black laborers.

These were the early, uncertain days of war. It was eye opening to see how folks on the West Coast were jittery after the Japanese attack on Hawaii. Movie mogul Jack Warner had workers paint camouflaged colors over the entire Warner Brothers studio. The glamorous life of Hollywood carried on, however, and I sampled of it. Entertainer and friend Etta Moten Barnett was in town and made sure I got the royal treatment during a visit to MGM studios. "Some very close friends of hers who write for MGM sent a car and chauffeur around to pick me up," I confided to Hastie, "and from that point on one would have thought I was no less than Secretary Stimson." Lunch on the MGM lot was followed by a dinner party at the estate of Etta's friends Wilkie Mahoney and his wife. Mahoney was one of Hollywood's leading gag writers. He counted Red Buttons among the top comedians for whom he had written jokes. Mixing work with play "amidst gorgeous surroundings" as I enjoyed the good food and several games of badminton, I assured Hastie, "I got in some good licks for the employment of Negroes in the moving picture industry."

General Davis met me in Los Angeles. African American writer Carlton Moss, who was detailed to the Army Motion Picture Section, had Davis stop at the home of Ira Gershwin, George Gershwin's brother. And he put me up with Yip and Eddie Harburg. Yip was a movie producer with *Stormy Weather,* starring Lena Horne and Ethel Waters, among his credits. He also was a talented lyricist, whose most famous lyrics are found in the song "Brother, Can You Spare a Dime?" He wrote the score for the Fred Astaire movie *Bloomer Girl.* Hollywood's A-list was assembled at Gershwin's home for a party for General Davis and me. Johnny Mercer played the piano for this gala. Amid the clinking of ice in cocktail glasses, I was introduced to the intellectual and politically active liberal elite of the motion picture industry.

The Harburgs, along with the Gershwins, had emerged as leaders among Hollywood's glitterati in wanting to do something about racial attitudes in America and searched for ways movies could help that cause. Here was the nucleus of the Hollywood Ten, ultraliberal people, but not communists, who would be victimized in the ugly postwar red scare.

I ended up staying with the Harburgs six to eight times. Generous to a fault, they wouldn't hear of me overnighting in a hotel. On my second visit to Los Angeles, I had hardly checked into the Roosevelt Hotel when Eddie showed up to yank me out and drive me to their home. Through them, I met Paul Williams, an architect who had designed the Harburg home and the Saks Fifth Avenue store in Los Angeles. Williams introduced me to his friend Norman Houston, founder and CEO of Golden State Mutual, one of the great black companies on the West Coast.

On my third or fourth trip to Los Angeles, thanks to Joe Louis, I got to know Tommy Tucker, owner of one of the first interracial sports bars. The flashy nightlife of Los Angeles and the success of his bar introduced Tucker to mobster Mickey Cohen, and they were on friendly terms. Tucker liked to regale friends with a story about Cohen. The mob boss was dining with a gambler one night when a gunman opened fire on Cohen. The shooter missed Cohen but hit the gambler, who collapsed facedown into his plate of beef Stroganoff. One night Tucker spotted Cohen in his bar with a new girlfriend. "Tommy," Cohen said, "this is the stupidest bitch I ever met in my life." It turned out that he had just taken the young woman out to dinner, and she had ordered beef Stroganoff. "I didn't know!" the poor girl pleaded.

One of my most memorable trips to Los Angeles, again in the early days of the war when anxiety and at times near hysteria gripped the West Coast, found me on a plane with First Lady Eleanor Roosevelt. A rumor of an impending Japanese attack forced the Sleeper Boeing airliner to land at Cheyenne, Wyoming. As we all killed time in the airport waiting room, I found the courage to go up and introduce myself to the great lady. "I know your name," she replied. It turned out that black educator and New Deal administrator Mary McLeod Bethune had mentioned me to her. We chatted, mostly small talk, for fifteen to twenty minutes. I was awestruck. She, unlike her husband, had a genuine understanding of the plight of African Americans and never failed to speak up on our behalf.

But, oh, how the army hated her. Her many letters to the War Department demanded a fair deal for black soldiers. For instance, she wrote Stimson in 1942, "I have heard from one or two sources that the young Southerners were very indignant to find that the Negro soldiers were not looked upon with terror by the girls in England and Ireland and Scotland." She suggested doing "a little educating among our Southern white men and officers."[11] On another occasion she passed on to McCloy a letter from a soldier at Camp Claiborne, Louisiana, about black GIs being treated like "primitive illiterate children." Mrs. Roosevelt's comment: "It seems to me to ring true."[12] After she had visited hospitals in the South Pacific, she complained about discriminatory bus service for blacks in Louisiana. "These colored boys lie side by side in the hospitals in the southwest Pacific with the white boys and somehow it is harder for me to believe that they should not be treated on an equal basis, after my recent trip, than it was before. . . . [T]hey get killed just the same as the white boys."[13] Black Americans never had a better white friend than Eleanor Roosevelt, and I felt myself privileged to get to meet her.

The sunny interludes of my trips to Los Angeles were brief. Back in Washington, horror stories accumulated. In March, a cop in Little Rock, Arkansas, pumped five bullets into Sergeant Thomas B. Foster while he was lying helpless on the ground, killing him. Secure in the knowledge that no grand jury would indict him, the officer filled his pipe and nonchalantly smoked it with Foster's body lying nearby. On July 28, in Beaumont, Texas, a black private was arrested, put in a police car, and then shot twice by cops. On September 12, two police officers in Montgomery, Alabama, beat black nurse Lieutenant Norma Greene, breaking her nose, blackening her eyes, and inflicting bruises on her body. On October 15, the local authorities in Mobile, Alabama, looked the other way after a bus driver shot and killed a black soldier. In October, a couple of black soldiers found that obeying the southern custom of riding at the back of the bus wasn't good enough in Norfolk, Virginia: police arrested, handcuffed, and beat them when they refused to give up their seats to whites; the seats were supposedly reserved for blacks. On November 4, Private Larry Stroud was fatally shot through the back of the head by a police officer in Columbia, South Carolina; a coroner's jury exonerated the cop when he said the soldiers had stooped over as if to pick up a rock.[14]

The troubles weren't confined to the United States. Brigadier General Benjamin O. Davis, on an inspection tour in Europe, found black-white tensions so inflamed that a white MP had killed a black soldier in "an affray" in Northern Ireland. While the British treated black soldiers well, American whites openly bristled at the absence of Jim Crow societal norms and segregation in the British Isles. As Mrs. Roosevelt had noted, white southerners found particularly galling the friendliness of British women to black soldiers. Racist attitudes on the part of white GIs had some blacks asking Davis, "Who are we over here to fight, the Germans or our own white soldiers?" The general recommended that army commanders be held responsible for race relations in their units and the conduct of troops under their command.[15]

As the year drew to a close, racial violence flared in a place where it had occurred at the beginning of 1942—Alexandria, Louisiana. On November 1, a Louisiana state trooper murdered Private Raymond Carr in a crime so blatant that Secretary of War Stimson, at the urging of an outraged Undersecretary Patterson, called on the U.S. Department of Justice to prosecute the police officer.

State police in Louisiana had carved out a reputation as being particularly hostile to African Americans, even by southern standards. Alexandria seemed ripe for trouble. Its prewar population of thirty thousand had mushroomed to eighty thousand civilians, and more than one hundred thousand soldiers, as many as twenty thousand of them black, were stationed in the area. "Tension is great, and both civilians and soldiers constantly live in a strain," reported G. Maynard Smith, sent there by the Justice Department to investigate the Carr murder.[16]

The case against the cop, Dalton McCollum, was strong. Nine eyewitnesses described a cold-blooded murder, and a mortally wounded Carr had made a dying declaration of what had happened to two hospital nurses. He and another black MP, armed only with billy clubs, were on duty that night when they intervened in an argument between two civilians, a man and a woman. McCollum and another state trooper showed up, and the woman said the man had hit her. Carr reported that he had not seen a blow struck. That "incensed" the troopers, who considered Carr to be interfering with them. They ordered the two MPs into a car and said they should consider themselves under arrest. Carr and the other MP declared they were on duty for the United States Army and could not leave their post. The two troopers left but returned shortly with two more officers. Carr ran, was chased down, and was shot in the abdomen by McCollum.

Smith reported that the government's eyewitnesses were black and said, "The colored witnesses are above average in intelligence, and they make very frank, fair statements about how the crime occurred and are the type that will stand up very well under cross-examination. They are not inclined to be 'smart-alecks' but impress you with the truthfulness of their story."

With the exception of a few allies of the state troopers, no one entertained any doubt that a terrible crime had been committed. Even so, tensions in town ran so high that the commander of Camp Beauregard, one of the area army training camps, argued against prosecution, saying it would undermine the harmony between military and civilian authorities. It speaks volumes about that time for this officer to talk about harmony when a police officer had just murdered a black soldier. The commander, Smith reported, "feels that a great wrong has been done and one that deserves punishment no doubt, but he is looking to the future and what might happen without the whole hearted support of the state and municipal police authorities." The commander's view fortunately was not shared by other military officers.

Despite Stimson's urging of a federal prosecution, U.S. Attorney General Francis Biddle recommended the case be turned over to state authorities. Biddle wrote a telegram, sent out over Stimson's signature, to Louisiana governor Sam Houston Jones recommending state prosecution of McCollum. Of course, nothing happened; McCollum wasn't prosecuted for a minute.

Hastie and I were outraged. He wrote Stimson urging that Alexandria be declared off limits to all military personnel and that MPs be armed with guns with orders to defend themselves "against any interference with the performance of their duty." It was long past time for the army to abandon its stance of being "unwilling to risk offending the sensibilities of the Negro-hating elements of the South." He also proposed that legislation be sought from Congress to make violence against military personnel a federal crime.[17] Of course, that didn't happen.

However, by this time, the War Department had become alarmed enough about continuing racial violence and the challenge that utilization of black soldiers presented the army to form a special committee to deal with these issues. The committee became the focus of my efforts to confront the injustices black soldiers faced while serving their country.

9

Negro Troop Policy

The curious thing about the War Department's decision to create a special committee on black soldiers was that nobody told Bill Hastie, the army's point man on African American issues, about it. The panel had been in business for a month in the summer of 1942 before Hastie finally got wind of it. "The creation of this board, without notice to him or participation by him, has caused him a good deal of uneasiness, and it is one of the factors that has led him to question his usefulness as Special Aide to the Secretary of War on Negro Affairs," Undersecretary of War Patterson complained.[1] Hastie put it down as just the latest in a growing string of slights and insults from the army. After further provocations, his anger finally boiled over and he quit the War Department on January 6, 1943.

Whatever little progress may have been achieved in his two years as civilian aide, Hastie came to believe that nothing more would come from working inside the Munitions Building. The department's supposed commitment that all racial issues and decisions would be routed through his office had proven to be "as much honored in the breach as it was in performance."[2] Secretary of War Stimson had no understanding of the problems of race in America, and that grated on Hastie. Once in discussing the Army Air Corps, Stimson said to him, "Mr. Hastie, is it not true that your people are basically agriculturalists?"[3] General Hap Arnold frustrated Hastie at every turn over the goal nearest to Hastie's heart—integration of the air corps. Arnold argued that integration wouldn't work because, for example, if a plane flown by a white pilot were to crash because of mechanical failure, black ground crews would be blamed and there would "be hell to pay."[4]

In fact, it was the army's decision to segregate training of ground crews—yet another decision kept from Hastie—that erupted as the direct cause of his resignation. Having lobbied hard for integrated ground crew schools and having been misled about the air corps' intentions, Hastie learned from reading the St. Louis newspapers that a segregated school was planned for Missouri.[5]

"Changes of racial policy should be made but will not be made in response to advocacy within the Department but only as a result of strong and manifest public opinion," he wrote in a memorandum to Stimson. "Therefore, it has seemed to me that my present and future usefulness is greater as a private citizen who can express himself freely and publicly."[6]

No one was more surprised by Hastie's resignation than I. Though I labored as his top assistant and occupied the office next to his, he gave not a hint to me that he contemplated resignation. That hurt. Still, I had come to accept that Hastie had an aloofness in his character that set him apart. He didn't socialize with other black government officials. One reason, perhaps, stemmed from his unhappy marriage, which kept him from joining social occasions with the rest of us and our wives. (Ultimately he divorced and married a much younger woman.)

The War Department made me acting civilian aide and then looked around for someone else for the job, considering college presidents and state and federal government officials. For a time, the department took a hard look at Charles Houston, Hastie's law partner, a counsel to the NAACP, and a Phi Beta Kappa graduate of Amherst when John McCloy was also a student there. Houston didn't get the job, and after spending half a year with the word "acting" in front of the title, I finally was named permanently to the post on September 21, 1943.

Hastie wasn't the only one kept in the dark about the August 27, 1942, creation of the Advisory Committee on Negro Troop Policies. Judge Patterson heard about it from Hastie. "This was news to me, although I have been charged with discussion of matters concerning negroes with Judge Hastie," Patterson told Assistant Secretary of War McCloy.[7]

What's more, Patterson allowed that he didn't know the purpose of the committee. McCloy himself wasn't clear about that either, according to military historian Major Ulysses Lee.[8] Which was kind of strange since a memorandum floated around the Munitions Building specifying the panel's brief as confronting "social questions involved, personnel problems and training, and use of Negro Troops."[9] Five days after Patterson complained, he and Hastie were instructed that "the committee had been set up to consider strictly military problems in the use of negro troops and that the broader social problems were only incidentally involved." The memo informing McCloy about this reported that Patterson "was more upset than seemed necessary!"[10] Such was the War Department's cavalier attitude toward those of us entrusted with representing African American interests in the army. Patterson's formal role in issues relating to African American soldiers pretty much ended when the advisory committee went to work, meaning black Americans lost for several years the possibility of help from this sympathetic government official.

McCloy might not have had a clear idea of the purpose of the committee, but Brigadier General Benjamin O. Davis Sr. certainly did. He declared that the panel should have as its mission "the breaking down of the so-called 'Jim-Crow' practices within the War Department and on the military reservations, and the securing of the cooperation of the communities near reservations to that end." Furthermore, he asserted that the War Department should announce that "military necessity requires a closer unity and comradeship among all races" and that "steps be taken to bring about better race relations within our country and to secure to all citizens, regardless of race, color, or previous conditions, the privileges guaranteed to all citizens by our Federal Government." Army orientation courses should provide a history of African American contributions to society, white soldiers should be made aware of their responsibility to improve race relations, and commanders of white and black units should confer on the best way to accomplish this mission. And whenever a designation of race was required, the term "colored" was preferred to "Negro."[11] Use of the word "Negro," Davis felt, could too easily deteriorate into "nigger."

Davis became a member of the committee, made up of military officers but chaired by McCloy and thus known as the McCloy Committee. McCloy, a Wall Street lawyer, would rise to several prominent posts in government service, including high commissioner for occupied Germany, and would land prestigious civilian jobs, including president of the World Bank, chairman of Chase Manhattan Bank, and chairman of the Ford Foundation. Two and a half months after Hastie quit, McCloy invited me to sit in on meetings of the committee.

McCloy's office was just a few doors down. I met with him frequently. He was terse, stern. I always reported, in writing and in person, on all my trips for the War Department. I traveled virtually every other week, usually on my own. It was a lonesome experience. The guys in the units did not know what to do with me. At Fort Benning, Georgia, the commander always referred to me as Dr. Gibson. I said no, I had a JD from the University of Chicago, but I didn't use it. He never called me Mr. Gibson. It was a very small thing but significant in subtly but clearly defining the racial boundaries of the day.

During my visits to army posts, I couldn't appear to be fraternizing with black units and be accused of being overboard in voicing black complaints, or I would have had my credibility assailed. Post commanders were wary of me, as were the African American soldiers on occasion. Enlisted men sometimes would say, "We know you can't do anything about conditions here." I would reply, "Go ahead and get it off your chest."

I traveled by train and plane. At army camps in the South I stayed at the bachelor officers' quarters and on the West Coast in hotels or at the home of friends. I never frequented segregated officers' clubs, though I did do inspections of PXs and theaters.

Occasionally I would travel with a group, as I did in the spring of 1943 with fourteen black newspapermen to observe maneuvers in Louisiana by the Ninety-third Division, one of two black infantry divisions. The tour produced good publicity for the army and was proof that my arguments that more open and direct dealings with the black press would pay big dividends for the War Department.

A *Chicago Defender* headline announced "93rd Division Nearing Combat Shape, Louisiana Battle Shows." The story under the headline confided, "It won't be long now before the 93rd Division gets 'hot.' In curt army parlance, getting 'hot' is another way of stamping the 'ready for combat' label on an outfit."[12] Accompanying photos showed General Davis getting a briefing on the maneuvers, and black soldiers from Chicago, Philadelphia, and towns in Mississippi manning a tank, a light mortar, and a machine gun. In an editorial, the *Washington Afro-American* noted that this marked the first time the War Department had sponsored such a tour for black newsmen. The editorial deemed the press tour a huge success: "It gave the newspapers an opportunity to see what progress the army and the men have made in military training. It gave the officers and soldiers themselves the distinct impression that the army is interested in their welfare. And not the least important, it demonstrated to the department that the folks back home can help the army do a better job."[13]

Another tour of black newspapermen took us to Mississippi, but this trip turned out to be memorable for what happened after we got back to Chicago. We had been flying on the same plane, a Consolidated B-24 transport, that had carried Wendell Wilkie on his two-month tour of the Middle East, China, and the Soviet Union as a special envoy for President Roosevelt in 1942. After we deplaned, the aircraft taxied away from the Midway Airport terminal and took off. Then something went terribly wrong. As it lifted off the runway, the B-24 suddenly veered off course and, as we watched in horror, slammed into a huge gas tank on the periphery of the airport and exploded in flames. All eight or ten people on board were killed. It was pilot error, of course. The shocking images of death and destruction have never left my mind.

Still, in those days, with war raging in every corner of the globe, death and destruction had grown to be a daily part of life. I was soon back in Washington coping with the complexities of race and army policy in the War Department. The key personality with whom I had to deal in that job was McCloy, and he turned out to be a complex individual. During my experience with him throughout the war years, McCloy didn't show his hand regarding his true feelings. I now know he remonstrated with Army Chief of Staff George Marshall and Secretary of War Henry Stimson about the abuses stemming from segregation. He saw black troops as a resource not properly utilized by the War Department and as a resource essential for the war effort. I think my memorandums and meetings had an effect on him. One time when McCloy did show a soft side came in 1942 when we traveled to Pittsburgh where the *Courier* had arranged a dinner and reception for the Ninety-ninth Squadron. Weather delayed the Ninety-ninth, and McCloy and I found ourselves whiling away the hours in his hotel suite. Affable and engaging, he and I chatted about this and that, nothing of great significance, for a couple of hours. I recall it as a most pleasant evening, a bit of relief from the formality that governed our relationship.

However, that pleasant passage of time was the exception. On another occasion, Mercer Cook, the head of the romance language department at Howard University, had returned from a civilian mission to Havana, Cuba, and presented me with two fine cigars. Well, I knew McCloy liked a smoke, so I sent them in to him. He never said thank you. After the war, I sent Morris MacGregor's book on the integration of the armed services to McCloy with a note saying he had started it all, but I heard nothing back from him.

The promotion to succeed Hastie and my ex officio status on the McCloy Committee plunged me directly into the most vexing issues confronting African Americans trying to serve their country. Hastie had gone public with his long list of grievances, and they were getting wide play in the black press. I told McCloy it was vital that the army do something about Hastie's complaints. I dug out the long overview of the status of blacks in the army, written by Hastie in 1941 after ten months of research by him and me, and submitted it to Charles Poletti, special assistant to the secretary of war. I added margin notes to update some of its key points. For example, policies to protect segregation and ensure that no white officer had to salute an African American meant that black officers served as lieutenants in only two divisions, the Ninety-second and Ninety-third, the two designated Negro infantry combat units. The War Department still had not written governors asking them to make sure that white civilians and local authorities respected the rights of black soldiers. On the other hand, blacks were now being employed as MPs. However, at no place had the armed forces made a beginning at using black troops without the restrictions of segregation.[14]

You couldn't say any one issue topped the list of complaints about treatment of black soldiers because the problems were all atrocious in their own right. At the root of all of them was the corrosive, bigoted philosophy of black inferiority. One committee member, Brigadier General Millard G. White, sought the views of the commander of a black regiment, the 350th Field Artillery. It's worth quoting at length from the reply of Lieutenant Colonel James H. Leusley:

> I doubt if the average negro soldier is physically as brave and strong as the average white soldier. History shows, however, that there have been individual cases where the negro was just as brave, strong, and courageous as any man. I believe, on the average, he is perhaps a little more obedient, and endures hardship with less growling than the white soldier. On the other hand he is slow to learn, lacks initiative, and I believe would be easily stampeded in case of surprise or heavy concentration of fire. . . . I have seen them stay up all night and occasionally lean against a tree or truck and "cat-nap" rather than go to bed in their tent when we were in the field, simply because they were afraid of the dark. . . . I doubt if the negro officer has the qualities needed for successful leadership. . . . I firmly believe that a negro unit on strange soil and under new officers, which is bound to happen once combat is joined, will be of little military value.[15]

However, to his credit, Leusley closed with this comment: "I do think that as an aid in solving the negro question, after the war, negro combat units must be given the opportunity to either prove or disprove the fact that they can 'take it' in action."

This officer's attitude was central to one of the first and most critical issues that the committee and I found ourselves confronting. The panel had begun meeting more frequently because Hastie's resignation was inspiring ever increasing complaints from African Americans. Most black soldiers hailed from the South, where they had been denied anything approaching adequate schooling. The army constantly equated lack of education with low inherent intelligence. For example, a memo prepared for General Dwight Eisenhower in the spring of 1942 asserted,

"The lower average intelligence rating of colored selectees is an obstacle to broad employment of colored soldiers throughout a modern, highly mechanized army. . . . Lack of an educational background, plus the apparent lack of inherent natural mechanical adaptability, almost prohibits satisfactory training of mechanical specialists from colored units." And "the low average intelligence of the colored selectee will call for longer periods of training."[16]

Newly inducted soldiers were given the Army General Classification Test (AGCT) to determine their educational levels and abilities, with the highest scorers rated as Class I and the lowest as Class V. Given the meager education resources devoted to blacks in the South, no one would be surprised to learn that 47.5 percent of African Americans finished in Class V against 8.9 percent of whites, and 30.4 percent of blacks scored in Class IV, meaning three-quarters of black soldiers ended up in the bottom two educational ratings, against 30.5 percent of whites.[17]

What to do about this? When I finally gained a hearing at the advisory committee, I found it considering a proposal to kick thousands of African Americans out of the army and distribute most of the rest into menial duty in white units. It had somehow been concluded that 9 percent was the magic number for the percentage of Class V personnel with which a combat unit could function. Therefore, it was proposed that each black unit be stripped of Class V personnel above 9 percent of its ranks and that they be replaced with higher-scoring African Americans, who would mostly hail from northern cities. Some of the Class V blacks could be distributed among white units for the most menial of jobs.[18] The rest would be discharged, with the army assuming they would be welcomed back to farm chores in the South. Rather than waiting to test new soldiers at reception posts, it was suggested that the AGCT be administered at induction centers to screen out all but 6 percent (another magic number based on what—I never found out) of the Class V men. The Class V and IV soldiers would be assigned to development battalions where they would alternate days of work with days of training to increase their abilities and then be assigned to a combat unit. The result of all this would be that "the Army might well take the necessary reduction (which will amount to 600,000 men at most) on the grounds that it is better to have quality than quantity."[19] The committee was told that this was a "constructive step . . . ridding the Army of its present misfits and preventing the enlistment of men unsuited for military service."[20]

"Aghast" would be a mild description of my reaction. Only the proposal to create development battalions made any sense. At least Class V troops would get training. The rest was bunk. Above all, the AGCT made no claim to be an intelligence test. In fact more than 30 percent of Class V black troops given a nonverbal test placed in higher classifications—with some even jumping to Class I. No study had determined the workable ratio of Class V troops acceptable to a unit. Common sense dictated that some units, such as sanitary or construction outfits, could absorb higher—in some cases much higher—levels. Requiring all draftees to take the AGCT at induction centers likely would gum up the induction machinery. I was also deeply suspicious of the idea that the rural South would welcome discharging thousands of blacks into the region at a time when more and more white husbands and fathers were being drafted.[21]

Open-minded white officers working with black troops came to distrust the AGCT as an accurate barometer of performance. The army incorporated new screening techniques at induction centers and special training units for low-scoring draftees. No mass rejection of Class V men materialized. That turned out to be wise policy as it became increasingly apparent that the number of soldiers required to fight a war around the globe made impossible the luxury of excluding hundreds of thousands of able-bodied men.

Another egregious policy resulting from the inferiority philosophy came out of the Red Cross. It announced on January 21, 1942, that it would accept blood donations from African Americans, but, it added, "in deference to the wishes of those for whom the plasma is being provided, the blood will be processed separately so that those receiving transfusions may be given plasma from blood of their own race."[22] This policy, it said, had the approval of the secretaries of war and the navy. Indeed, McCloy was told this was War Department policy.[23]

That, I noted, would merely divert public protest from the Red Cross to the War Department.[24]

My attempts to get the advisory committee to change this policy ran into the edict of "don't rock the boat" on social issues. The army acknowledged no scientific justification existed for the policy but referred to "a disinclination on the part of many Whites . . . to have Negro blood injected into their veins."[25] Reminders that the separation of blood plasma was developed by the eminent African American medical researcher Charles R. Drew didn't matter. The policy should be quietly abandoned because it "coincides with the Nazi philosophy of superior blood," I asserted. "It seems to me utterly preposterous to go on the principle that men dying on a battle field would request or in fact have indicated any preference for any particular kind of plasma."[26] This issue likely would have resolved itself under the medical demands of treating the wounded on the battlefield had black troops been committed to combat, but they had not, as General Davis complained to the McCloy Committee on March 22 and April 2, 1943.[27]

Drawing on two and a half years in the War Department and visits to army posts across the land, I wrote McCloy that racial issues urgently needed his attention. "There is a serious and immediate need for some expression calling attention to the responsibilities of commissioned personnel for the proper treatment of Negro officers and enlisted men." I took note of the army's position that the military couldn't solve the problem of race in America but added, "Unfortunately, racial attitudes are unpleasant facts that must be dealt with and met by the army. They cannot be dismissed as social problems." The army had failed to develop consistent instructions to officers so that they were falling back on civilian, that is, racist, approaches to dealing with African Americans. "The issue, in my opinion, is not one of changing fundamental attitudes. It is little more than getting the attitude across to our civilian Army that all soldiers engaged in a common task should be treated as soldiers regardless of race."[28] I urged the War Department to instruct commanders to recognize and protect the rights of black soldiers, an appeal I would make many times.

The army refused to issue specific, written instructions to commanders. "Letters of the kind proposed by Mr. Gibson are, in effect, letters from the Chief of Staff telling a commander in the field to comply with War Department instructions," said Brigadier General White, the assistant chief of staff. "The value of such letters is questioned. . . . We will have the Inspector General check up on compliance with War Department instructions rather than have the Chief of Staff write to commanders asking them to comply."[29]

Violence-prone bus drivers; inadequate transportation; a paucity of movie theaters, post exchanges, and clubs; and segregation of recreational facilities were issues Davis and I brought up time and again. He told the committee no race problems arose in the mixing of white and black soldiers in the early 1900s but that the trouble began with the policy of "everything equal but separate" in 1918.[30] I complained about reliance on white southerners to be officers for Negro troops, segregation in officer mess halls, and the army's failure to formulate policy for including black women in the Women's Army Auxiliary Corps.[31] I wrote McCloy that the army's policy "restrict[ed] the assignment and promotion of Negro officers solely because of race in violation of well established principles governing Army promotions." Promotions and assignments should be based only on merit and the needs of military units.[32]

I told Charles Poletti, special assistant to Secretary Stimson, that the air corps was so haphazard in training black pilots that it would fail to deliver on Stimson's promise to have "a complete [black] fighter group" combat ready by June 30, 1943. "The assumption of the Army Air Forces seems to be that Negroes cannot be developed into Army pilots." The army was dragging its feet in training African Americans for anything other than single engine aircraft. Even if blacks demonstrated they could command bombers, "the war would have long since ended before any plans could be developed for any effective utilization."[33]

While often failing to address the real grievances of black soldiers, the committee and the army brass developed a near obsession with criticisms, complaints, and negative observations about the army from the African American community. The black press was a constant object of anger among white officers. They accused black newspapers of publishing inflammatory, unpatriotic, and false accounts of life in the army. Inflammatory they may have been, and inaccurate they may have been in details, but the overall picture the papers portrayed of black soldiers under siege in the army was certainly true. At any rate, black servicemen didn't need newspaper stories to tell them about the injustices and violence directed against them. Disturbances and riots erupted not because of newspaper stories but because of actual grievances and wrongs.

A Commerce Department survey in 1940 counted 210 black newspapers, of which 117 had been around for at least a year, with a combined circulation of 1,276,600.[34] A poll of black Americans by the Office of War Information—kept secret for reasons I couldn't understand then or now—found that more than 72 percent of Negroes nationally, and up to 85 percent in some cities, read black newspapers.[35]

What these black newspapers published got under the army's skin. The commandant at Fort Lee, Virginia, complained that the *Baltimore Afro-American* and the *Norfolk (Va.) Journal and Guide* had published articles "subversive of the soldierly mood and attitude not only of soldiers of the colored race, but those of the white race."[36] When the *Chicago Defender* wrote that "it is not necessary to be a military person to understand that some of the time required for planning a jim crow army may detract from planning an offensive of the whole army," Hastie pointed the editorial out to McCloy. He didn't like what he read. "What I urge upon the Negro press is to lessen their emphasis upon discriminatory acts and Color incidents irrespective of whether the White or the Colored man is responsible for starting them," McCloy said. "I believe that papers like the *Pittsburgh Courier* and, perhaps, some others, serve to take the mind of the Negro soldier and the Negroes generally off . . . the basic issues of this war."[37]

An officer touring army bases in Louisiana reported to the army's inspector general that white officers in black units believed "the negro press of the country has contributed materially to the racial unrest existing in the armed forces today by publication of highly inflammatory and exaggerated articles printed under glaring headlines. Many minor incidents are magnified or distorted to appeal to the racial emotions of negro personnel."[38] Field commanders wanted the army to take legal measures against black papers, but the advisory committee wisely rejected that course. Instead it suggested the army's public relations bureau do a better job of serving the African American press, making sure it got all the information it wanted and inviting African American reporters to events featuring black soldiers or units.[39]

By the end of the year, I could report that "relations with the Negro press have never been better" and that black newspapers were urging black men to be the best soldiers they could be. "All will be lost by Negroes generally if our soldiers fail to measure up" was the message emanating from the columns of the black press. This would be short lived as the African American press was like all media in being notoriously fickle in its attitude toward authority, and I would find out personally how the press can turn on you.

Some months later the War Department began supplying the McCloy Committee with regular reports on the content of black newspapers. Often these reports tried to measure the attitudes expressed in the African American press. For example, the report dated April 17, 1944, surveyed 347 articles in fifty-four daily and weekly black newspapers and found that 65 articles, or 19 percent of the total number, were unfavorable in their coverage of the army, while 204 stories, or 59 percent, were favorable, with the remainder neutral. Negative stories included accounts of the reassignment of black cavalry units in service duty, of black soldiers killed in Alabama and Louisiana, and of black reaction to comments by Secretary of War Henry Stimson considered detrimental to the quality of black soldiers. On the plus side were stories about black soldiers fighting in the South Pacific, African American pilots in action in the Mediterranean theater, and the impending release of the motion picture *The Negro Soldier*, the War Department's project to portray the contributions of black soldiers to the war effort. This memo even broke out the negative and positive impact of photographs and cartoons.[40]

The problem for the army, of course, was that the black press reflected the attitudes of African Americans about the military. I knew that from the voluminous mail we got at the War Department. Shortly after succeeding Hastie, I got an earful from Roy Wilkins of the NAACP when he wrote to me in the spring of 1943:

> The Army is going about the country, and even outside the country, stamping new patterns of segregation and humiliation upon Negro Americans. This business of setting up separate posts [and] theaters, based on race, in areas of the country where no such segregation exists in civilian life is but adding to the wall of segregation which Negroes will have to try to surmount after the war is over. Moreover, the army is teaching millions of white Americans, soldiers and civilians who probably never gave a thought to this item before, that segregation is the only way to handle the Negro.
>
> It may be that nothing can be done about it, but I hope attempts will be made to combat it. At any rate, it is a dead certainty that the practice is not improving the morale of Negro soldiers; it is not making them enthusiastic fighters for democracy; and it is adding to the cynical bitterness in the Negro civilian population.[41]

Of course, Hastie and I had been hard at work trying to combat the army's racist policies, and I tried to convey that to Wilkins in my reply. "Efforts are being made within the army to specifically meet the theater and post exchange situation." Still, I pointed out that we also had to deal with the reality that not every cry of discrimination was valid. "We have got to call our shots and be sure of our ground before proceeding. I know that this sometimes causes an irritating delay but too often wholly erroneous conclusions are drawn that do inestimable harm." I went on to say, "The whole matter of treatment of grievances is, as you realize, a very difficult one. Mixing as it does a universal tendency in the Army to complain plus an element of racial prejudice which sometimes exists and which at other times does not. Too frequently personal deficiencies are explained by yelling race prejudice."[42]

Looking back six decades later, my response sounds defensive, but Hastie and I had to battle the close-minded bureaucracy of the War Department and then defend ourselves from criticism that, while well meaning, did not always take into account the full weight of the burden under which we labored.

Some of that came across in Wilkins's next letter to me: "My attitude in this matter is that it is not my duty to lean over backwards and be too judicial. I am a protagonist for the citizen and the Negro soldier. I will not take up every fanciful tale, but neither am I spending any extra time thinking up excuses and defenses for the War Department, whose policies and basic procedure I know to be restrictive and discriminatory so far as the Negro is concerned. In my book, it is up to the War Department to prove it is not guilty."[43]

Wilkins did express sympathy about my plight:

> I know that every member of the press to whom I have talked has admiration for you personally, that they all understand the difficulties of your position, that they want very much to cooperate with the War Department and with the whole war effort (and are doing so), but that they feel that the War Department is not doing the things it could easily do to give the Negro soldier some of the justice to which he is entitled and to bolster the morale of the Negro civilian. Not only is this opinion held by the Negro publishers, but it is held by the vast majority of the Negro population and, understandably, by the men in uniform.[44]

Still, he offered up criticism of the work Hastie and I had done. He wrote that during a visit to an army post in an unnamed southwestern state, African Americans had told him that whenever Davis or I showed up, we were given a snow job inspection by white officers and never found out about "things that are sticking in the craw of every enlisted man and officer." Furthermore, he said that the troopers told him that when General Davis visited he was always surrounded by white officers and so busy with official interviews that he never heard from black soldiers.[45]

While saying there was "no personal animus" toward me, Wilkins wrote:

> I believe there are men in the War Department who want to be firm and uncompromising. I believe you want to be firm and uncompromising. But the fact remains that the War Department, instead of putting its foot down squarely, has pussy footed. It has catered to civilian

> prejudices. It has bowed to community ideas. It has transferred to the army community patterns and has not been satisfied with transferring the community pattern of Albany, Georgia, to the army post at Fort Benning, Georgia; but it has transferred the community pattern of Albany, Georgia, to the Middlewest, the East, the Northwest, and the Pacific Coast.[46]

Naturally, some of those were sentiments I could not let pass unanswered. I observed in my letter of response:

> Any sensible person would agree with many of the things you said about [the] War Department. In fact, many persons in the Army do so agree. It would perhaps surprise you to know that specific steps have been taken on nearly all of the items raised by you and others in addition. Particularly would I like to call your attention to the sponsorship of legislation in Congress by the War Department to cover the treatment of all soldiers in civilian communities near army camps. No legislation was ever enacted. Do not get the idea that there is any wholesale agreement in the War Department with the practices of segregation. Do not think that General Davis agrees with the idea. After having closely observed him in the south for three weeks and seeing his recommendations in writing, I can assure you that he feels as strongly as you and I about the practices which prevail in too many places on military reservations.[47]

I also rebutted the allegations about our visits to military camps: Notices were posted inviting soldiers to talk to us. Those conversations took place out of sight and hearing of white officers in buildings where the troops could not be seen entering or leaving. "When people tell you that officers and soldiers cannot get near us when we go out, they are just not telling the truth."[48]

I went on, "Certainly there is no denying that there is a great deal wrong in War Department attitudes. We all will have to fight like hell together to correct these conditions. . . . I will try humbly Sir not to present too vocally the War Department point of view."[49]

Wilkins's letter telegraphed to me the uncomfortable truth that I was becoming a lightning rod absorbing all the venom that the army's racist policies would understandably generate among African Americans.

Throughout 1943, tension and violence persisted on army posts and erupted in rioting at Camp Van Dorn, Mississippi; Camp Stewart, Georgia; March Field, California; Camp Breckinridge, Kentucky; Camp San Luis Obispo, California; and Fort Bliss, Texas, to name just a few.[50] The army was reaping what it had sown by adhering to the rule of Jim Crow. "Not only have race riots interfered with and crippled war production in civilian communities," I wrote General Davis, "but they are rapidly spreading within the Army to the detriment of the entire military organization."[51] At Camp Stewart, a black officer led his battalion during the rioting, even orchestrating the removal of wounded men while under fire. In Charleston, South Carolina, black MPs joined the rioters. Black soldiers looted PXs and stoned and overturned buses at Camp Claiborne, Louisiana. The post commander at Camp Clark, Texas, was booed and hissed by black troops. Rocks were hurled at the car of the Ninety-second Division commander at Fort Huachuca, Arizona, smashing all the windows, resulting in flying glass injuring one officer; the commander was not in the car.[52]

The smoldering unrest and violence, I noted, reflected an attitude among black soldiers that "if I've got to die it might as well be here as overseas."[53] The complaints were familiar: discrimination in bus transportation, abusive police, limited recreational facilities, separate drinking fountains and toilets, army release of black soldiers for trial in civilian kangaroo courts sure to convict them on charges such as rape of a white woman, and use by officers of epithets such as "nigger," "boy," and "darkey."[54] A songbook sold at the PX at Camp Claiborne, Louisiana, included the song "Watermelon Advice," containing lines like, "Oh, Ise a great big nigger." In late June, the advisory committee set up a subcommittee to make recommendations "for controlling the race problem."[55]

That panel, which included Davis, quickly responded, and the McCloy Committee passed on most of its recommendations urging the army chief of staff to pass the word down that commanders were responsible for keeping atop the racial situation in their units, detecting and defusing unrest, following army racial policies to the letter, and securing cooperation from civil authorities to correct causes of friction.

Furthermore, the committee recommended that "the Commanding Generals of the Air, Ground and Service Forces be directed to submit specific recommendations with regard to changes in War Department policy treatment of Negro personnel: use of facilities; organization of Negro soldiers into units and employment of Negro units." But the panel backed away from a subcommittee recommendation that black combat units be committed to combat as soon as possible, instead recommending they "be dispatched to an active theater of operations at an early date."[56]

A month later the McCloy Committee considered disseminating a survey of attitudes of black soldiers. There was some resistance to the idea, but Davis and I persuaded the panel to publish the survey and use it in preparing guidance for commanders of African American troops. "The truth or falseness of the grievances is not as important as the attitudes of the soldiers," I said. Even white lieutenants "do not know the attitudes of their soldiers, and it's most important that they should." General Davis agreed, observing that African American enlisted men didn't have much confidence in their white officers. "The white officer has a five times harder job commanding Negro troops than white troops," I added. "It is important that junior officers understand Negro soldiers."[57]

Of course the army brass kept insisting that discrimination did not exist. For example, I complained to McCloy that, except for a few token cases, black soldiers were being denied the opportunity for foreign language training.[58] The army rationalized that since it didn't know where black soldiers would serve overseas, it couldn't know what languages to teach them.[59] Black soldiers could be trained for administrative jobs in occupied territories in many areas of the world, I responded. In fact, the army's relegating African Americans to service jobs underscored the need for language training. "Negro truck organizations, Port Battalions and other service troops come in more intimate contact with civilian populations than any other troops in the Army."[60] McCloy insisted that "there is no disposition to ignore the employment of Negro personnel wherever and whenever they can be appropriately placed."[61]

A blow from an unexpected corner came that fall in the form of an attack on the combat capabilities of the air corps' Ninety-ninth Pursuit Squadron. I was surprised because the summer had brought mostly good news. Its commander, Colonel Benjamin O. Davis Jr., the general's son, had led the squadron in air operations in Sicily and in October had been called home to take over and complete the training of the 332nd Fighter Group. I arranged for him to meet the Washington press corps on September 10.

After providing background on the Ninety-ninth Squadron's training and deployment overseas, Davis talked of the additional training his men had received in P40 fighter planes from Lieutenant Colonel Philip Cochran, a famous aviator immortalized as Flip Corkin in the *Terry and the Pirates* cartoon strip. Davis said that he believed no unit had gone into combat better trained or equipped than the Ninety-ninth, although he acknowledged its one weakness was the lack of combat experience by himself and other flight commanders. In June, the squadron got its initiation into the war with missions over Pantelleria Island, dive-bombing attacks, and escort duty for bombers attacking Axis targets. Captain Charles Hall was credited with the unit's first kill.

The fighting had inspired increasing religious fervor. Davis told of a pilot knocked out of the sky and stranded in a dinghy for twenty-four hours in the Mediterranean who reported that "when you sit out there that long, shivering from cold at night and trying to hide from the heat of the sun by day and always hoping against hope that somebody is going to see you and pick you up, you just pray automatically." Davis concluded his report to the press by saying he had returned home for reassignment confident that "the men that I left behind instead of being the fledglings they were on the first of June are now seasoned veterans of a combat experience that all of us may well be proud."[62]

Davis went on to observe that the men knew they bore a heavy burden. "All members of this organization were impressed at all times with the knowledge that the future of the Negro in the Air Corps probably would be dependent largely upon the manner in which they carried out their mission. Hence, the importance of the work done by this squadron, the responsibility carried by every man, be he ground crewman or pilot, meant that very little pleasure was to be had by anyone until the experiment was deemed an unqualified success."

Days later, however, came the first signs of trouble. *Time* magazine carried an article asserting that while the Ninety-ninth "seems to have done fairly well," it had seen comparatively little action and that the high command "was not altogether satisfied" with its performance.[63]

Then on October 13, the squadron was trashed in a report to the McCloy Committee. While Colonel Davis was praised, the squadron was condemned for lacking aggressiveness, failing to show eagerness for battle, lacking a will to win or reach its objectives, and not possessing the stamina required of fighter pilots.[64] "Their formation flying has been very satisfactory until jumped by enemy aircraft, when the squadron seems to disintegrate," declared a report of the "combat efficiency" of the unit. "Attempts to correct this deficiency so far have been unfruitful." It cited a mission where the Ninety-ninth was directed to attack German bombers over Pantelleria but "allowed themselves to become engaged" in dogfights with the bombers' escorting fighter planes. Another damning allegation was that "on numerous instances when assigned to dive bomb a specified target in which the anti-aircraft fire was light and inaccurate, they chose the secondary target which was undefended." The Ninety-ninth peeled off from attacking one target in the toe of Italy citing weather, but another fighter group had pressed the attack, substantiating that weather was not a hindrance. These observations came from Colonel William W. Momeyer, the widely respected commander of the air group including the Ninety-ninth.[65]

"Although excellent pilots, they seem unable to fight as a team under pressure," concluded another officer quoted in the report.[66] It was recommended that the Ninety-ninth be assigned to backwater duty off the coast of Africa and that any black fighter group formed in America be assigned to homeland defense to free up a white unit for combat in Europe.[67]

This negative report landed like a bombshell for General Davis and myself. The report about the Ninety-ninth Squadron, written by Major

General Edwin J. House in Europe and forwarded to the committee by that foe of black pilots, General Hap Arnold, was described in the minutes of the meeting as "a secret letter."[68]

"White squadrons have done worse," I noted, frustration and anger welling up within me over the air corps' continued bigoted notion that blacks were incompetent by nature. "If the present Air Force attitude continues, Negroes should not be used in the Air Force."[69]

Lacking any real information from the squadron itself, the general and I did the best we could to parry the accusations. The squadron had not been assigned flight leaders with combat experience, I asserted, aware that Colonel Davis had identified that as a weakness for a unit about to experience its first taste of air war. I recommended calling Colonel Davis to appear before the committee to answer these very serious charges, a suggestion McCloy soon accepted.[70]

"The inference of the report is that Negroes are not good flyers," I said. "Suggest we get all the facts."

"You can't make veterans in one campaign," General Davis agreed. "The War Department goes on the theory that colored flyers are inferior; put the squadron in with a veteran group."

Fuming and growing ever more angry by the second, I poured out sarcasm: "The basic issue is lack of guts."

"Rather a lack of judgment," responded Brigadier General Millard G. White. "The white pilots respond automatically."

"Lack of courage; lack of judgment in a tight situation," I shot back, again in sarcasm. Then I noted, "The Air Force opinion was first, the Negro could not fly; now, he does not have the judgment to fight. There is no need to go on with the bomber and fighter units if the Air Force believes Negroes lack the necessary qualities."

Brigadier General Ray E. Porter asserted that "Negroes are reluctant to follow Negro leaders" and suggested that a division be developed under white officers.

General Davis knew exactly what that meant and protested vehemently. "While Negro leadership is limited, it would be discouraging to officer a division with white officers. Training Negroes in the South puts two strikes on them. They would rather train in 40 degree below zero weather than in the South. Don't send Negroes to places hostile to them."[71]

A few days later the committee met again, and Colonel Davis was there with a spirited defense of his men. "The squadron was handicapped in that no one in the squadron had had combat experience," he observed. The Pantelleria incident marked the squadron's first mission. "If there was a lack of aggressive spirit, it was at first; later we had it." He went on to add: "The report is a surprise to me—that the squadron disintegrates when jumped was brought to my attention only one time. . . . The reason for that failure was inexperience; I have no excuse."[72]

The squadron had been accused of failing to dive-bomb a German target. Colonel Davis said weather forced the planes to turn back. He added, "We were never given a secondary target."

Then Colonel Davis unleashed the facts. Only twenty-six pilots were assigned to the Ninety-ninth, compared to thirty or thirty-five for other squadrons. He continued, "We arrived . . . and began running patrols continuously. . . . On heavy days we flew three missions, some six." In other words, the black pilots had every bit as much stamina as any other flyer.

"What is your feeling about the group?" McCloy asked. "Will it be able to take its place?"

"I have no doubts about it," replied Davis.

"How good were your flight leaders?" McCloy asked.

"Our best men."

Davis voiced his respect for Momeyer and worried that "if his opinion is correct, there is no hope. . . ."

Then it came out that Momeyer acknowledged that he had never seen the Ninety-ninth "in a good fight," meaning a full-scale air battle, that "it hadn't been proved."

Colonel Davis was surprised to be learning about the criticism only now. "What's so disturbing—this impression was not given me over there. I carried out my mission—if given a mission to bomb a target, I went ahead and bombed it."[73]

But as the unit gained experience, it also saw its confidence, its morale, and its fighting ability grow and mature. Joining the more experienced Seventy-ninth group in Italy, the Ninety-ninth picked up precious knowledge of flight and fighter tactics. Success bred a heightened sense of commitment. Soon pilots who had finished fifty missions making them eligible to return home were requesting longer tours of duty, and the army had concluded more black squadrons should be brought in for a true test of the abilities of black pilots.[74] The Tuskegee Airmen were starting to write themselves into the history books.

As 1943 wound down, the army might point to a constructive letter to commanders here and a favorable tweaking of procedures there, but the fact was that segregation continued to be king, and its impact was poisonous. Especially was this true in the export of racial separation to a place unfamiliar with it: Great Britain. What's more, white officers there were being instructed that to be successful in handling African American troops, they "should be Bible-spouting, fatherly masters who recognize the primitive and child-like qualities of their Negro soldiers who in turn should be worked hard and given a reasonable amount of recreation along with pretty uniforms, medals and pats on the back."[75]

General Davis painted a dismal picture of conditions stateside:

> The War Department appears to regard the colored soldiers as separate and distinct and, as such, sets them apart. Fraternization or any kind of comradely association with white troops is discouraged. The War Department is making no appreciable efforts to lessen the Jim Crow practices, which are by far the greatest factor in the morale of the colored soldier. Many colored units are kept in localities from which many of the families of the men composing these units left in order to escape Jim-Crow practices. If the Department cannot change the attitudes of these communities, it can refrain from locating colored units in the communities hostile to them. Both colored and white soldiers are given the same intensive training, inculcated with the same desire to serve their country with honor—the privilege of every free citizen of any nation. It is the duty of the Department to demonstrate to the world the principle of tolerance toward our own colored group. [What's more,] the War Department has failed to

> secure to the colored soldier protection against violence on the part of civilian police and to secure justice in the courts in communities near-by to Southern stations. . . . Officers of the War Department General Staff have refused to attempt any remedial action to eliminate Jim-Crow.[76]

Although it was not then known, the war was half over. Except for the Tuskegee Airmen, black troops had not been committed to battle. How long could this intolerable failure continue?

10

A Demand for Combat

Anger over the failure to commit black ground troops to combat exploded on the floor of the Congress in early 1944. Representative Hamilton Fish, Republican from New York, had led brave black troops into battle in France in World War I, and now he demanded to know why African Americans were being denied the opportunity to do their part in the fight against fascism.

The fuse on Fish's explosive outburst had been lit nearly six months earlier. The first inkling that the army was reneging on its commitment to let African American soldiers fight for their country came in a letter to me from Lieutenant Colonel Marcus H. Ray, himself later the civilian aide in the War Department but then the commanding officer of the 931st Field Artillery Battalion at Camp Forrest, Tennessee. His letter revealed the disturbing news that 484 enlisted men in his battalion were being transferred to quartermaster, headquarters, and postal units—being relegated from combat duty to service work. Though a couple of cadres of men would remain, the "transfers are tantamount to a dissolution of the organization," Ray wrote.[1]

The 931st had proved itself to be an exemplary unit. All its men hailed from Chicago, so I had a special interest in it. "This battalion had passed every test for combat, including the firing of all weapons and physical conditioning tests," Ray noted. Placed on alert status, the soldiers had every expectation of departure for a combat theater. Hope of getting into the fighting had sustained the morale of the African American troops and motivated the building of their fine record. "The training job accomplished with the group we are losing was possible only because they had in mind release from the insults, discrimination, and segregation by an early move to a combat theater. Ironic, isn't it, that men should be willing to face death for a people who hate them. In addition to the racial implications in the transfer of black artillerymen to the Quartermaster service, there is a waste of training and education that I can't understand," Ray observed. Artillery teams, gun mechanics, survey men, and radio and telephone operators were being thrown away to perform mostly menial work. "I don't know that anything can be done about the matter as . . . transfers have already been effected, but I would like to know the reasons behind it all."[2]

More bad news followed immediately. Just a few days after the Ray revelation, Lieutenant Colonel Wendell T. Derricks of the 930th Field Artillery Battalion at Camp Butner, North Carolina, showed up in my office to report that "a train load of enlisted men" from his unit had been reassigned to a quartermaster battalion in Massachusetts and more than three hundred men were transferred to similar duty in Illinois. The 930th and 931st boasted the proud lineage of the fighting spirit of the Eighth Illinois Infantry.[3]

"Two combat units that have been in training for more than two years are suddenly stripped of their men who have been sent to service organizations," I told McCloy. "Nothing could be better calculated at this time to revive the arguments that the War Department did not intend to use combatant troops than a move such as this."[4]

I hardly had those words down on paper when word came that the 795th Tank Destroyer Battalion at Camp Hood, Texas, "has likewise been stripped of large numbers of enlisted men." The sarcasm of my next observation was couched in the best diplomatic language I could muster. "This is brought to your attention because these moves will be made known to Negroes generally and a probably unwarranted connection made between them."[5]

McCloy's reply was unsympathetic: "I believe that this is only one of the vicissitudes of war. It is a heavy blow to any unit that has been organized as long as it has to have its personnel so greatly cut down and transferred to a service unit. I hope these units can be promptly brought up to strength."[6]

Before it was all over, nearly eighteen thousand African American soldiers had been transferred from artillery, tank destroyer, antiaircraft, and other combat-related battalions to service units. As I had forecast, the black press erupted in rage, especially since no replacements had been shipped to the black combat battalions. "The continuation of these units as paper organizations draws heavily on Negro civilian and soldier morale," I wrote McCloy.[7]

A few months later Walter White of the NAACP, on an overseas inspection tour, visited the Second Cavalry Division, which had been reassigned to service duty, in Algeria.[8]

"I never saw more depressed troops," he told the McCloy Committee.

McCloy again evidenced little sympathy. "There are times when you have to cannibalize."

White pressed on, "The agony is increased by the paucity of Negro combat troops. Men who carry shells get no recognition."

The decision on the Second Cavalry was "soundly made," McCloy insisted.

"The belief," White countered, "that Negroes are used in a mediocre capacity is an important matter."

Irritated, McCloy complained, "We are under the lash—everything done to colored troops is alleged to be on account of race."

White responded that blacks didn't mind service duty so long as there are African American combat troops.

This hardly represented a fresh insight, as General Davis noted. "What Mr. White has said, I said two years ago. It would help the morale of colored civilians if there were a larger number of colored combat troops in the European Theater of Operations."

The conversions reinforced black opinion that African American soldiers were not destined for battle. Also, in what amounted to a blatant admission that it had no real interest in committing African Americans to combat, the army said personnel had been transferred only from units "that were in low priority for shipment overseas." In other words, the army brass had picked on men that it had no intention to commit to battle. Furthermore, the black combat units could not be rebuilt anytime soon. Army Ground Forces Headquarters acknowledged there were not enough black troops available to fill the depleted ranks of the African American combat organizations.[9] "It is regrettable," McCloy told me "that the filling of the depleted units cannot be accomplished as rapidly as morale considerations might dictate."[10]

The unspoken truth was that the hard facts of that era's bigotry condemned African Americans in a rigged game. The War Department had imposed a quota to restrict African American participation in the army to the 10 percent ratio blacks constituted in the nation's population. With so many African Americans consigned to service units, the quota held down induction of enough blacks to reconstitute the combat units.

Having black soldiers fighting on the battlefronts emerged right from the start as a primary goal of African American politicians and press, indeed of the black population generally. Yet 1943 ended, two years into the war, with nothing having been done to get black combat troops into action, and there was, to my knowledge, no policy about doing so, I told McCloy. "Complete candor forces me again to the observation that some decision should be made and implemented by action on the use of Negro soldiers in the army. The present situation is one generally of confusion."[11]

Against that backdrop, the reassignments of the combat soldiers to service duty throbbed like a boil, and the outcry mounted, climaxing when Representative Fish took the floor of the House of Representatives in February 1944. He had written Secretary of War Stimson on February 1 demanding to know more about the transfers and asking whether black soldiers were deliberately being kept out of the fighting. Stimson's February 19 reply sparked Fish's angry remarks to Congress.[12]

The secretary had started out by declaring that the African American units had unsatisfactory records, an assertion flatly contradicted, at least in the case of the 931st Artillery by the record presented by Ray. At the start of the war, Stimson wrote, fear of an Axis attack on the homeland and worries about enemy superiority in aircraft and tanks prompted the army to emphasize defense. So it had organized a large number of antiaircraft artillery, coast artillery, and tank destroyer units. With most of the army training in America, there was not the demand for the large commitment of service units that overseas combat required. However, now—with the Allies on the offensive, Nazi and Japanese airpower severely damaged, and homeland defense less of a concern—the "necessity of fighting a global war on many fronts has required provision of service units on a tremendous scale." White soldiers suffered such reassignment as well as blacks, he said, but assignment had to be based on the capabilities of the soldiers available. Of course the low Army General Classification Test (AGCT) scores indicating poor educational levels piled disproportionate numbers of blacks into service work. Stimson closed with a defense of the army's record on race. "Permit me to emphasize, in conclusion, that any implication that the War Department is deliberately attempting to avoid sending overseas, or to keep out of combat, troops of the Negro or any other race, is entirely without foundation. Our personnel is distributed and employed as required, on duties individuals are qualified to perform, regardless of their racial derivations."

Fish wasn't buying any of it. Within one year of the U.S. declaration of war in 1917, he had been commanding black troops on French battle lines. But, he stated, here it was twenty-six months into World War II and, with the exception of the Ninety-ninth Squadron and a few antiaircraft units, virtually no black Americans had been thrown into battle in Europe or the Pacific. Stimson had ignored his request, Fish said, for a clear reason why the combat-trained Twenty-fourth Infantry Regiment was loading and unloading supplies at docks twenty-one months after embarking from California for the South Pacific.

> I do not understand how it is that four separate colored regiments made such gallant fighting records in the last war . . . and yet no colored infantry troops have been ordered into combat in this war. The educational standards of colored people have improved in the last 25 years and I cannot agree with the Secretary of War's inference that colored soldiers' efficiency ratings are so low that "many of the Negro units have been unable to master efficiently the techniques of modern weapons." I believe many American Negroes will resent bitterly

> this broad indictment of their people and the discrimination against their use in combat units in defense of their country.[13]

The battlefield proved Stimson's assertions wrong, Fish argued. "It seems passing strange that French Senegalese or whole British divisions from India have been fighting so superbly with our allies and that Russians with low educational qualifications have been the heroes of this war, and that even the Japanese with lesser educational qualifications than American Negroes have been found to be brave and efficient soldiers."

In a thundering declaration that African Americans all over the country would have applauded with a loud "Amen!" Fish said, "Any American who is good enough to wear the uniform of his country, regardless of race, color, or creed, must be treated equally and be afforded an opportunity to serve, fight, and die in defense of our free institutions, our constitutional form of government, and for America itself."

Stimson's letter had turned out to be a huge fiasco, and I told McCloy and the Advisory Committee on Negro Troop Policies as much. It would confirm the worst suspicions about the army. Reassignment of blacks on grounds that they were too dumb for the artillery would be politically explosive, reducing "War Department policy with respect to Negroes to very simple terms that cannot be misunderstood." Stimson's letter "is most unfortunate and will, in my opinion, accentuate the greatly increasing criticisms and resulting resentments which have already reached alarming proportions," I told McCloy.[14]

Sure enough reporters and editorial writers in black newspapers expressed raw rage over it. "Troops Resent Stimson's Slur on Ability of Negro Combat Units," shouted a front-page headline in the *Chicago Defender.* The *Defender* story stated:

> From widely separated camp areas comes the report that morale has taken another deep nose dive—that underneath an outward calm colored soldiers are burning mad over the secretary's statements, which reflected upon their qualities as fighting men. . . . Men and officers feel they've got a dirty deal. One officer [at the reassigned 931st Field Artillery Battalion] is quoted as saying, "There are any

> number of us who will resign before we'll accept assignment in the engineer corps as glorified foremen to a road gang." . . . The storm of resentment among Negroes, which has thundered across the country, crystallized into positive action this week when over a thousand citizens here in Chicago pledged themselves to start the machinery to get over two million signatures on a petition demanding Congress to impeach Stimson.[15]

The keynote address for a meeting of black Republicans in Chicago devoted its entire message to the insults in Stimson's letter. African American Democrats convening in Washington revealed themselves no less angry. Democratic congressman Bill Dawson of Chicago told the Washington meeting that "the failure to use Negro Americans to the fullest in this war is the diabolical work of a reactionary and prejudiced clique within the military establishment."[16] Dawson later called for Stimson's resignation, as did the Chicago Citizens Committee of 1,000 and the National Negro Council in a resolution declaring that getting rid of Stimson was necessary "for the good of the morale of all true Americans regardless of race, creed or color."[17]

It was obvious that "serious political repercussions" likely would follow, I warned. This wasn't a new theme for me. Several months before, I had warned McCloy that the treatment of blacks by the military portended to be a critical issue in the 1944 elections.[18] Columnist Frank R. Kent of the *Washington Star,* then a conservative and influential voice in the nation's capital, placed "extreme importance on the Negro vote in the eight or nine key states north of the Mason-Dixon Line." Another conservative paper, the *Chicago Tribune,* had adopted the same position. What's more, this important midwestern paper "already had on its payroll for some time an exceedingly clever ex-New Dealer who has been making numerous speeches attacking the Army."[19] The Republican Party had warmed to the possibilities of such a campaign issue.

To me, the lesson was clear: "There is in fact every present indication that the treatment of Negroes in the armed forces will constitute the most important issue in the general effort to capture the Negro vote." The Democrats and the army ignored the potency of this issue at their peril. "Undoubtedly, much of what will be said about the Army will be political in nature and hence essentially untrue," I wrote in another diplomatic tactic aimed at relating the facts while not offending the army's sensibilities. "The essential fact is, however, that the present situation is such that the statements will be believed implicitly."[20] The most telling issues were the violence directed against black GIs by civilians in the South and the failure of the army to commit African Americans to combat.

I noted that the black pressure during the 1940 campaign forced President Roosevelt to commit the army to including blacks in the air corps and to establish the office of civilian aide. Next came my political analysis. "If Mr. [Wendell] Wilkie, or Mr. [Thomas] Dewey either for that matter, obtains the Republican nomination, no effort will be made by the Republicans to break into the solid south. On the other hand, the south will have little choice but to vote for the president, so that a number of actions now considered impolitic might not seem so in the midst of a campaign to secure the control of eight or nine states and particularly states like New York, Pennsylvania, Michigan and Illinois." The appropriate actions, I suggested, included committing black units to combat, getting the Congress to pass legislation to protect black GIs from southern civilians, and, wherever possible, getting black soldiers out of the South.[21]

Now that it was 1944 and Fish had laid the issue of combat before the American people, the War Department came under tremendous pressure over its policies toward African American GIs. Blacks everywhere concluded that the War Department had condemned the Negro soldier to a service role. Army attitudes had not materially changed since a 1925 War Department study that declared, "A temporary embarrassment will occur in the drafting of a certain few National Guard colored units which now have Negro officers. A solution may be found in the employment of these units in the Zone of the Interior until such time as the machinery of reclassification, separation, etc., is in operation. Negroes in the Reserve Corps holding commissions should be assigned to noncombat units of Negro personnel."[22]

Stimson seemed to be saying that AGCT scores, not military necessity, governed the battalion conversions, I asserted. That was damaging to the morale of the very vital service organizations, leading them to believe "only illiterates and misfits are sent to their units." Furthermore, "in what regard will combat engineer units be held when it is blandly stated that men too dumb for field artillery for which they have been trained for three years can be sent into combat engineer battalions?" I also suggested white America might be unhappy if work in service units meant black America didn't suffer its share of battle casualties.[23]

Dawson, my old friend from Chicago and the only black member of Congress after succeeding Arthur Mitchell, followed up with his own letters to the War Department. Stimson's views represented "a repetition of the attitude of the Army that has been all too familiar to Negroes." Dawson told McCloy, "I say to you frankly that the political enemies of the Commander in Chief of our armed forces are seeking to place responsibility for this un-American attitude squarely upon his doorstep."[24]

His letter unanswered, a few days later Dawson wrote McCloy that he had received "hundreds of communications from every section of this country" denouncing Stimson, calling for his removal and demanding a "sweeping investigation of the entire military situation with a view of finding out the sources" of the attitudes reflected in the secretary of war's letter. The secretary's letter "is widely regarded as a direct insult to every Negro in the country and a gratuitous slap in the face to many thousands of Negro soldiers in the Army." The wholesale conversion of black units to service duty "is the gravest danger to the morale of the Negroes in the Army and out of the Army."[25]

This time McCloy replied, after conferring with me, offering a much more measured response, advancing some arguments I would later elaborate on in another Stimson letter, and asserting that "the War Department has adhered to the principle that Negroes should be permitted to participate in combat in this war as they have in all of the wars in which our country has been engaged."[26]

The Stimson letter to Fish, I observed, was "one of the most stupid statements ever to come out of the War Department." It tarred all department personnel, even those like myself fighting every day to bring change. I knew that I had become a lightning rod for African American criticism of the War Department, but even so I was not prepared for a letter I received in mid-March from my friend Claude A. Barnett of the Associated Negro Press in Chicago. Stimson's letter sounded so much like one or two speeches I had given, Barnett wrote, "I would have sworn you wrote it [Stimson's letter]." I found myself having to write back assuring Barnett that I had nothing to do with the letter. I hadn't even seen it before it was sent out. Any reference I had made in speeches to the AGCT scores only highlighted the problems blacks face in the army and in no way implied giving the army a pass on its offenses against black soldiers. "Not even my severest critics among the newspaper boys" had voiced Barnett's sentiment.[27]

"I am sorry indeed if my letter gave form to an expression which pained you," Barnett replied. But in his own conversations, he had used my observations about the AGCT, accepting my "version" that low educational standards held back blacks and were reflected in the deficiencies of some black officers. "There is no lessening in my appreciation of you, I assure you."[28]

McCloy believed, or at least said he believed, that Stimson's letter had been twisted through "considerable misinterpretation by the American press, both white and colored." Stimson held a news conference with black reporters to attempt to give statements in his letter "their proper interpretation."[29] He acknowledged that a high educational level was not necessary for a good combat soldier.[30]

But the storm showed no sign of abating. Fish followed up with a letter asking Stimson "why the famous old Colored Cavalry Regiments, known as the 9th and 10th Regulars created by Acts of Congress in 1869–70" with a record of heroic service with Teddy Roosevelt's Rough Riders in Cuba and with General John J. "Black Jack" Pershing in World War I, had been broken up into service units.[31] Bill Hastie had also complained about the conversions of the black combat units: "The truth of the matter is that these original Negro combat units have been the problem children of the Army for more than two years, not because they were incompetent, but because no one wanted them."[32]

Hastie's complaint prompted another letter from Stimson. Assuming his reply to Hastie would be widely circulated among African American opinion leaders, Stimson wanted to clarify his statements in the Fish letter and, most of all, avoid another public relations disaster. The last time he didn't even bother to run his letter by me. This time, I was asked to draft the reply to Hastie. It was a tricky exercise for me, walking the fine line between explaining and justifying War Department policy and not betraying my own outrage over Stimson's attitudes.

First up, I addressed Fish's very specific request for what was going on with the Twenty-fourth Infantry Regiment in the South Pacific. As luck would have it, press accounts reported that these black soldiers had seen action in the battle for Bougainville Island, and I had the letter point that out. While Stimson had been correct in observing that poor educational backgrounds were a problem for black soldiers, he failed to say the army was confronting this issue. His AGCT observation simply reflected the fact that from June to December of the previous year, nearly 80 percent of African American inductees scored in the bottom two categories of the test. However, this time I made sure the letter added that a new army training program had in its first six months of operation kept 90 percent of the lowest-scoring blacks, numbering twenty-nine thousand men, in the military and sent them on for advanced training. "Many excellent soldiers have been developed out of men who had initially made low scores in their tests. This program better than anything else bespeaks the determination of the Army to make the best use of its Negro soldiers."[33]

The letter to Hastie also corrected and clarified several other points. Nowhere in his Fish letter had Stimson written that black soldiers were fit only for defensive action. Now, I had him stipulate, "No plan now exists for the conversion of all Negro combat units and certainly none is contemplated." Five times more white than black combat units had been converted to service duties required as U.S. troops marched further into once enemy held territory. The overriding goal of the War Department was "the early and successful termination of the war" and this guided manpower decisions, although Stimson acknowledged that mistakes certainly had been made. "I make no pretensions to perfection on behalf of the War Department even in the matter of the utilization of Negro troops. However, I do assert that we in the War Department have approached the matter objectively and with good faith."[34]

Of course, all the damage done by the Stimson letter couldn't be undone with another letter. Stimson's mistakes would haunt the army. Still, I was able to write the letter in good conscience because I believed change was coming. As a result of the roar of anger from the African American community, the committee and Stimson concluded the United States had to commit black troops to battle as soon as possible. As I told Barnett a few weeks later, "Obviously I cannot comment for publication on future plans but I can assure you that there will be Negro ground combat units in substantial numbers in the European Theater of Operations."[35] The Ninety-second Infantry Division, the famed "Buffalo Soldiers," was in training in Arizona, and elements of it would start embarking in a few months for Italy where the Allies were locked in a hard fight against the Nazis.

In the meantime, the problems inherent in segregation and the tensions it fostered continued to monopolize my time. I constantly looked for ways to drive home to white America the contribution black soldiers had made to the country and could make in this war. That endeavor propelled me into one of the more pleasant experiences of the war, my involvement in the making and distribution of the movie *The Negro Soldier.*

AUTHOR'S COLLECTION

I was the first African American to be awarded the Presidential Medal of Merit.

AUTHOR'S COLLECTION

I worked with the committee to reelect President Roosevelt in 1940, and his son, Franklin D. Roosevelt Jr., came out to campaign in Chicago. I'm standing to Roosevelt's left.

AUTHOR'S COLLECTION

Bob Weaver, Bill Trent, and me (*left to right*) in Chicago in 1940 when I was contemplating joining the War Department.

ASSOCIATED PRESS

Joe Louis (*right*) and I (*left*) discuss his round-the-world boxing exhibition tour in 1943 with Colonel Stanley J. Gorgan, the acting director of the War Department's Bureau of Public Relations.

AUTHOR'S COLLECTION

Benjamin O. Davis Jr. in a cadet's uniform in 1933 when he attended West Point.

A. W. Williams, president of Unity Mutual Insurance, served as secretary-treasurer of the American Negro Exposition of 1940 and exercised tight control over expenses.

DAVID JACKSON

A 1947 reunion of the black cabinet in New York. Seated are (*left to right*) Frank Horne of Interior, Campbell Johnson of Selective Service, Bob Weaver of Interior, Bill Hastie of the War Department, Bob Ming (who wasn't in the cabinet but advised many of its members), and Ralph Bunche of the State Department. I'm standing (*fourth from right*); also standing is the great NAACP leader Roy Wilkins (*seventh from left*), and to his right is Ted Jones, my business partner, who served on the Fair Employment Practices Committee with Wilkins.

BILL ANDERSON

U.S. ARMY

U.S. ARMY

U.S. ARMY

Above and facing page: The Ninety-second Division training around Fort Huachuca, Arizona.

AUTHOR'S COLLECTION

Visiting Lockbourne Army Air Corps base at Columbus, Ohio, in 1944 with (*left to right*) Anthony "Spanky" Roberts, Colonel Benjamin O. Davis Jr., me, and unidentified officers.

MARSHALL FIELD STUDIO

Secretary of War Henry Stimson pins the Presidential Medal of Merit on me.

HARRY S. TRUMAN LIBRARY

President Truman receives the universal training report from commission members *(left to right)* Edmund Walsh, Chairman Karl T. Compton, Sam Rosenman, Anna M. Rosenberg, me, and Dan Poling.

DAVID JACKSON/JOHNSON PUBLISHING CO.

I found myself on a fishing outing with Thurgood Marshall during his honeymoon in the Virgin Islands. (*Left to right*) Cecilia (Cissy), his second wife, me, Thurgood, and the captain of the fishing boat.

DAVID JACKSON/JOHNSON PUBLISHING CO.

I try my hand at deep-sea fishing while Cissy Marshall looks on.

AUTHOR'S COLLECTION

The heyday of the International Boxing Club often found me *(third from left)* conferring with *(left to right)* Harry Markson, Jim Norris, and Arthur Wirtz.

BRITISH OVERSEAS AIRWAYS CORP.

The high life of the International Boxing Club meant I enjoyed the early days of transatlantic jet travel. I'm boarding a British jetliner for a trip to Europe in 1958.

CALTOA PHOTO

My father (*left*) with baseball legend Jackie Robinson.

WILLIS PHOTOGRAPHER

My father and me with boxing great Sugar Ray Robinson (*left to right*).

H. S. RHODEN

With my mother and father in April 1954.

AUTHOR'S COLLECTION

Each year the International Boxing Club sent a Christmas card to the boxing writers and television production personnel.

AUTHOR'S COLLECTION

Beautiful Pat Wymore had to endure a lot married to the rake Errol Flynn, but she came out on top in the legal fight over his estate.

11

The Negro Soldier

Trying to make segregation work tied the army up in knots. Time and again the War Department and the McCloy Committee searched for ways to reconcile this odious practice with the challenge of organizing African American soldiers for the war effort. The army was determined not to violate the lowest civilian conventions, that is, the views of the South, but bristled at being under siege from black and liberal white opinion revolted by the injustices done to African American soldiers. That left the military brass grasping for something that would make segregation work and improve the lot of the black soldier.

As 1943 wound down, Colonel J. S. Leonard, secretary to the Advisory Committee on Negro Troop Policies, was asked to prepare proposals to improve race relations in the army. His report began with a catalog of all the complaints from African Americans about the army: Jim Crow reigned on military posts without a peep of protest from the military command. The army didn't protect black soldiers from the wrath of racist civilians. Mess halls, theaters, and recreation facilities were segregated, with the insulting practice at some posts of painting white the facilities for white GIs and covering with tar paper the ones for black soldiers. Horror over the prospect of a white man saluting an African American stood in the way of promotion of black officers. Blood plasma segregation and enlistment/draft quotas persisted. No black GIs had been shipped overseas for combat. Leonard stated the obvious: "The elimination of segregation, in its various forms, is the primary objective of the Negroes and the basic cause of most of the serious complaints."[1]

His report ended with four recommendations. The first was a tactic that universally signals a lack of will to actually make change—set up another committee to study the problem. Another recommendation was to issue "a statement of approved policy concerning Negro personnel . . . for the information and guidance of all concerned." Perhaps that was why on January 10, 1944, the War Department forwarded to the army's director of training a "Digest of War Department Policy Pertaining to Negro Military Personnel." It had been compiled by Leonard.

Another recommendation, aimed at removing African Americans from hostile environments, suggested transferring black soldiers to "unoccupied camp facilities in localities that are especially suitable for Negro troops." Just where such places might be, Leonard didn't say. Earlier he had noted that the South wasn't the only place not welcoming to African Americans. "For example, Senator [Joseph Christopher] O'Mahoney of Wyoming protested vigorously the assignment of a maximum of 10,000 Negro troops to Fort Warren."[2]

The one recommendation that did have promise was Leonard's proposal for issuing a manual for officers charged with commanding black troops. Certainly there was nothing new here. On several occasions over more than a year the McCloy Committee considered this idea, and the research branch of the army's Special Service Division had actually produced one. Given the ignorance and poor records of so many white officers, and the tensions and unrest they helped generate, such a manual would seem like a logical development—but not to some elements of the army. While the manual got favorable comment at McCloy Committee meetings, some officers on the panel objected to the inclusion of data about the attitudes of black soldiers and the "questionable" conclusions and "controversial statements" included in the booklet. Alternatives were proposed, including lectures by white commanders who had successfully led black troops and publication of their case histories.[3]

A reading of the booklet finds a lot of sensible observations and recommendations, given the times and the army's adherence to the basic fallacy of segregation.[4] While repeating the oft-recited chorus of army brass that the military can't experiment with social reform, it did impose on white officers the responsibility for understanding the historical background of black troops under their command. Officers had to be aware of "beliefs, attitudes and traits most likely to cause trouble in the handling of Negro troops." For any white officer who didn't understand these things, terms including "boy," "darky," "uncle," and "nigger" were named as offensive, as was the pronunciation of Negro as if it were spelled "Nigra." Race-based jokes about blacks were prohibited. "Colored soldiers are quick to learn whether their officers look on them as members of a childlike, mentally limited, primitive, or even vicious race, or whether the officers expect them to be good and useful troops." Low expectations would be rewarded with low performance from black soldiers. Likewise, blacks do not like to be tagged with "special, highly regarded talents," such as a supposedly inborn ability in music and dancing or advantage in running, jumping, boxing, and some other sports. These, like derogatory attributes, attempt to place blacks as a race apart, the manual noted.

Then the booklet strayed in offering a defense of segregated units. Citing a 1943 survey of white and black soldiers, it noted that about the same percentage of African Americans (38 percent) favored separate outfits for whites and blacks as those who said both races should serve in the same outfits (36 percent). These results, the manual said, in no way indicated any degree of black acceptance of the idea of segregation, that in fact "the *idea* of racial segregation is disliked by almost all Negroes and downright hated by most." (Emphasis in the original document.) Rather the survey simply illustrated, in the army's view, that a sizable portion of black soldiers desired to avoid the friction they felt would come in serving in the same outfits as whites. Eighty-eight percent of white soldiers favored separate outfits, but again, the manual's authorities put a very narrow interpretation on this. "What the findings [for both races] do indicate is no more and no less than that the odds are very much in favor of less interracial friction if colored and white enlisted men continue to be organized in separate military units." Subsequent history would prove of course that racial issues disappear in the foxhole. The manual noted, uncritically, the fig leaf the army placed over segregation of recreational facilities. Service clubs, theaters, and PXs were not to be designated for use by any race but classified for use only by certain units. Since units were segregated, of course these facilities were segregated.

Back to the plus side, the booklet stated that the rights of black soldiers must be respected by civilian authorities as well as by the military. "Responsibility for the proper treatment of Negro military personnel is always on the shoulders of the commanding officers. . . . Every effort should be made to instill and enforce principles of mutual respect, courtesy and cooperation between Negro and white soldiers." Furthermore, the "problem of relations between Negro soldiers and civilian communities adjacent to their stations is a matter of military importance and is the responsibility of the post, camp or station commander."

According to the booklet, also incumbent on officers was the task of heading off unrest and violence:

> Investigation has shown that every case of serious interracial trouble has been fed by rumors, and that these rumors are never accurate. Colored soldiers have been angered into mob action by stories of mistreatment. White soldiers have been similarly goaded by distorted and utterly false tales about Negro behavior. The antidote for such inflammatory rumors is to be found neither in oppressive censorship nor in overzealous repressive discipline. Malicious rumors should be met squarely with the truth so stated that it cannot be misunderstood, ignored or doubted. This should be done as quickly as possible, just as soon as the responsible officer learns that dangerous tales are circulating or that there is a focus of dissatisfaction among his men.[5]

Probably no sadder commentary on the lack of commitment of some members of the advisory committee to their jobs could be found than the panel's report early in 1944 that only two members had read the draft of the manual. This "indicates a lack of initiative on the part of all the members . . . and should be corrected immediately or a new committee appointed," recorded an addendum to the minutes of the January 4, 1944, meeting. "There is a tendency on the part of the committee to maintain a status quo and let a problem solve itself."[6] Accurate, but a far from encouraging observation about the advisory committee. Still, in actuality, it reflected the army's profound reluctance to do anything that even suggested rocking the boat when it came to the issue of race.

If there existed any doubt about the need for better training of white officers, it would be eradicated by a reading of the letters, complaints, and memos crossing my desk. German prisoners of war (POWs) got better treatment than black soldiers at the dispensary and hospital at Camp Lee, Virginia, wrote Private Adolphus Pruitt. "The way the Medical Officers talked to us was awful and discouraging. Why, we are being treated worse than dogs."[7] POWs had the run of the theater at Godman Field in Kentucky while blacks were restricted.[8] At Camp Barkeley, Texas, German POWs shared latrine facilities with white American soldiers, while black GIs had to use a segregated section of the latrine. "Seeing this was honestly disheartening," said Private Bert B. Babero. "It made me feel, here, the tyrant is actually placed over the liberator."[9] Babero's complaints about filthy quarters, inadequate bus transportation, one small PX for blacks, and malicious treatment of African American GIs by civilians fell on deaf ears with the company commander, "himself a Texan and probably accustomed to the maltreatment of Negroes." His complaints about German POWs getting treated better than black GIs got Babero labeled a troublemaker.

White bus drivers continued to assault and kill black soldiers with impunity. Private Edward Green, a black soldier, was shot to death by white bus driver Odell Lachnette at Camp Claiborne, Louisiana, on March 14, 1944. An army investigation found "no justification moral or legal" for the shooting. "Of course, nothing was done to Lachnette," I reported.[10] Master Sergeant Joseph T. Daley boarded a bus in Hattiesburg, Mississippi, to find the black seating section filled. Another soldier moved the Jim Crow sign one seat forward, and he and Daley took seats. Bus driver B. F. Williams told the soldier to "leave that Goddamn sign alone" and later told him to straighten it. When he refused, Daley, trying to defuse a tense situation, straightened the sign. "You son of a bitch," bellowed Williams, who then drew a revolver and shot Daley in the abdomen, critically wounding him. Williams had killed a black passenger several months earlier.[11] Negro officers were herded out of the post theater at Camp Forrest in Tennessee at gunpoint, and black soldiers were kept out of the post library.[12]

Camp Gordon Johnston on St. James Island, Florida, was described as a particularly repulsive place where black soldiers feared beatings and worse at the hands of white soldiers and civilians. Primitive outhouses located near the barracks left the camp stinking of human waste. Men who in civilian life had been schoolteachers and skilled tradesmen were regularly detailed to carry pails from these outhouses. Refusal to do this duty meant stockade time. "I have spoken to about 15 or 20 men, who are yet working on these pails, and I have never seen a more dejected looking group of men," Corporal Rupert Trimmingham wrote. "These men have a haunted look in their eyes—a look of fear as though they were afraid of their very lives."[13]

I asked the adjutant general to investigate after a soldier from Davis-Monthan Field at Tucson, Arizona, wrote me that black soldiers were deprived of access to programs for training to become aerial gunners, bombardiers, navigators, pilots, and bomb-sight mechanics. "Thus we see that the maintenance of the ideology of 'white supremacy' resulting in the undemocratic practices of jim-crow and segregation of the Negro members of the Armed Forces brings about the condition on Davis-Monthan Field whereby 80 percent of the whole Section is removed from the fighting activities on the base."[14]

Now as bad as these complaints were, I was soon to hear worse. The army intelligence services began making regular reports about racial conditions across the country. One in the fall of 1944 found plenty of trouble.[15] The Ku Klux Klan was organizing in Jacksonville, Texas, and "The Order of the White Cross" in Spartanburg, South Carolina. Police in Los Angeles and East St. Louis, Illinois, were girding for possible rioting. Rioting had occurred between white and black soldiers at Camp Patrick Henry, Virginia, leaving one white dead and three African Americans wounded. Fifty black soldiers angry about overcharges from black businesses rioted in Durham, North Carolina. Tear gas was used to disperse five hundred black soldiers rioting in Tallahassee, Florida. Unrest or violence was reported at Camp Sutton, North Carolina; Camp Claiborne, Louisiana; Fort Benning, Georgia; Camp Shanks,

New York; Seattle, Washington; Gary, Indiana; Richmond, Virginia; Spartanburg, South Carolina; and elsewhere. Blacks in Chicago, Harrisburg, Pennsylvania; Norfolk, Virginia; and Cincinnati, Ohio, were arming themselves. "Get guns and get ready," a black minister in Cincinnati was alleged to have told his congregation. Especially disturbing to me were the report's allegations of rape of white women by black soldiers.

While I wholeheartedly agreed with the assessment that racial tensions were rising, I found the army's intelligence reports biased to the point of distorting what was going on. "The lists consist almost entirely of a repetition of crimes by Negroes which apparently go to the belief that the present situation is due to the fact that Negroes are committing acts that will inflame and arouse whites," I told McCloy.[16] No attention was paid to background causes. "This approach dangerously oversimplifies a complex problem. The basic underlying assumption apparently is that conditions have deteriorated because of Negro criminal aggression against whites."

A dead giveaway to the flawed nature of this document turned up in its allegations of rape of white women by African Americans. The report painted a picture of all sex crimes committed by blacks. The worst, most poisonous stereotypes of Jim Crow had broken into what purported to be an objective account of racial problems. Indeed, but for a couple of references to the Klan, the army's intelligence services painted a "pessimistic, one-sided and decidedly out of balance" picture of black soldiers responsible for all acts of indiscipline and violence, I wrote McCloy. This "manufactured crime wave" rendered "impossible the consideration of any preventative action other than harsh, repressive measures to curb unruly and criminal Negroes."[17] I was convinced that arrest and conviction records from the Judge Advocate General's Department and the collection of statistics from a variety of sources, including black newspapers, would provide a more comprehensive picture. Employment of blacks by the Intelligence Division in collecting information about racial conditions would help bring a broader perspective.

While there was plenty that was wrong with the intelligence reports, the fundamental premise that racial tensions were rising could not be denied. Time after time, the War Department flinched when other black leaders and I practically begged army officials to tell civilian authorities in no uncertain terms they had to respect the rights of black men and women in uniform. Hell, the brass failed on too many occasions to get that message to the white officers commanding African American troops. A more indirect approach, educating white America about its black citizens, seemed like the only alternative. I certainly wasn't against this tactic. After all, I had played a major role in recruiting talent for the 1941 radio broadcast *America's Negro Soldiers.*

A year after that broadcast we launched a much more ambitious project. The mistreatment, abuse, and violence directed against black troops by white civilians and police sickened Undersecretary of War Robert Patterson. In his view, the injustices were bad for the morale of African Americans, but, more fundamental to his heartfelt sensibilities, what was going on throughout the South was just flat out wrong. Aware that the army's special services branch had in the works a series of motion pictures under the broad categorical title of *Why We Fight,* Patterson saw an opportunity to present the case for African American soldiers to America.

Patterson introduced me to Colonel Frank Capra, the Hollywood director who was producing the *Why We Fight* movies intended for both military and civilian audiences. Capra later recalled that "Gibson opened up a thick dossier of sickening acts of discrimination against Negro troops in the South."[18] The movie genius knew he faced a daunting challenge. "To my knowledge, no documented film on the American Negro had ever been attempted. The subject was dynamite. If my film inflamed passions, or hardened existing prejudices, it would be shelved."[19]

The result was *The Negro Soldier,* produced by Capra, directed by Stuart Heisler, and written by the black writer Carlton Moss. Moss had some impressive credentials, having worked with Orson Welles and John Houseman in promoting the Federal Theatre's production of a black *Macbeth* in Harlem. He not only was responsible for writing *The Negro Soldier* but acted in it, playing a preacher whose sermon narrates episodes of black history. Heisler, the white director, had directed white and black actors in *The Biscuit Eater* in 1940.[20]

The Negro Soldier told the story of African Americans with an emphasis on military accomplishments. It related the slaying of Crispus Attucks by British troops in the Boston Massacre of 1770. If that sounds familiar, it's because the film picked up on themes highlighted at the American Negro Exposition in Chicago in 1940. Advancing beyond the expo, the film touched on more-recent black achievements and war heroics. The scientific breakthrough of Charles Drew in developing and storing blood plasma was revealed to audiences. Navy mess man Dorie Miller epitomized valor at Pearl Harbor by shooting down half a dozen attacking Japanese warplanes. Hugh Mulzac captained a Merchant Marine ship, the SS *Booker T. Washington,* in convoys churning through the German submarine-infested North Atlantic. The trials, tribulations, and combat successes of the Tuskegee Airmen were displayed on the silver screen. And of course that all-American hero Joe Louis exemplified the commitment of black America to the war effort. While Moss and Heisler were not allowed to mention Jim Crow, they filmed army life as it was, and the reality for black soldiers was splashed across the silver screen.[21]

The Negro Soldier received its first showing to an audience of black troops in the Pentagon in January of 1944. Given the bad experiences they had had in the army, some in the audience expressed amazement that the army had made this movie. *Time* magazine noted, "At first they froze into hostile silence. But after 20 minutes they were applauding. For just about the first time in screen history their race was presented with honest respect."[22]

Langston Hughes, who was among two hundred black publishers, editors, and writers who saw the movie at a special showing in January 1944, called it "the most remarkable Negro film ever flashed on the American screen." Writing in the *Chicago Defender,* he said, "It is distinctly and thrillingly worthwhile."[23] The *Pittsburgh Courier* exulted that "the 45-minute picture might easily prove to be one of the most outstanding and factual characterizations of the Negro ever made. . . . If the film—which by the way is available to movie houses free—is properly distributed throughout the nation, it will be worth its weight in gold."[24]

To get that kind of distribution, General Davis and I flew to Los Angeles in April 1944 to screen the picture for the captains of the motion picture industry. I wrote McCloy to report on our trip. I told him we lobbied tirelessly for the movie, emphasizing the hundreds of thousands of blacks serving in the armed services, talking about the black GIs being shipped overseas, stressing that the more open environment they found in Europe would influence their attitudes upon returning home, and expressing our dismay over continued segregation, intolerance, violence, and murder directed at African Americans. Unless America gets the true picture of its black citizens, I wrote, the war would end with hardened attitudes of intolerance. "Unless steps are taken, we pointed out, many white persons will be stronger in their determination to show that the Negro soldier is still 'just a nigger.' "[25] I stressed that the best step to combat such attitudes would be wide distribution of *The Negro Soldier.*

The premier for the movie moguls on April 13 was a big success. "You may quote me as saying this picture is the greatest service film made to date," declared Harry Cohn, the Columbia studio magnate. "I think a letter ought to go out to every exhibitor expressing the urgent necessity for running it," said Hollywood legend Darryl Zanuck. "I have seen the film and think it is great," asserted movie trailblazer Jack Warner, who instructed his company's first-run theaters to show the film. Joe Schenck immediately got it into a couple of theaters in Los Angeles and Hollywood.

A few quibbles were voiced. All the movie moguls agreed that the film, at nearly three-quarters of an hour, was too long to fit into the standard show lineup of cartoon, short subject, and Hollywood featured film. Warner and Zanuck promised a "vigorous exploitation" of the film if it were shortened. Warner feared that the title might run into resistance from distributors and suggested renaming it *One in Every Ten.* But, I noted to McCloy, "significantly, no one had any objection to the content of the picture."[26] In fact, some suggested we needed to get additional footage shot showing black soldiers in combat theaters. Davis and I stuck by the name but did suggest the movie be shortened.

One night later, Warner had the movie screened for distributors in California. "These men, unaware of our presence in the screening room, applauded the picture despite the fact that viewing films is their business," I reported.

A few days later, *The Negro Soldier* was shown at Fort Huachuca, Arizona, home of the black Ninety-second Division, inspiring all manner of questions from the African American GIs. Why weren't the combat troops pictured in the film actually in combat? Given the treatment of black soldiers in the South, what did they have to fight for? Several questioners noted Secretary of War Stimson's infamous letter to Congressman Fish. Others wondered how the army could persist in keeping its fighting men segregated by race. "I fail to see any essential difference between Hitler and traditional U.S. attitudes toward Negroes," complained one soldier. A white officer who summarized the questions for the War Department had this to say: "Answers to the above questions, comments regarding same that can be used in further indoctrination, information of enlightening nature is respectfully solicited."[27]

It turned out that the movie moguls were right about shortening the movie, at least as far as general audiences were concerned. The longer version did not do well at the box office in 1944. When it was shortened to twenty minutes from forty-three minutes, white audiences liked it. Sixty-seven percent of white soldiers surveyed by the army registered a highly favorable view of the movie. Capra biographer Joseph McBride went so far as to assert that the movie "played a significant role in the breaking down of the Army's racial prejudice and helped pave the way for the desegregation of the Army in 1948." Historians Thomas Cripps and David Culbert said that by depicting black soldiers as part of the fabric of American life, the film indicated change within the army and posed the question, Why not also in the civilian world?[28]

I rejoiced in the good press *The Negro Soldier* garnered. Unfortunately, I had had some bad press of my own. In the summer of 1944, *Time* magazine, in an article on black soldiers, described me as "a not-too-insistent" advocate on behalf of African American troopers.[29] P. L. Prattis, executive editor of the *Pittsburgh Courier*, responded in a letter to *Time*, not for publication unfortunately, with a spirited defense of my work:

> I have spent a quarter of my time in the last three years in the War Department. I have carried the complaints there, to Judge Hastie and to Mr. Gibson. Mr. Gibson has never failed to investigate any proper complaint lodged with him. He has never, to my knowledge,

> truckled or compromised. He has had the good sense not to move in when he had nothing. But when he thought he had a case, he has insisted that something should be done. I write this about Mr. Gibson because there are many Negroes who feel that a Negro leader who is not ready to fight at the drop of the hat on every issue, good or bad, is "not-too-insistent." These people will welcome *Time's* description of him and use it to lessen the provocative influence he now enjoys in the War Department.[30]

Such good notices for me from representatives of the black press were to prove fleeting. For all the good that *The Negro Soldier* achieved, 1945 opened with a stunning setback for the black fighting man. It was a chapter in the history of World War II that remains controversial to this very day and one that plunged me into a firestorm of criticism.

12

Buffalo Soldiers

Early in February of 1945, soldiers of the black Ninety-second Infantry Division launched an attack against the Germans' notorious Gothic Line in northern Italy. After several days of hard fighting against Axis troops commanded by Field Marshal Albert Kesselring, the assault failed. Blame fell on black GIs who had "melted away" in big numbers from the battle. In the eyes of the army brass, African Americans had lived down to expectations and demonstrated that black GIs could not be counted on in a hard fight. I rose to the defense of the soldiers only to find myself vilified in the black press. It all added up to a depressing chapter in the history of African Americans in World War II. It's a complicated, tangled story that began far away from Italy, in the Arizona desert at a place named Fort Huachuca.

Everything wrong with the army's treatment of black soldiers converged on this big training facility. It was ground zero for the collision of the conflicting demands of a war to save democracy and American society's commitment to segregation. Caught between these irreconcilable forces were the Buffalo Soldiers of the Ninety-second Infantry Division. "Buffalo Soldiers" was the name American Indians gave to the troopers of the Ninth and Tenth Colored Cavalry Regiments of the Indian wars in the West because of the buffalo hides they wore during the harsh winters. The Ninety-second inherited this colorful appellation.

Black public opinion and agitation in the late 1930s and afterward ensured that hundreds of thousands of African Americans would serve in World War II. Ever mindful of civilian prejudices, the War Department was loath to congregate too many black soldiers in any one place. Time and again towns and cities in all areas of the country objected to black units being assigned to nearby camps. Among the places that registered complaints about having African American troops stationed nearby were Rapid City, South Dakota; Albuquerque, New Mexico; Spokane, Washington; Las Vegas, Nevada; Battle Creek, Michigan; and Morehead City, North Carolina.[1] Blacks lobbied against assigning African Americans from the North to training camps in the South, but, in fact, most of the posts were located in the southern tier of states.

Army policy stipulated that no black unit larger than a brigade could be stationed in an American post.[2] The exception was Fort Huachuca, Arizona, which had been utilized for black troops as far back as the days of the Indian wars. The simple reason for the choice of Fort Huachuca stood out in its isolation from any town of any size. Tucson, Arizona, was eighty-one miles away; Tombstone was twenty-six miles; and Bisbee, thirty-nine miles. Nogales, on the border with Mexico, was sixty-five miles down the road.[3] The nearest town of any size was Douglas, sixty-three miles away, or as Allen Joiner, a Chicagoan who trained with the Ninety-second at Fort Huachuca, put it, "Douglas was a twenty-five dollar cab ride away, and twenty-five dollars was a lot of money in those days."[4] These towns had small black populations, further limiting off-duty opportunities for GIs from Fort Huachuca. Of course, the Southwest was no haven from racial bigotry.

Adjacent to Fort Huachuca stood the miserable little town of Fry. Military historian Major Ulysses Lee labeled it "dirty, unsanitary and squalid."[5] The only things it was good for were liquor and prostitutes. At one point, the army tried to tackle a serious venereal disease problem by fencing in the shacks used by the prostitutes, an area that came to be called the Hook, but the effort ultimately was abandoned.[6] By the time the Ninety-second arrived, Joiner recalled, "they had little huts one right after another out there on the line just outside the post, and that's where the hookers were and where they did their business. You'd get a pass, go out of the post and get drunk. You could fill a grip full of whiskey like Old Granddad, take it back to the fort, and sell it for thirty dollars a fifth. And I'll tell you something, it was sold as soon as you got on the post."[7] One army venereal disease control officer observed that no army post in America had "vice and corruption at its front door" like Fort Huachuca.[8]

Adding to the insult of isolation came the injury of the worst segregation practices—separate hospitals, officers' clubs, civilian quarters, and other facilities—and the most corrosive of all, the entrenched rule that no white officer could serve under a black officer. Some of these wretched practices would be duplicated overseas when the Ninety-second shipped out to Italy.

All this made me question whether Fort Huachuca constituted a good place to train black soldiers, and I said as much in a letter to the fort's commanding officer, Colonel Edwin N. Hardy. While acknowledging the problems of isolation, his reply insisted the post had compiled a good record of turning out disciplined black soldiers. "We have not had a single concerted action against authority, riots or any racial clashes," Hardy wrote. "The people of Arizona have come to be less prejudiced against Negroes and are showing more confidence in them."[9]

Hardy clearly was in denial, but then you might expect that, considering how he had carved out the kind of life he wanted at Fort Huachuca. He was a horseman, an old bowlegged cavalry man, and at the post he commanded the black Ninth Cavalry, a show regiment that he led in performances throughout the West. Having built a very pleasant way of life for himself, Hardy came to resent the intrusion of the war and the duties, responsibilities, and headaches imposed on him by having big forces like the Ninety-second and Ninety-third Divisions concentrated at the camp for training.

However much Hardy enjoyed the place, there was no denying that Fort Huachuca remained a desolate, isolated camp. So dire was the absence of recreational facilities for the soldiers at the post that I came up with the idea of building a recreation center/beer hall there. Back in Chicago, my father organized some business friends, and they chipped in thirty-five thousand dollars. My new Los Angeles friend, architect Paul R. Williams, designed the facility. Since the beer hall would be built on government land, it had to have approval of the War Production

Board. I drafted a letter for Colonel Hardy, explaining to the board that the facility was needed because the "remote and isolated location of this Post makes the usual community resources unavailable for the many thousands of Negro troops now being trained here." I seconded Hardy's suggestion that he write the governor of Arizona seeking his support "so that the aimless wanderings of the soldiers in the towns may be kept to a minimum."[10] The Green Top, as the beer hall became known, was fondly remembered by Joiner as a place for a relaxing drink.

The Green Top wasn't the only Chicago contribution to the camp. We staffed the station hospital with guys from Chicago, led by my old friend Lieutenant Colonel M. O. Bousfield, the head of Negro health studies for the Julius Rosenwald Fund. Bousfield became a regular correspondent reporting to me on problems at the fort. Chief among them was the division of the hospital into white and black sections. Bousfield described himself as "completely inconsolable" over the failure of the Surgeon General's Office to issue orders on the organization of the Fort Huachuca hospital. "All this has left us pretty helpless in the organization of the hospital here on the Post, which has resulted in one single hospital with two sections," with the white side being better treated.[11] About six months later, Bousfield wrote, "The question of two separate hospitals *seems* now to be pretty well established [his emphasis]."[12] The white hospital had 222 beds, while the black one counted 944 beds. The hospital situation reflected the army's rank discriminatory policies on promotions: the smaller white hospital was officered by four lieutenant colonels, while only one, Bousfield, supervised the black hospital, which was nearly four times larger.

Into this miserable hellhole arrived the Ninety-second in the spring of 1943. Fort Huachuca first had been home to the Ninety-third, the other all-black division designated for combat duty. That unit had to start moving out before there would be enough room for the Ninety-second. That meant that when the Ninety-second was activated in October of 1942, its troops had to be spread around four camps—Fort McClellan, Alabama; Camp Robinson, Arkansas; Camp Atterbury, Indiana; and Camp Breckinridge, Kentucky—since Fort Huachuca remained the only post where an African American unit larger than a brigade could be stationed.

Trouble quickly followed the deployment of the Ninety-second to Arizona. Bousfield wrote me of discriminatory treatment of black officers. Fifty-one African American officers had been disciplined by being sent to the "School of Application and Proficiency," ostensibly for training, while not one white officer suffered this treatment. "One poor fellow," wrote Bousfield, found himself sentenced to the school after he complained to a white officer about ordering black GIs to fall in by shouting "Fall in, you monkeys." These black officers "are put through long hikes with full packs and are drilled in front of the enlisted men who laugh at them being treated like privates."[13]

A black chaplain and his wife visited a restaurant where they and other African Americans had eaten before, but this time when they sat at a table with three white officers, a white colonel at another table told the black couple to move. Bousfield reported on camp gossip about the wife of the Ninety-second commander, Virginia-born Major General Edward M. Almond. The camp was abuzz with talk that she had called a telephone operator with the Women's Army Auxiliary Corps "a nigger" and that she thought separate shopping days should be set aside for the races at the PX.[14]

Challenging the notion of segregation wasn't allowed. In opening an art exhibit at Fort Huachuca, Almond declared that "controversial issues must not be raised in the 92nd else one will be considered unpatriotic!" During a review of officers, Almond addressed the whites by their rank, as in "Captain Blank," but when Captain Homer Roberts, an African American whom I had known in Chicago, was presented to him, Almond greeted him with "Hello, Roberts."[15]

Separate officers' clubs existed, the one for blacks called Mountain View and the white one Lake Side. Lake Side of course was the one with a swimming pool, and procedures were installed to preclude black kids from swimming there. Segregation of recreational facilities supposedly was verboten, so Almond covered up the fact that the post had two clubs for the races by forbidding public notices on bulletin boards announcing events such as dances, Bousfield told me. "This is the apotheosis of the Virginia method of handling race relations," he observed. "Almond is pretty stupid about race relations."[16]

Bousfield wrote me twice on May 27. The first letter was full of complaints. But in the second, his morale was buoyed. Bousfield reported that the better officer at Fort Huachuca was Colonel Hardy. He had called Bousfield, Homer Roberts, and another officer in, and the racial issues were discussed "pretty freely." Apparently Hardy had had a "heart-to-heart talk" with Almond, who now understood that his comment at the art exhibit was a mistake, as was the concentration of black officers in the proficiency school. The colonel was unaware of the insult to the chaplain and his wife at the post restaurant but said he deplored it. Furthermore, Hardy was arranging a barbecue for white and black officers with "instructions that they are not to bunch up, but that they are to mix." Bousfield praised the half-hour meeting with Hardy as "just about the finest thing which has happened on this Post." In addition, "It is very good to realize that Hardy has the guts to take such a stand as this, to recognize the problem, and frankly to make an attack on it, even carrying it to people of higher rank."[17] Unfortunately, it turned out to be a short-lived moment of enlightenment, and in the end nothing of significance changed.

By the summer of 1943 I was reporting to the War Department that Fort Huachuca should be counted among the military bases experiencing "considerable unrest." One white officer suffered cuts from flying glass when black GIs threw rocks smashing the windows of the division commander's car. The commander himself, Almond, was not in the vehicle that day.[18] In another incident, a white captain had been attacked and beaten to within an inch of his life. I suggested to General Davis, who had served with the Ninth Cavalry at Fort Huachuca before the war, that he and I visit the post.[19]

We made an inspection tour of the base in mid-July, talking to officers and enlisted men. Both of us wrote reports, and although we tried to accentuate the positive where we could, we found signs of trouble everywhere and widespread disaffection, resentment, and anger among African American enlisted men.

The most dramatic indicator of how wrong things were going at Fort Huachuca came when we accompanied Almond to the dedication of a new baseball field and the game that followed. About ten thousand soldiers, most of them black GIs from the Ninety-second, filled the stands. As Almond rose to address them, he was greeted with disorder, boos, and catcalls. Astounded by this display of disrespect and disturbed by what I had been seeing and hearing at the post, I couldn't help adding my own dig at Almond. "General," I said, "such popularity must be deserved." He didn't say anything, only scowled while waiting for the booing to die down. General Davis described Almond as "greatly shocked" by the outburst from the GIs. Davis believed that the show of disrespect "was not altogether personal, but was an expression of resentment" from the men over conditions at Fort Huachuca.[20]

In his report to the army's inspector general, Davis related a sad but familiar story. "The promotion policy of the War Department as applied to colored officers is considered as discriminatory and unjust. . . . The segregation of colored officers in a regimental mess at Fort Huachuca also had a demoralizing effect." Particularly galling was the objection by white officers when the black chaplain and his wife showed up at the post restaurant. The assignment of only black officers to the "School of Application and Proficiency" was "regarded by the colored officers as discrimination and punishment, rather than an attempt to help the below-average colored officer." Black and white officers rarely met to discuss professional issues. Black chaplains found white officers "too prejudiced to be fair." The stoning of the commanding officer's car wasn't the only violence. A white officer sleeping in a tent during field exercises was attacked and severely injured by a blow to the head from a shovel.[21]

My account of the visit for Assistant Secretary McCloy reflected those same problems. I made a point of emphasizing that we didn't go there soliciting complaints. "At no time were the enlisted men mollycoddled. General Davis constantly reminded them of their obligations and responsibilities as well as the necessity of initiating complaints through proper channels to proper officers who possess the power to institute remedial action."[22] And we passed on our findings and related what black soldiers were thinking and talking about to the officers commanding the Ninety-second and Fort Huachuca without embellishing them with our own personal opinions. The officers responded to the complaints, though "rather strong exceptions were at first noted to the facts which we presented." One of the things we emphasized was that the GIs' attitudes were important whether or not their opinions were based on fact. For instance, we heard black soldiers express outrage that a white lieutenant had gotten away with beating and injuring a drunken African American enlisted man, even though the truth turned out to be that the lieutenant had faced a court-martial.

So bad were things at Fort Huachuca that the black enlisted men had lost confidence in their white officers. African Americans entered the service with the preconceived notion that the army was going to discriminate against them because of their race, and that conviction was confirmed by the attitudes of white officers, especially the younger, lower-level, more inexperienced officers.

"Negro infantry officers in one of the Negro regiments were segregated in one of the officers messes immediately upon their arrival," I told McCloy. That was a National Guard unit from Massachusetts, where of course African Americans weren't acquainted with the code of Jim Crow. The army's promotions policy rankled black soldiers. Almond and other white officers blamed black newspapers and black officers for the unrest. Indeed Davis and I talked to several black officers totally unfit for service. Furthermore, we reminded all African American officers that the "irresponsible actions of a few could irreparably harm them all."[23]

The show of disrespect, the violence, the poor morale, and the pervasive segregation caught General Davis by some surprise. Earlier in the year, he had made several visits to units of the Ninety-second scattered among four bases, and the picture then had been decidedly different. The division's morale rated superior with "the best of feelings existing between the colored and white officers." He had heard no complaints about discrimination. Black and white officers sat together at several tables in the headquarters mess, displaying "the best of comradeship." African American and white officers turned out at a reception for him at Fort McClellan. All officers had the highest respect for Almond. "The colored officers were especially profuse in their praise of him for his fairness and deep concern for their advancement and welfare" because of his interest "even in their comforts and entertainment."[24]

What had happened between Fort McClellan the previous winter and Fort Huachuca the next summer?

Black officers and men interviewed by Davis and myself attributed Almond's change of attitude to his being "unduly influenced by some officers" in the Ninety-second Division. Focusing on "mechanical perfection in the execution of training missions," Almond at Fort Huachuca overlooked the human element and paid too little attention to working toward racial understanding between whites and African Americans. Davis found that Almond interpreted smart execution of military exercises as a sign of good morale. That was never true with the black soldier. "He can be driven to perform without necessarily having a high morale," Davis reported. "Due to long suffering and working under conditions highly distasteful to him, he has developed, as a defense mechanism, the ability to present a calm outward appearance."[25] Resentment over his unfair treatment seethes beneath the surface in the black soldier until some seemingly small incident sparks anger and behavior out of proportion to the incident.

Still, Davis and I made sure to include in our reports praise of Almond as an able officer who, now aware of African American grievances, could be expected to attack the underlying issues of unfairness and discrimination at the root of the resentment. That is, all issues but one—the unfair, discriminatory policy on promotions of black officers. Only the army high command could do something about that, and it had no real intention of doing so. I made the further point that white officers, especially the inexperienced junior officers, should be given more information about the special circumstances of blacks serving in the military. "Particularly were we impressed with the lack of recognition of the fact that Negro soldiers are affected by conditions that happen outside of camps as much as by the incidents that take place within the limits of the camps to which they are assigned."[26] That included incidents occurring far away and reported by black newspapers.

It couldn't be denied that black newspapers occasionally carried inflammatory, inaccurate articles. A case in point was a story, based on an anonymous letter, headlined "Fort Huachuca Is Hell on Earth" supplied by the Associated Negro Press and carried by fewer than ten small

African American newspapers in late summer of 1943. Now, Huachuca certainly qualified as hell on a number of points. However, this story spewed a couple of accusations so wild that the *Baltimore Afro-American* and *Pittsburgh Courier* refused to publish it, and Carl Murphy of the *Afro-American* even called the Associated Negro Press to say he knew from personal knowledge that most of the accusations were unfounded. Those included charges that Almond referred to soldiers as "niggers" and that obsolete weapons were given to the Ninety-third Division.

I wrote the editors of the newspapers knocking down those claims. While at Fort Huachuca, General Davis and I had investigated allegations that Almond used "nigger" in remarks at a school for cooks and bakers. Interviews with several hundred men did not turn up one statement that he used the epithet. I did note that Almond used the southern pronunciation of Negro, "which sounds like Negra." Because of that we had urged Almond to use the word "colored" instead of "Negro." As for the other allegation, it would be foolish and expensive for the army to alter its weapons procurement and distribution system just "to get at some 20,000 Negroes." I had seen bazookas, automatic weapons, and field pieces sent to the Ninety-third and knew the charge was false.[27]

The publication of these accusations by even a relative handful of black newspapers distressed Colonel Hardy. When I heard about that, I wrote him saying I didn't think this episode was "particularly serious."[28] He responded with a letter of thanks. "After laboring so earnestly for more than a year to obtain a constructive attitude and relationship, I was indeed discouraged when this outbreak occurred." He voiced optimism about the Ninety-second and its capabilities. "I believe we are progressing here and I hope that the time will not be far distant when this Division will be given an opportunity to meet the enemy. Even in my humble position, it would afford me the greatest pride to have the troops which trained at this station make a glorious record in campaign." He also reported the encouraging news that he had finally won authorization to construct a swimming pool for the black officers' Mountain View Club and a larger one for the enlisted men.[29] It was not hard to see why Hardy made a much more favorable impression with Bousfield than Almond had.

Hardy's hopes for the Ninety-second getting into the war reflected the wishes of black leaders, and the explosion of anger against a recalcitrant War Department exposed by Congressman Hamilton Fish early in 1944 finally produced results. The Advisory Committee on Negro Troop Policies on February 29 recommended to Secretary of War Stimson that, "as soon as possible, colored Infantry, Field Artillery, and other combat units be introduced into combat." If present organization or training of black troops would not permit that, "steps [should] be taken to reorganize any existing units or schedules so as to permit the introduction of qualified colored combat units, as promptly as possible, into battle."[30]

During the meeting that produced that recommendation, McCloy distinguished himself as an enthusiastic advocate of getting black GIs into combat. He opened by saying that in a discussion with Secretary of War Stimson and Army Chief of Staff Marshall, "I said I thought we ought to have on the record the use of Negro Combat Troops in war." As the meeting went on, McCloy elaborated his view. "In some situations we have to dictate, as when National policy is involved," he declared. "This is such a case. Ten percent of our people are colored and we have to use it. We make a farmer out of a clerk. It is a vital National policy to make a military asset out of that part of our population."[31]

McCloy added more fuel to the committee's recommendation in a separate memo to Stimson. He stated that because of the lower educational attainments of African Americans and the problems that entailed for black units, those units get passed over when the army picks troops for combat. Thus far, the army had done nothing to find "new means" to get black units into shape for battle duty. "With so large a portion of our population colored, with the example before us of the effective use of colored troops (of a much lower order of intelligence) by other nations, and with the many imponderables that are connected with the situation, we must, I think, be more affirmative about the use of our negro troops."

Stimson wrote at the bottom of this memo, "I concur with the recommendation. H.L.S."[32]

All this clearly demonstrated that the War Department brass did not think the Ninety-second Division as a whole was up to the challenge of battle against the Nazi war machine. McCloy followed up with a note to General George Marshall, the army's chief of staff, suggesting that the best men be selected from the Ninety-second to form a special team to be sent into combat. The experience gained from this could be used "to bring the balance of the division up to fighting quality."[33] That was the genesis of the 370th Regimental Combat Team, formed from infantry and artillery battalions of the Ninety-second and shipped to Italy, arriving at Naples July 30.

These Buffalo Soldiers joined the Allied army fighting its way up the peninsula of Italy. The unit saw some action, but at this point the Nazis were mostly fighting rear guard action as they were withdrawing to the formidable Gothic Line in the mountains north of Florence. From the start, battlefield commanders grumbled that the 370th men, while willing, were lacking in training and motivation. Still, the men's behavior appeared to be no different than any other green troops facing the shock of combat for the first time.[34] In October, black GIs joined attacks against Axis positions in the Northern Apennines mountain range toward the Italian city of Massa. Fighting in the hills in autumn's rain and mud confronted the soldiers with much tougher challenges than the summer advance up through Italy. Complaints about the 370th piled up. There was no lack of individual heroism, but commanders found a "tendency to mass hysteria or panic . . . much more prevalent among colored troops."[35]

In the meantime, the rest of the Ninety-second was arriving in Italy, bringing with them what Major Ulysses Lee, the military historian, called the "accumulated problems of Fort Huachuca and the training period."[36] Its soldiers disembarked and assumed positions in the Allied line. Soldiers of the Ninety-second occupied positions from the coastal plain in northwestern Italy into the Serchio Valley in the mountainous terrain before the Gothic Line.

Back in Washington, I was becoming alarmed at the reports about the black soldiers and that a negative spin was put on them at every opportunity. I asked Major Oscar J. Magee of the Intelligence Division, on his way to Italy, to report back on the Ninety-second Division. His report in December contained the first reference I had heard of a phrase that was to stick to the Ninety-second like a curse. "Too frequently the infantry 'melts away' under fire and an abnormal number of men hide in cellars until they are routed out by their officers." With the important exceptions of infantry patrol and attacking, the Ninety-second was performing satisfactorily. Only an all-out attack by, or offensive against, German troops would truly determine the Ninety-second Division's mettle, Magee concluded.[37]

After reading Magee's report, I told McCloy, "I was not only impressed with the difficulty of the problem but also with the extreme care that must be constantly exercised so that an accurate picture may be obtained of Negro troop activities. Apparently there is so much conflicting evidence available that a person with any bias could prove just about anything he wanted to."[38]

For four hours I interrogated Magee and turned up the ugly stench of bigotry emanating from commanders in Italy. White officers detailed to black units felt they were doing penance. The ranking officers in the division had no faith in the black GIs they commanded. "I don't trust Negroes," Major Theodore Arnold was quoted as saying. "There have been many examples of individual heroism on the part of Negro officers and soldiers," said Colonel William J. McCathery, the chief of staff for the Ninety-second. "However, I believe that the Negro generally cannot overcome or escape his background [of] no property ownership, irresponsibility and subservience. The Negro is panicky and his environment hasn't conditioned him to accept responsibilities." What would be the effect on fighting morale of officers who disliked their assignments and didn't believe in the troops they commanded?[39]

Magee had returned with an invitation from Lieutenant General Mark W. Clark, commander of the Fifth Army in which the Ninety-second served, for me to come to Italy to see firsthand the Ninety-second Division in action. I told McCloy we should talk about my accepting his invitation.

In the meantime, Clark filed his own report on the first elements of the Ninety-second to engage the enemy, and it was disturbing. It contained only a couple of lines of faint praise. "They have performed excellently in supply and administrative matters and in such tactical [combat] operations as do not require sustained demonstration of initiative and aggressiveness on the parts of junior leaders and of the rank and file." He said that most of the junior officers failed to show the "leadership, initiative, responsibility and aggressiveness" needed for "offensive combat against determined opposition." The enlisted men "exhibited more nervousness and less aggressive will to fight in the face of danger than do white soldiers." When they did take ground, they failed to hold it against counterattack. "Experience so far has shown that unless the men are under the immediate control and guidance of effective leaders they are apt to shrink from danger and to fall away from their units as they close with the enemy. The most flagrant cases are malingerers who, in several instances, have been found to have hidden rather than go forward."[40]

Clark did not use the phrase "melting away," but it was already being applied to what commanders called the tendency of soldiers from the Ninety-second to abandon battle. By the time of his report, fifty soldiers already had been court-martialed for "misbehavior before the enemy." Clark cited the example of a November 24 incident in which 411 enlisted men from the Ninety-second attacked "over moderately difficult mountainous terrain with open sloping hillsides and comparatively good roads and trails." Twenty-four hours later, only seventy men were left although casualties numbered just one dead, fifty-nine wounded, and "four exhaustion cases." Still, he acknowledged that the division's combat experience was "so brief that impressions gained thus far are not conclusive."[41]

It was not hard to see that preconceived army prejudices against black soldiers were being expressed and reinforced.

The negative reports coming in from Italy distressed and angered me. After seeing Clark's comments, I told McCloy they raised the question of why black soldiers showed a lack of aggressiveness and will to fight. "An easy answer is that Negroes possess certain inherent racial characteristics that make their use as combat soldiers impossible. The more difficult one is that our training methods with respect to Negroes have been inadequate in several important respects." I, of course, stressed the training problem, pointing to the attitudes of white officers, the stationing of black GIs in the South where they were soldiers on the post but "niggers (and all that goes with that term) in nearby communities," and the army's discriminatory promotion policies.[42] The only encouraging thing in Clark's memo was that he showed he intended to keep committing black troops to battle in Italy. Clark had concluded his report by stating that the Buffalo Soldiers would get the chance to prove their fighting prowess: "It is my intention to give the division increasing opportunity to assume combat responsibility and to demonstrate its ability to carry a full load in offensive operations."[43]

That opportunity came in early February 1945, when the Ninety-second hurled into the Gothic Line. Alas, the attack failed after several days and the word reaching us in Washington was that the black soldiers had "melted away" under fire from the Germans. It was time for me to take Clark up on his invitation. McCloy wrote him that I would be visiting Europe "to observe the performance of Negro troops, their attitudes, and the attitudes of their officers towards them."[44]

This of course was before the age of jetliner travel. Getting from Washington to Italy proved to be a grueling journey. A five-hour commercial airliner flight put me in Brazil, where I boarded an Army Air Corps DC-3 and it took off over the Atlantic Ocean. I was strapped into a far-from-comfortable aluminum bucket seat, and I bounced around in it as the plane transited the Atlantic, stopping in the Canary Islands for refueling before heading on to Casablanca. There I was introduced to Old World attitudes about personal hygiene. The toilet was a hole in the floor. Then I spied a queer-looking contrivance, which someone finally educated me by identifying it as a bidet. At least I got a few hours of sleep in a bed. Then it was back to the metal bucket seat for the final leg of my journey. The flight across North Africa exposed us to occasional shelling before we finally landed at Caserta, Italy, on February 26.

My old friend from the War Department, Major General Otto Nelson, now deputy commander of the Mediterranean theater of operations, greeted me upon landing. With only the brief bit of sleep hours before in Casablanca, I was dog tired, but there was no time for rest. Otto hustled me into an army sedan, and we sped to the grounds of the king of Naples's winter palace, then the headquarters for the Mediterranean theater of operations, where I met theater commander Lieutenant General Joseph T. McNarney.

The general handed me a report which he said he had received from General Clark. I gave it a quick scan. It said the division had been capably commanded by Almond and praised the regimental and battalion commanders, that is, the white officers. Everything else was negative: The Ninety-second wasn't equal to the seven other U.S. divisions in northern Italy. Black GIs failed to stand fast under enemy counterattack as well as mortar and artillery fire. The troops were unwilling to close for hand-to-hand combat and had often retreated. Entire units had disintegrated under artillery fire. The noncommissioned officers and the junior commissioned officers, that is, the black officers, had failed. The Ninety-second had achieved some success before—here's that damning phrase again—the "melting away" began. The Ninety-second under fire had been characterized by repeated withdrawals, panicky and disorderly retirement, and the absence of offensive fighting spirit.

I immediately objected, noting that by praising only the white officers, complete responsibility for the failure of the offensive fell on the black officers and men. The logical conclusion of all this was that black men could not be made into efficient soldiers and officers.[45]

McNarney said the Ninety-second had fouled up, and his officers had recommended that the division be pulled out of the line. I protested that I hoped he would stop that. No, he said, the order was awaiting his signature. I implored him to wait. McNarney refused.

Otto then took me to General Clark, who also refused my request to rescind the order to take the Ninety-second out of the line. The failure of the Ninety-second had stalled the entire Allied effort to breach the Gothic Line, said Clark, who had recently been promoted to commander of the Fifteenth Army Group.

Next Otto took me to General Lucian K. Truscott Jr., who was Clark's successor as Fifth Army commander and who would write his own devastating report about the Ninety-second. Again my plea not to take the Ninety-second out of the line was rejected.

Our last chance, Otto told me, was to get to the battlefield commander, Major General Willis D. Crittenberger. Then came one of those peculiar episodes that make the recounting of history so enjoyable. Crittenberger said he would help me out if I could give him a hand with a problem he had with Major General Joao Baptista Mascarenhas de Morais of the Brazilian Expeditionary Force. Those troops had been "bloodied," and afterward the general would not visit them.

"What can I do?" I asked.

Crittenberger produced two bottles of cognac and said, "Let's go see him."

So off we went to the Brazilian command. Otto and I were introduced to Mascarenhas, and Crittenberger pulled out the bottles, opened them, and poured a glass for everyone. Then commenced one toast after another. We toasted President Roosevelt, the president of Brazil, Secretary of War Stimson, the Brazilian minister for war, General Crittenberger, Otto, and finally I was treated to a toast. The bait had been taken.

Then Crittenberger dropped this one: "Truman, would you like to review the Brazilian troops?" The trap was sprung.

I said yes, working up all the enthusiasm I could. How could Mascarenhas refuse!

We piled into a jeep, and off we went. Unknown to us, the Germans were watching through high-powered binoculars. The wind blew Mascarenhas's parka back, exposing the gold on his cap. The Germans saw they had a high value target, and one of their eighty-eight guns belched out a shell. It exploded close to us, fortunately not harming anyone but leaving us all with a good scare.

Well, I had done my part, and Crittenberger delivered on his end, dispatching a recommendation that McNarney hold off on signing that order until I had conducted my investigation. McNarney gave me two weeks to supply him with any pertinent information that might change his view, including the influence of racial attitudes on the performance of the enlisted men and officers of the Ninety-second in combat.

From March 1 through March 8, I spent my waking hours with the Ninety-second Division, traveling from Leghorn to Viareggio. In all, eight hundred officers and hundreds of enlisted men were interviewed. The company officers said there was little or no pattern in the tendency of many—but not all or even a majority—of the enlisted men to melt away. Either an entire company or platoon would fold, or, conversely, the entire unit would not break. The officers had no trouble identifying the source of some of the panicky and disorderly retreats. More than twenty-six hundred replacement soldiers recently moved into the Ninety-second came from service organizations and had had no combat training, many having never even fired an M-1 rifle. "No other single observation was repeated [by company officers] in more instances than this one," I told Nelson. No white soldier had ever been sent into combat without undergoing the infantry basic training courses. Of course, Almond denied that untrained troops had been sent into battle. Furthermore, 89 percent of the replacement troops fell in the two bottom categories of the Army General Classification Test. The Ninety-second was manned by many troops who had the bare minimum of schooling and who were illiterate.[46]

Beyond that, the racial attitudes of segregated America played out to devastating effect. Discriminatory promotion policies convinced the black GIs that the high command had no confidence in black officers and wounded the division's fighting spirit. Since no white officer could serve under a black officer, junior inexperienced white soldiers were vaulted into command positions. I found that dozens of black second lieutenants had much more experience than their white counterparts. White officers scapegoated black troops with all the prejudices of men who didn't want to command African Americans. In addition, too often promotions were made not on the basis of merit, skill, or daring but rather went to subservient African Americans who lived up to stereotypes and did not challenge the authority or competence of the white officers.

The blight of Fort Huachuca was duplicated in Italy through segregated officers' clubs. One white captain who had the temerity to invite two black officers into his club was officially reprimanded for having "an improper social attitude," and the two African Americans were asked to leave. The white club boasted having dances; women were not permitted in the black club. As I later reported, "Unfortunately, the pattern of incidents overseas reflects closely the situation which General

Davis and I found to exist at Fort Huachuca in 1943."[47] It was difficult to inculcate pride in self, combat spirit, or love of country in soldiers trained in the hostile environment of the South.

After outlining those findings, I suggested a number of recommendations. At the top of the list was the vital need for a fair promotion policy that elevated officers on the sole basis of ability. Separate officers' clubs had to be abandoned. The army should stimulate race pride in black troops. Training courses for replacement troops should be strengthened to account for black troops coming from service units. Finally, the Ninety-second Division should be reorganized so that it could stay on the front line.[48]

The failed attack made news back home. *Newsweek* magazine told its readers that the most extensive effort by the army to get black troops in the war had "so far been more productive of disappointment and failure than of anything else." The Ninety-second troops were "trigger-happy," shooting American patrols and Italian civilians. The February attack ended with the black troops forced back to their original positions.[49] The *New York Times* wrote, "Something should be noted now that has been troubling headquarters for some time: how to handle the division's public relations in view of the supersensitivity of some Negro papers at home, which have unquestionably tended to overemphasize the division's accomplishments and the inevitable racial aspects of the situation."[50]

Next came a day I would rue for many years. Over my protests, the army scheduled a news conference for me in Rome. I did it for only one reason: I knew that all the newsmen knew about the shortcomings of the Ninety-second, and I wanted to make sure they knew the reasons behind the division's reported failure against the Gothic Line.

When I entered the room, the correspondent for the *New York Times,* Milton Bracker, a red-haired, arrogant, nasty guy, sarcastically shouted out, "Now we're going to hear about the glorious Ninety-second." I replied that if that was his view and that of the other reporters, we were wasting our time. But, I said, if they were actually interested in what had gone wrong, the underlying reasons for the division's problems, I'd proceed. And I did: The fault of the Ninety-second Division's failure lay with the army. A segregated army by its very nature destroyed fighting morale in black soldiers. Jim Crow officers' clubs had a corrosive effect, as did the discriminatory promotion policy for black officers. Service troops were assigned to the Ninety-second without combat training.

The *New York Herald Tribune*'s report on the news conference said that I had found that the division "labors under the handicaps of excessive illiteracy and inadequate training . . . while Negroes are always sensitive to incidents which revive race prejudices, and many of them lack a clear conviction of what they are fighting for." It also said I "had tried to find out why Negro troops so often 'melt away' in the face of the enemy."[51]

Bracker's story in the *New York Times* pretty much reflected my views. The headline read "Negroes' Courage Upheld in Inquiry," with the deck below it reading "Gibson Lays the Difficulties of 92nd in Italy to Its High Illiteracy." It quoted me as saying, "If the division proves anything, it does not prove that Negroes can't fight," and "not all straggling and running has happened in the 92nd Division." I was quoted as stating, "There is no question in my mind about the courage of Negro officers or soldiers, and any generalization on the basis of race is entirely unfounded." In going into the reason I gave for the Ninety-second's behavior, Bracker emphasized the issue of illiteracy, failing to report what I said about the army's embrace of segregation being the central culprit. His story also included that I had conceded that certain units of the Ninety-second Division had engaged in "more or less panicky retreats, particularly at night when the attitude of some individual soldiers seemed to be 'I'm up here all alone; why in hell should I stay up here?' "[52] Other news reports followed this line and ignored my explanations and concentrated on my acknowledgment of the reported failures of the Ninety-second.

The stories in the white press about the news conference produced a storm of anger against me back home among black Americans. No one seemed to notice that I had laid the problem at the feet of the army and its segregationist policies, or they just ignored it. "It is hard to believe that any responsible Negro spokesman would discuss the record of Negroes in the service without first of all drawing a strong indictment against the indefensible policy of the army in giving Negro soldiers the kind of inferior training which is inevitable under the army jim crow system," said Lester Granger, national secretary of the National Urban League. Of course, I had done exactly that. Oscar DePriest, a former congressman and now a Chicago alderman, declared, "My actual reaction to the statement that Negro troops 'melt away' in the face of the enemy could hardly be printed. I can't understand how Mr. Gibson could make such a statement." Representative Charles Skyles of the Illinois House of Representatives pledged to seek my removal from office.[53]

"Somebody's Gotta Go!" screamed the headline on the editorial page of the *Chicago Defender.* I was an "Uncle Tom" who had decided not to join Bill Hastie in resigning in protest of segregation in order to get myself "a soft job." "Gibson last week in Rome, Italy, put on an unpardonable performance that has shamed and embarrassed every Negro with the least bit of pride in his race." "Negroes have fought bravely and valiantly in all American wars without the generalship of Truman K. Gibson Jr." Then the editorial listed battles in wars from the Revolution to World War I in which black soldiers had fought without melting away. "Yet, no sooner does Truman Gibson Jr. come upon the scene, the Negro troops start 'melting away' in the face of the enemy."[54]

In response, I wrote the newspaper's editor saying that I was only trying to cope with the reality that it was well known to white newspaper war correspondents that things had not gone well in the attack. "The reason given by many was the familiar one—Negro soldiers are no good. What I felt I had to do was to orient them on the reasons for the failures and place the responsibility where it belongs and that's not on Negroes. . . . We can only correct matters when we drag them out into the open."[55]

A few papers offered kinder, more understanding accounts. The *Defender* did publish a letter rising to my defense. "If the 92nd did fall back, why lie and paint the situation rosy merely to satisfy our self chauvinistic minds?" asked Dr. George Frazier Miller Jr. "Now, Mr. Gibson, after having reported the facts, he then very admirably attempted to rationalize his report in regards to causation. . . . Your paper owes

Mr. Gibson an apology for the unjust, unfounded and unwarranted attack."[56] No apology came.

Still, few rose to my defense. My most prominent defender turned out to be Secretary of War Stimson. In response to U.S. Senator H. Alexander Smith, who had passed on a complaint from a constituent that I had slandered black soldiers in the Rome press conference, Stimson wrote that I "at no time generalized about Negro soldiers; nor have any statements to this effect been attributed to him by any responsible publication. He stressed the fact that the Command in that theater in attempting to get at some of the basic causes of the failure of small units and individuals in the 92nd Division had wholly disregarded unscientific generalizations about racial characteristics."[57]

I must add that during this time of duress, I never heard from Bill Hastie, the man who had brought me into the War Department and one who knew the roadblocks and hurdles of the job and the crippling effect of segregation on troops. He didn't rise to my defense in any way at a time when terrible things were being said and printed about me. That really hurt. At one point during all this, my wife suggested that I just quit. I never seriously entertained that idea, and she wasn't really pushing it. I had a responsibility to African Americans exposed to the nightmares of war and racism, and I didn't intend to abandon them.

I wasn't the only one to trace the poor performance of some units of the Ninety-second to the conditions at Fort Huachuca. After the war, my successor, Marcus Ray, noted that as an officer in the division he had "observed the development of those morale-destroying factors which made good combat performance an almost certain impossibility." He also came to my defense. "I do believe that he was sincere and honest in his press report in Rome but that the basic reasons he gave for the failures of the 92nd were not given proper notice. I suspect that the bald statement of a Negro unit's failure would make much better reading without the addition of underlying and correctible causes."[58]

All the vitriolic anger directed at me hurt. Months later, I was still confronting it. In response to a sympathetic letter from a medical officer in the Ninety-third Division, I wrote, "You are quite right about my bumps as a result of my visit to the 92nd Division. However, from bitter experience, you know how the cards can be stacked against any so-called Negro unit. I think it is incumbent on us who know the situation to yell loudly in order that basic conditions can be corrected. . . . One cannot spend much time around any of the large segregated divisions without becoming impressed with the fact that this system is not only morally wrong, but is unsound from a military point of view. Of course, many of our people want to have their cake and eat it too. They want to say that segregation is wrong and yet that the end product, segregated divisions, is all right."[59]

On August 9, I noted, "The attacks on me have not yet been thoroughly quieted. The brethren are still breathing maledictions for my statements and the failures of some small units in the 92nd. They apparently overlooked the point of what I was saying, which was as long as you have the fundamentally vicious system of segregation these failures will inevitably result and not because of individual failures either. The real problem ahead of all of us is to get those responsible for planning to realize that such failings as have occurred are not due to any racial characteristics but to the improper utilization of Negro soldiers."[60]

After the war, General McNarney attempted to distance himself from some of the harsher judgments he made about the Ninety-second. Writing in the *Pittsburgh Courier,* I recounted those miserable days in Italy and said that McNarney had found African Americans to be failures as soldiers except for certain units such as artillery battalions. But he said that in his discussions with me he had been talking about leadership. "It was intended as a frank admission that the leadership qualities evident were below the standards required for the efficient performance of certain types of combat duties, and an equally frank statement that for some time to come the Negro soldier would need new and wider opportunities in order to develop the standards of leadership required." McNarney said that I had characterized his statements as ridicule of black soldiers. That was not true. I acknowledged that McNarney "did agree that there were contributing causes, resulting from unequal opportunities for Negroes in civilian life, to some of the incidents reported to him." I noted that an army board of officers had considered his official reports and "rejected their validity."[61]

All in all, the experience of dealing with the Ninety-second and the Italian campaign had been one of the rougher periods in my life. However, I was satisfied that I had done my duty to explain why the Ninety-second had failed the test of battle.

But was that true? Were the soldiers of the Ninety-second Division responsible for the failed American offensive in early February?

13

The Ninety-second Vindicated

The phone in my eleventh-floor Chicago apartment on Lake Michigan rang on a beautiful, clear, warm day in the summer of 2003. On the other end of the line was Carlo Binosi, a friend of many years from Italy. As I listened to what he had to say, I found myself being drawn back to northern Italy, the winter of 1945, and the Ninety-second Division. What Carlo told me turned the world upside down. He had come across what to me appeared to be revisionist history of the long-ago battle against the Gothic Line.

I searched my memories of those unfortunate days six decades ago. I realized that I had been told the barest of information about the February offensive. Upon my arrival in Italy, General McNarney had handed me a report on the battle. The urgency of trying to stop him from taking the Ninety-second out of the line, combined with my bone-weary tiredness from the long flight across the Atlantic and northern Africa, meant that I could give the report only a cursory glance. McNarney and the others told the same story: The Ninety-second had gone into battle and, under fire, its soldiers had melted away, dooming the attack to failure and stalling the Allied advance against the Gothic Line. With so much army brass sharing their judgments with me, I was left with the only conclusion possible: The Ninety-second had failed. I saw that my job was to explain to the generals and the American public why this had happened—and, most urgent, to keep the Buffalo Soldiers in the fight.

I was aware only of a sketchy picture of the February offensive. The Gothic Line loomed as the objective, a rugged defensive position across the top of Italy that had to be breached for the Allied offensive to surge northward. To that end, thousands of black soldiers had launched a three-pronged attack. Along the coastal plain, black GIs crossed the Cinquale Canal toward the town of Massa. To the east, other troops assaulted the Strettoia hills, and still further to the east, African American soldiers charged into the mountains aiming to capture important German defensive positions. Hard fighting over four days had produced heroism by many black troops, but unfortunately many others had panicked under the stress of combat and left the battlefield in disarray. That constituted the picture painted for me then and remains today the judgment on the Ninety-second Division's combat record.

The telephone call in the summer of 2003 started filling in the blanks in that picture. Carlo told me he had come across an account of the battle written by Italian historian Lido Galletto. What he said sent me looking for other information. That led me to *Buffalo Soldiers in Italy* by Hondon B. Hargrove, an exhaustive account of the Ninety-second Division in action in northern Italy; *A Fragment of Victory in Italy* by Colonel Paul Goodman that gave the army's account of the Ninety-second; the autobiography of Vernon Baker, a Ninety-second Division soldier belatedly awarded the Congressional Medal of Honor in 1997 for heroism in northern Italy; and, of course, Major Ulysses Lee's *The Employment of Negro Troops.* Together they filled in the blanks of my knowledge of the February offensive and painted a much more complex picture than the one I carried into my investigation in March of 1945.[1]

First of all, the Gothic Line stretching from the narrow coastal plain in the west to the Strettoia hills to the east and then to mountains of the Apennine range, also called the Apuanian Alps, presented a formidable if not insurmountable barrier that in the winter of 1945 would have challenged and likely defeated the best troops the Allies could throw against it. Baker recalled "trenches and gun emplacements . . . invisible and impenetrable with logs, dirt and rocks" and a "labyrinth of escape tunnels that rendered our most intense shelling and bombing useless." German soldiers holed up in caves were protected from harm from U.S. artillery shells and bombs, which usually missed their targets because of "masterful" German camouflage. On one of the mountains was Castle Aghinolfi, employed by the Germans as one of the forts controlling the passes through the Apennine Mountains. To the castle's medieval fortifications of four-foot-thick stone walls, the Nazis added barbed wire, minefields, and trip wires that fired flares to expose intruders and illuminate them as targets. German artillery and mortar spotters used the castle to direct fire on the Ninety-second.[2]

Goodman describes the Mount Folgorito–Mount Cauala area as rugged and ideal for defensive purposes. "Deep ravines cut through the towering peaks so that rock walls are nearly perpendicular. Only shrubs and small trees spotted the landscape; the rest was rock and shale. . . . Emplacements for machine guns, mortars, cannon and anti-tank guns were hewn out of solid rock."[3]

Hargrove provided an even more detailed account of the fortifications. "All these hills were studded with a series of enemy strong points, which included interlocking and mutually supporting steel and concrete fortifications for machine guns, mortars and observation posts. Barbed wire abounded throughout the hundreds of carefully planted mines covering all anticipated approaches." In the mountains, "mine fields, concrete and re-enforced steel bunkers and dugouts . . . provided protection and flexibility of movement for the defenders. Heavy and light machine guns were placed so as to deliver devastating mutually supporting cross fire."[4]

From Galletto I learned of Skoda cannons belching shells from the hills and mountains into the lines of the Buffalo Soldiers. Even more ominous were huge menacing naval guns taken off Axis warships, two of them from a cruiser, and placed in impervious rocky cliffs and heavy concrete bunkers at Punta Bianca near the naval facility at La Spezia to the northwest of Allied positions. These cannons added up to an artillery capability more powerful than anything on the Allied fleet in the Ligurian Sea, which consequently couldn't take on the Nazi batteries. Air strikes failed to damage them. Think of the big artillery pieces of the motion picture *The Guns of Navarone.*

Later General Almond, the Ninety-second commander, reported that these weapons "have proven their ability to deliver extremely effective fire on our positions without fear of retaliation" and had inflicted heavy casualties on the Ninety-second.[5] These monstrous weapons rained death and destruction on the Ninety-second throughout the offensive of February 8–11, 1945, especially on the soldiers attacking across the Cinquale Canal in the coastal plain. Galletto recounted that observation posts in the hills and mountains directed pinpoint accurate fire on the helpless black GIs from the coastal naval guns and German artillery from the hills and mountains.

The accounts of the four-day offensive describe desperate fighting. Hills would be taken at tremendous cost only to be abandoned to the brunt of ferocious German counterattacks. Black GIs would claw their way up mountainsides only to be thrown back by the enervating fire from the hidden and supporting German machine guns and artillery. Baker described German artillery unleashing a "cloudburst of explosives" in "a wall of fire" that marched up and down hillsides and mountainsides, leaving Buffalo Soldiers helpless to do anything but die. He called the battle an "all-out massacre."[6]

Along the coastal plain, Allied tanks were devastated by mines and artillery fire, especially from the coastal guns at Punta Bianca. The mouth of the Cinquale Canal turned red from blood.[7] Galletto described American tanks exploding and the bodies of soldiers hurled into the air like dolls. Machine-gun fire raked through the survivors, killing and wounding many Buffalo Soldiers and pinning down many more. Recalled an Italian partisan, "The Americans were sending their black troops straight into the front of the German lines, instead of around to the side. And there was no reason for it. So the Americans sent these soldiers to die."[8]

The Americans enjoyed air support the first day with Allied planes pounding German and Italian positions. Bad weather moved in on the second day, and the enemy troops inflicted terrible punishment on the Americans. Finally, on February 11, Almond called off the attack, and the troops found themselves mostly at their jumping-off lines of four days earlier.

What of the melting away? Goodman said "straggling," as the army termed the disorganized falling out of men from combat, was negligible in the mountain fighting. But elsewhere he found a different story. At one point in the battle in the Strettoia hills, one unit of eight hundred men had been reduced to eighty by straggling. "Stragglers were routed out of houses, caves and cellars." The coastal attack also suffered "excessive straggling." Overall, Goodman wrote, "straggling was excessive and disorganization was evident in nearly every unit across the division front." He put the total number at 2,182 stragglers.[9]

This was the army's position, and it was disputed by a number of defenders of the Ninety-second. Baker said none of the men in his platoon ever "faded away" or retreated in disorder. "When I went forward under fire, they followed."[10] This would be consistent with what I was told—that some units stayed together while others melted away.

Of course, the fact of the matter was that straggling occurred in every big battle. Caught up in the terror, death, bloodshed, and confusion of combat, some soldiers panicked and became stragglers. Sometimes, the chaos of battle separated soldiers from their units, and many of these stragglers ended up trying to reunite with their companies. Officers and military police manned "straggler lines" to catch men fleeing battle.

Hargrove believes the army applied different standards to black troops regarding straggling. He compared the offensive against the Gothic Line to a battle in the south of Italy a year earlier. Then troops, white soldiers, had mounted an attack across the Rapido River under observation and fire from Germans on Monte Cassino and other mountains. Sounds familiar. Those were similar conditions to the ones the Ninety-second faced, and the result had been the same: heavy casualties and a lot of straggling. In 1944, the army brass used the words "heroic," "brave," "determined," and "intrepid" to recount the action of the soldiers and "needless" to describe the losses. But the only term used to recount the story of the Buffalo Soldiers under fire was "melting away." Only the Ninety-second Division was ever tagged with straggling as such a major problem that it merited the special term "melting away."[11]

Still, military authorities said much had been gained from the attack despite its overall failure. They learned important intelligence about the strength and manning of the Gothic Line. Enemy artillery positions had been exposed for the first time. Heavy losses had been inflicted on the Germans.[12] General Almond similarly praised the division's intelligence work and lauded its artillery as "magnificent." Furthermore, he noted the division had been subjected to a hard fight in difficult terrain against a strong foe.[13]

The army's propaganda arm made sure to put the best face on the story. A War Department press release stated, "One major drive, launched in February, gained some ground before the Germans sacrificed much in men and materiel in pushing the division back to its original starting point."[14] In one honest appraisal of the fight, the press release took note of the many challenges facing the division: "The 92nd was confronted by the loftiest peaks and mountains in the Apennines. . . . The wily Jerry, who used natural mountain barriers masterfully, made all maneuvering for the attacking elements just about the toughest in modern warfare." It cited a couple of Buffalo Soldiers for heroism. Staff Sergeant Mansfield Mason of Baltimore, Maryland, had attacked a German position "in the face of withering machine gun fire" and captured five Germans, one of them an officer. First Lieutenant William E. Porter of Indianapolis, Indiana, won the Silver Star for advancing into "a hail of machinegun fire" to knock out a machine-gun nest. And it spotlighted an element where everyone indeed did agree that the Ninety-second performed admirably—the artillery. "Time and again . . . perfectly placed artillery fire shatter[ed] hostile emplacements and [broke] up repeated and determined German counterattacks."

Despite the public relations hype, the army's verdict declared that the Ninety-second had come up short. Morris J. MacGregor Jr., an eminent military historian sympathetic to the cause of black soldiers, noted that black journalists and others had refused to accept the view that the Ninety-second had performed less capably than white divisions. But, he said, "such an assertion presupposed that hundreds of officers and War Department officials were so consumed with prejudice that they falsified the record."[15]

Well, I don't know about that, but I do know that the army had a stake in trying to prove that black soldiers couldn't fight. The Ninety-second was the epicenter of the black experience in World War II. For the army, the failed attack showed that the prejudices of the generals, the ones based in the venomous notion of white superiority, were right—you couldn't rely on black troops in the ultimate test of battle. To justify its policies of segregation, the army had to prove the inferiority of African American troops, and it claimed to have the goods in Italy. The War Department latched onto the army's account of the Ninety-second's record there to justify reassigning the African American Ninety-third Division from combat duty to service-and-support functions in the Pacific theater.

A close look at the events in Italy that February reveals a problem more serious than that of straggling. Reading all these accounts of the battle dredged up from the recesses of my memory something that looms much more important now than it did to me in 1945. Upon arrival in Italy and learning of the failed assault against the Gothic Line, I had been met by my old friend from the Munitions Building, General Otto Nelson, who was now deputy commander of the Mediterranean theater. As we sped in an army sedan to my meeting with the Italian campaign commanders, Nelson turned to me and said, "Why don't you ask McNarney if, in his long experience in the Army, anyone above the grade of first lieutenant had ever made a mistake?"

I had taken that as a challenge to me to question the structure of the division, the Jim Crow officers' clubs, the poor training, and the discriminatory promotion policies. Now, six decades later, the realization came to me that Nelson was prompting me to probe the planning for the battle. He was prodding me to go to the heart of the matter—the strategy of battle and the orders given to the Buffalo Soldiers. The official reports said only junior officers and enlisted men had erred, not commanders. I don't think Nelson believed all the bad reports about the Ninety-second and was trying to push me into questioning the generals. Now, after all those years, I realized I had been told nothing about the big naval guns at Punta Bianca, nothing about the Skoda cannon belching death from heights above the Ninety-second fighters, nothing about soldiers assaulting entrenched positions without air cover the second day of the battle, nothing about brave soldiers marching up hill slopes and mountainsides that offered little or no cover into the torrent of rifle, machine-gun, and artillery fire from supremely fortified positions.

Foolish seems the only word to describe the decision to send the tanks and infantrymen swarming across the Cinquale Canal in clear view of spotters for the big naval guns at Punta Bianca and the fortified artillery and machine guns looking down from the Strettoia hills. Would not a focused attack on the mountain stronghold or the Strettoia hills have had a better chance of success than a three-pronged attack across a broad front? That question seemed much more urgent and pertinent than "straggling."

In 1945, I had left the War Department, scarred by the racism of the army, embittered over the ravages of segregation on the fighting spirit of black soldiers, and battered and bruised by the vicious attacks on me in the *Chicago Defender* and other African American newspapers. I'd put all that behind me, and now in the summer of 2003, it had flooded back.

Still, no easy answers availed themselves. None of the hundreds of interviews I had done with the Ninety-second officers and enlisted men had produced denials that a lot of straggling had occurred. My reading now only confirmed the corrosive effect in those long-ago days of segregation and racism of the African American fighting spirit. Baker recalled ugly memories of Fort Huachuca: white officers hating their assignment with the Ninety-second coming and going as quickly as "Mae West changed lovers," the humiliating snubs black officers endured, black draftees turned sullen and unruly because they knew they weren't wanted, Almond bringing in a buffalo as the division's mascot and naming it "Buffalo Bill" after the white showman Bill Cody, and the animal disgracing the Ninety-second by plopping "buffalo pies" at the most embarrassing moment.[16]

One ludicrous example of the politics of race concerned Edward Wimp, who had been in my brother Harry's class at the University of Illinois. In those days, the rules of race denied African Americans the opportunity to enroll in the Reserve Officers' Training Corps (ROTC), but Wimp was an African American of the Walter White variety, meaning he had fair skin. When he showed up for ROTC training, no one thought to ask him his race. No one asked, and he didn't tell. However, once in Italy, somehow his race became known. Well, he may have looked white, but that wasn't enough to let white officers serve under him. The color line had to be respected even when you couldn't see it. The army solved this problem by assigning Wimp to an Italian farmhouse with a detachment of two men to fire an artillery piece at the Germans twice a day. This assignment provided him all the comforts of home, which he enjoyed to the fullest.

Allen Joiner, the Chicagoan who served in the Ninety-second, recalled that bitter disputes and feuds traveled to Italy from Fort Huachuca. Joiner recalled a white captain, two black lieutenants, and a black sergeant being shot by their own men, such was the bitterness engendered in the Arizona desert. "I remember a kid named Nichols from North Carolina who said he was glad to go overseas. I asked him why? 'There's a whole lot of officers and sergeants I'd like to get even with.' Nichols was killed trying to bring wounded men down from a mountain during a December attack. That proved to me that God don't like ugly."[17]

Almond also appeared to carry a grudge. Baker reported that when elements of the Ninety-second were ordered overseas for combat duty, Almond's chief of staff told them, "All these years, our white boys have been going over there and getting killed. Well, now it's time for you black boys to get killed."[18] A similar story was related by Hargrove. Officers of a Ninety-second Division regiment arriving in Italy recalled Almond telling them and their men, "Your Negro newspapers have seen fit to cause you to be brought over here; now I'm going to see that you suffer your share of casualties."[19]

Later Baker would have his own embittering encounter with Almond. After the Gothic Line was finally breached, Baker won the Distinguished Service Cross for heroism in the breakthrough battle. As it happened, at the same time Almond was awarded an oak-leaf cluster on his Silver Star. Now, in awards ceremonies the position of honor, at the far right on the line of the soldiers getting medals, goes to the man honored with the highest decoration. That was Baker on that day. But Almond took the place of honor for himself, leaving Baker boiling angry.[20] When I read that story, I recalled the time at Fort Huachuca where Almond had addressed every white officer by his rank but called the lone black officer only by his name.

That kind of attitude, so typical of the army's view of African Americans, had to have an impact on black soldiers, and it was impossible to ignore it. As I told people back then, you couldn't have it both ways, damning segregation and expecting the fruits of segregation to be unscathed by the experience.

So, what happened in February of 1945 before the Gothic Line? This question will be debated for years. I believe the answer to be complex. There's no doubt that poor planning threw the Buffalo Soldiers into a hopeless fight, into a battlefield with little or no cover, against a seasoned German war machine dug into impregnable natural and man-made fortifications, into a hurricane of artillery and machine-gun fire decimating platoons. No fighting force could have done better, as evidenced by what came to be known as the Rapido River fiasco where white troops a year earlier suffered the same fate as the Ninety-second in Italy. Still, what seemed true to me in 1945 seems true today: No group of men could be subjected to the horrors and humiliations of segregation, racism, and hate and come out imbued with the fighting spirit that would be needed to advance up the hills of Strettoia or across the Cinquale Canal into the teeth of a devastating torrent of artillery and machine-gun fire. At the Gothic Line, the brave men of the Ninety-second charged into a hell of poor planning and poor training, and somehow they had overcome all that. The fight was lost through no fault of theirs. Too many Buffalo Soldiers fought bravely and earned decorations, too many paid the ultimate sacrifice in heroics on the battlefield those four days in February for the Italian campaign to endure as a black mark against the Buffalo Soldiers.

The final evidence that poor planning ranked as the paramount reason for the failure of the offensive was soon to come. What often happens when a favored supervisor fouls up? Why, he gets promoted. It's the classic cover-up ploy. That's what happened here. Almond, who was related to Army Chief of Staff George Marshall, was promoted to the grade of lieutenant general and later assigned to a posting in Korea where I later heard he had brought along his baggage of derogatory views of black soldiers. The army had to prop up Almond in order to put down black soldiers. It sickens me to think about it.

The story of the Ninety-second in Italy didn't end in February. It ceased being a black division, though. The best black soldiers were organized into a regiment, with racially mixed officers, to serve alongside a white regiment and the famed Japanese American 442nd Infantry. In April the Ninety-second attacked with the objective being Massa. But unlike February when men charged across the Cinquale Canal to become cannon fodder for the big naval guns and the hill cannon, the Ninety-second aimed to clear out the mountains and hills first. What's more, rather than attack mountain fortifications frontally, the black GIs assaulted on the flanks. Baker won his Distinguished Service Cross—and five decades later a belated Congressional Medal of Honor—in this attack. He destroyed a German observation post, machine-gun position, and dugout. Later he covered the withdrawal of his men under fire, helped get severely wounded men out of harm's way, and, using hand grenades, wiped out two enemy machine-gun nests.[21] By the time the Italian campaign ended, the Ninety-second Division had suffered twenty-eight hundred killed and wounded.[22]

Joiner recalled that when the end of the Gothic Line came, it came quickly, but not before some harrowing moments. Normally artillery followed infantry, but this time Joiner's artillery unit somehow had leapfrogged ahead of infantrymen and found itself under point-blank fire from German cannons.

> Nine of us ducked into some kind of building. Then a shell hit the building. Four men were killed and three seriously hurt. I was covered with debris. I couldn't see for four or five minutes, and I couldn't hear. Another soldier, a Japanese American, and I took off running out the door. Outside we sat down. I spotted a puddle of blood on the ground. It turned out that blood was mine, streaming from a head wound. I put something on my head to stop the blood, and we took off. I found my outfit, and he found his.
>
> Then things got bad again. I was mighty tired and needed sleep. A colonel came up and started looking at a map. He got on a phone, and I heard him telling another colonel that the Germans were forming a

> horseshoe around us—they were putting a noose around us, encircling us. I got wide awake then. This was about six P.M. The colonel told us if we could get our guns dug in by four A.M., we could keep the Germans back.
>
> We got the guns dug in by one-thirty A.M. At two o'clock all hell broke loose on those Germans. Then things happened fast. By four o'clock in the afternoon I was forty miles away in Genoa half drunk on bootleg cognac. That's where they surrendered. We didn't give them a chance to dig in.[23]

Joiner was to have one last experience in Italy a month and half or two months after the war ended. Black soldiers had a rest center at Viareggio. Right behind it was a building where three hundred German land mines had been stored. Returning from a trip to a beach on a four-day pass, Joiner saw a mushroom suddenly plume on the horizon. "Then the sound got the whole earth just trembling." The mines had exploded, blowing up the rest center and killing ninety-one soldiers and some Italians and Red Cross workers. It couldn't have been an accident. "Somebody went there, got by the guard, got in there, and detonated those mines with a timer and got away," Joiner said. "It had to be a white officer, a captain on up. A white soldier wouldn't go there but an officer could go anywhere. He had to be a mine expert. We was three days digging them out. Only one, a soldier, was still alive. I guess he died later on. They ain't found out yet how that happened."[24]

It was an ugly ending for the African American soldiers' experience in Italy.

Fortunately for me, my trip to Europe didn't conclude in Italy, and the second leg of the journey would bring a pleasant surprise, a deliberate attempt by a son of the Old South to integrate troops on the front lines.

14

At Last!

When at long last black soldiers got to fight alongside white infantrymen in integrated units, the push for it came from a most unlikely corner, Lieutenant General John C. H. Lee, the grandson of that icon of the Confederacy, Robert E. Lee. Now this Lee was no champion of social equality of the races. Still, in his view, a soldier was a soldier, and that counted for something in late 1944 when the Allied forces in France needed men.

The war was devouring soldiers faster than the army could replace them. December had brought crisis to the western front in the form of the German offensive remembered as the Battle of the Bulge, turned back in fierce fighting exemplified in the heroic defense of Bastogne and the loss of nineteen thousand American lives. The German attack failed, and from the hindsight of history we know the German war machine was on its heels, that the war against the Nazis would be over in a matter of months, but the final push had to be fueled by manpower. Every soldier was needed. The days when black GIs were considered a kind of luxury to appease civil rights leaders in America had long gone.

Allen Joiner, the Chicagoan who served in the Ninety-second Division, recalled, in his own amusing style, just how much things had changed. Joiner was a reluctant warrior. Like some other black Americans frustrated by the country's racial history, he didn't see stakes in this war worth risking his life. "The Germans hadn't done anything to me." Still, he had been drafted and found himself at Fort Huachuca in

1944. “I tried to get out of going overseas,” he recalled six decades later. “At Fort Huachuca, my hemorrhoids came down on me. I figured I was going to beat the deal then—that was three weeks before we were supposed to go overseas. I remember being examined by the medical officer when I heard steps, a woman’s steps. I said, ‘Close the door.’ He said, ‘Aw, they’ve seen everything.’ I said, ‘They ain’t seen this one.’ Anyway, he went and got done examining me. I figured I wasn’t going to Italy. Then he called my outfit and said, ‘We’ll take him over as is and separate ’em when we get over there.’ I just stood there and shook my head.” Joiner recounts that story with a hearty laugh.[1]

But the shortage of manpower was no laughing matter for the army that winter of 1944 to 1945. Lee proposed freeing twenty thousand men from service units in his communications zone command in Europe and training them for combat. Furthermore, he recommended taking more than two thousand men from the Com Z black units and persuaded General Dwight Eisenhower, the supreme commander, and General Omar Bradley that this was a good idea. The day after Christmas, he sent to his commanders a call to battle to be distributed to the African American units. A “limited number” of black GIs were to be offered “the privilege of joining our veteran units at the front to deliver the knockout blow” against the Germans, his call read. “Your comrades at the front are anxious to share the glory of victory with you. Your relatives and friends everywhere have been urging that you be granted this privilege.”[2]

Embedded in this patriotic and somewhat patronizing call to arms were these revolutionary words: “It is planned to assign you without regard to color or race to the units where assistance is most needed, and give you the opportunity of fighting shoulder to shoulder to bring about victory.”[3]

Individual black men were to be assigned wherever they were needed. If an infantry platoon was short one man, a black rifleman would find himself fighting among white infantrymen, or two or three African Americans could be thrown into a unit once all white.

When Ike’s chief of staff, Lieutenant General Walter Bedell Smith, who arrived in the army via the Georgia National Guard and thus carried the attitudes of the South, saw these words, he immediately grasped their revolutionary nature. They threatened to overturn the War Department's die-hard policy of segregation. Smith objected to Lee, but the son of the South was unimpressed. Lee had a manpower emergency to confront, and a soldier was a soldier. Smith was sympathetic to Lee's view but said, "Two years ago I would have considered [Lee's call] the most dangerous thing that I had ever seen in regard to negro relations." Now it would still have "the most serious repercussions in the United States." But Lee "can't see this at all," Smith wrote Eisenhower. "He believes that it is right that colored and white officers should be mixed in the same company." Smith urged Ike to take the matter to the War Department.[4]

Eisenhower didn't, but he did rewrite Lee's call to black troops. The new version called for black volunteers for combat, saying that if the number of volunteers "exceeds the replacement needs of negro combat units, these men will be suitably incorporated in other organizations so that their service and their fighting spirit may be efficiently utilized."[5] That was pure sophistry. No black infantry combat units served in the European theater of operations, just artillery, tank, and tank destroyer organizations (the Ninety-second was in the Mediterranean theater), and Ike knew it. So the black volunteers would have to go to white organizations. As it turned out, there were plenty of volunteers—more than forty-five hundred had volunteered when the army cut them off after sending twenty-eight hundred for training. So eager for the chance to fight for their country were these black soldiers that noncommissioned officers agreed to return to the rank of private to get into combat.

Eisenhower, ever the political general, wouldn't allow integration of individual black soldiers, but he would permit integration of units. Black rifle platoons were organized, given a white lieutenant and sergeant, and assigned to divisions. By the time I got to the European theater, the integrated divisions had fought the Germans. As I later reported to Assistant Secretary of War John McCloy, the black rifle platoons had seen action in Remagen, Germany, and in fighting west of the Rhine River. "Their combat efficiency rating was 'excellent,' " I was pleased to report.[6]

I had arrived in the European theater of operations from Italy on March 16, 1945. I was there because Lee had written to McCloy saying he would welcome a visit by me. My instructions from McCloy were to "observe the performance of Negro troops, their attitudes and the attitudes of their officers towards them."[7] My trip took me to the Sixteenth Reinforcement Depot at Compiègne, France, where service troops were trained to be riflemen, as well as to General George Patton's Third Army headquarters and its African American tank units; General Omar Bradley's Twelfth Army headquarters; the Advanced Section, Communications Zone, at Namur, Belgium; army positions in Normandy, France; and to a hospital in the north of England where African American nurses treated American soldiers wounded on European battlefields.

I had never met Lee, a graduate of the Virginia Military Institute, the epitome of the old-officer establishment—those VMI guys were more West Point than the West Pointers. Lee was a strict disciplinarian; that and his initials of *C.H.* resulted in him being called John "Court House" Lee. Indeed, you were aware of a commanding presence when you were around him. However, just as impressive was his searching mind; he was one who gathered information and studied a situation before reaching a decision. In my conversations with Lee and my nosing around the command, I gleaned some details behind the integration that had finally come to the battlefield. As it turned out, Lee had discussed the idea of combining black soldiers and white soldiers on the battlefield with General Davis, but upon my arrival, I immediately became aware that Lee's ideas for individual integration had been frustrated.

How did this southerner come up with the idea of having black and white soldiers fight side by side? As I noted, Lee was no advocate of social integration. Far from it. In fact, he opposed off-the-battlefield integration because he believed social intermingling, which likely would involve liquor and women too, would inevitably lead to disturbances.[8] However, his attitudes about war zone integration had been influenced by a study given him by a colleague, Major General Frederick Henry Osborn, commander of the Information and Education Division of the War Department and before the war a trustee of the Carnegie Foundation. A friend of mine in the division from Chicago, Charles Dollard, who also had worked for the foundation, had told me about this report, which was a survey of how white troops would react to the idea of service with black Americans. I don't remember anything about this survey but its gratifying findings—the thrust was that white troops wouldn't give a damn if they were billeted with black fighters.

If white troops were open to the idea of combat with black soldiers, Lee knew African Americans were eager for it. His command included a battalion of black truck drivers who called themselves the Red Ball Express because they carried munitions and other supplies to the front along a route called the Red Ball Highway. Lee knew these men would volunteer to the man to get into a rifle company, which indeed they did. Only the intervention of Smith kept individual integration from being achieved.

Still, Lee was responsible for a signal advance on behalf of African American troops. "The reinforcement training plan is, in my opinion, the most significant forward step that has been undertaken by the army since [integration of] the Officer Candidate Training program," I wrote Lee. "It comes at a time when it is badly needed, to assure the public of the fact," and here I added some face-saving for Washington, "known to many inside the War Department, that the army is flexible and is making serious efforts to approach a workable solution to the difficult problem of race." And I was starting to look to the postwar period. "Experiences in the integration of Negro soldiers by platoons into combat organizations will be a source of valuable information for the guidance of the army in the development of future policies."[9]

Lee paid a price for his daring. His enthusiasm had won Eisenhower's agreement for his original plan. More familiar with Washington's tough line on race, Smith had saved Ike from carrying the army further than the War Department intended. Implementation of Lee's original ideas would have contradicted Washington's policy of not transgressing against civilian dictates against integration. Eisenhower had a close call, and Lee would pay for it. Eisenhower busted Lee for crossing the race line, retiring him and sending him back to Norfolk, Virginia, where he lived out his life as a deacon of the Episcopal Church.

That didn't happen until after I had left Europe, so I got to see a couple of other examples of Lee's exemplary attitude toward blacks. Lee pressed me for reports about the state of the European command. I had a memo about an incident involving African Americans in one unit of the Women's Army Corps (Wacs) in England. One of the Wac officers had earned a reputation for standing up to one particularly overbearing senior commander. During a visit to the unit, which was assigned to telephone switchboard duty, he imperiously demanded that all the Wacs turn out for inspection. Well, the demands of army communications had the women working long hours and getting little sleep. Their Wac officer refused to turn out women who were getting a brief bit of well-deserved rest or to have operators abandon the switchboards. "I'll have you up on charges," blustered the white officer. Lee had this martinet transferred to other duties. On another occasion, after visiting a hospital where black nurses worked, I quoted to Lee the complaint of a white officer unhappy about being attended by an African American nurse. Lee snapped that he didn't give a damn about the officer's beef.

What a pleasing development my visit to London turned out to be after the dismal experience in Italy. While in the European theater, Lee assigned as my aide a senior officer, Lieutenant Colonel Kenneth Campbell. Campbell and I had become friendly years before when we were among the handful of black undergraduates at the University of Chicago. He had married a Kansas oil heiress and gone into business with Homer Roberts, also an officer in Europe. They had run an auto agency in the Grand Hotel at Fiftieth Street and South Park Avenue in Chicago, selling Hupmobiles, a sturdy, durable car on the market for more than thirty years before going out of business just before World War II. Campbell knew the ins and outs of the European theater of operations and was invaluable to my inspection tour.

After London, I traveled to Paris to meet up with General Davis. Following a weekend there, I visited some units in the south of France. I was exposed to new and exotic alcoholic beverages several times during my time in Europe. In Italy, I had sampled cognac for the first time with General Crittenberger. Now in the south of France, someone introduced me to an apple brandy called calvados. It was pretty potent stuff—

it could warm your toenails. Some days later I found myself in Reims, France, with an old friend, Lieutenant Colonel Harvey Whitfield. He was a physician whom I had known in Chicago when he was in medical school at Northwestern University and who later would be one of my doctors in Chicago. (I had also represented his wife in mortgage litigation.) Whitfield, who always had the stump of a cigar stuck in his mouth, and I spent an evening endeavoring to deplete the stock of wine and champagne in Reims. We failed but not for want of trying.

I was carousing with Whitfield that night because he had sent me a startling message—General George Patton wanted to talk to me. Just why I never found out. Perhaps it was because he had tanks manned by black soldiers.

In any event, I soon found myself in Luxembourg, where Patton was recharging his Third Army for a hoped-for offensive across the Rhine. I was ushered into Patton's office, and I found myself facing the great man himself. He was striking—piercing blue eyes, erect military stance, burnished cavalry boots, and two ivory-handled 45-caliber pistols strapped to his legs. Standing behind him was an African American sergeant. Patton gestured toward him and said, "No one messes with me."

We talked for about an hour and a half, conversing on subjects ranging from military tactics to polo to the black men under his command. He stunned me right at the opening of our meeting. He asked me if I was familiar with his battlefield tactics. I confessed that I was not. Then he said words I'll never forget—"I developed the strategy and tactics when I served with Hannibal crossing the Alps." Hannibal of course was the Carthaginian general who had battled Rome a couple of hundred years before the birth of Christ, and here was Patton telling me he had marched with Hannibal to make war on the Romans! Hannibal's famous elephants were quick and effective in battle, and Patton said he had adapted Hannibal's methods of maneuvering elephants on the battlefield in his deployment of tanks in World War II. I thought, is this guy kidding me? But his manner persuaded me that he was dead serious.

Later the conversation turned to his men. Patton declared that he had no race problems in his army. When his black tank men delivered in a fight, Patton said he expressed his pleasure with their strategy.

When they didn't deliver, he treated them the same as white tank men who had not succeeded. I never doubted his sincerity. The army propaganda machine seized on this transparent characteristic of this famous general, and it was one of those times when army public relations accurately reflected reality. A War Department press release in the spring of 1945 recorded Patton addressing the 761st Tank Battalion, a black unit. "I don't give a damn what color you are as long as you get out there and kill those sons of —— in the green suits."[10] Anyone who has seen the great George C. Scott portray Patton in the eponymous movie has no trouble visualizing that scene.

My visit with Patton and the Third Army turned out to be a most memorable day. I'll never forget it or Patton. The visit I made to Omar Bradley's headquarters didn't bring an invitation to meet General Bradley, although Bradley was supposed to be the "GI's general." Patton may have been a man who believed he had walked the earth in ancient times, but he proved himself now to be a man ahead of his times.

Soon, it was time to head back to Washington. I boarded a military plane in Paris, and off we headed out over the Atlantic. Unfortunately, off the coast of Africa, the plane developed engine trouble, and we had to make an emergency landing in the Azores. After the rigors of Italy and the successes of northwestern Europe, I'd had about as much excitement as I could stand. I was happy when I finally found myself back in Washington.

I spent a lot of time assessing my visit with General Lee for the brass in Washington as well as writing a report for Lee. Besides praising the integrated combat units, I took care to tell Lee of other positive things I had seen during my visit to the European theater. Morale was high in the service units, due in large part no doubt to the fact that black GIs were in combat alongside white troops. Enlisted men in the Quartermaster's Depot were working around the clock on a voluntary basis. One sergeant told me, "We've got to keep the supplies moving, and all of us want to do our part." Black truck drivers, saying they "hated to see the doughs walk," drove white infantrymen deep into dangerous territory at night.

I did point out a couple of negative developments in one district in Normandy. No promotion was approved for any officer until he applied for transfer to the infantry, a policy that could only be discouraging to the morale of men remaining in service units. Another charge was that only white applications for officer training were being forwarded from this district. I closed my report to Lee by urging field commanders be instructed to report on their racial experiences.[11]

Once back in Washington, I met with Washington news reporters and again emphasized the positive developments in Europe. American commanders over there were "following in racial matters what must be the basic policy of any Army in any war, namely, that of utilizing most efficiently all available resources of men and material to defeat the enemy. Such a policy is working." White soldiers heaped praise on black GIs. I quoted one white noncommissioned officer "graphically, if ungrammatically," as asserting, "It don't matter who's firing next to you when you're both killing Krauts." I quoted a battle veteran commander as saying, "These men will fight because they have been trained and treated just like the other soldiers here and they know they are going to be used in the same manner, in the same divisions. They want to fight." The only two African Americans recorded as absent without leave later turned up on the front line ready to do battle. The black soldiers had proven themselves in fighting. I concluded, "Certainly the record being made by Negro soldiers gives the lie to any charge that Negroes cannot and will not fight."[12]

After Victory in Europe Day, the army surveyed white officers and enlisted men about their experiences with the experiment in integrating foxholes. The 250 white officers and noncommissioned officers had begun the experiment with reservations among 64 percent of both groups. Afterward, 77 percent of both groups recorded more favorable attitudes toward African Americans. Every one of the officers and 99 percent of the noncommissioned personnel rated the performance of black soldiers in combat as very well (84 percent of officers, 81 percent of noncommissioned officers) or fairly well. They often lauded the black troops for aggressiveness in attacking, effective use of firepower, adeptness in close-in fighting, and teamwork in battle. The few negatives focused on black troops going too rapidly and too far in attacking—in other words, an excess of zeal! How did they measure up compared with white troops? Sixty-nine percent of white officers and 83 percent of noncommissioned personnel said the black soldiers had performed the same as white troops. Their combat showing was rated better than whites by 17 percent of officers and 9 percent of noncoms. Majorities also said white and black soldiers got along well or very well away from the battlefield, with the best relations reported among troops who had shared the toughest fighting.[13]

The survey also questioned 1,710 white enlisted men. Of the white men who had had the experience of serving in companies with black and white platoons, only 7 percent said they disliked the arrangement, and 64 percent said it was a very or fairly good idea. Soldiers who had not had the benefit of serving with black troops were, not surprisingly given the times, more likely disposed against the idea. Interestingly enough, white men from the South made up about a third of both groups.

Significantly, the black volunteers registered only slightly better in education attainment and Army General Classification Test (AGCT) scores than the average among all black troops in the European theater.[14] The conclusions seemed clear: The AGCT was far from a perfect indicator of the potential for men in combat. Given the proper training and the right leadership, freed from the odious morale-busting stereotypes of race, and committed to battle alongside their fellow white citizens, African American troops proved they had the right stuff and performed in combat as well as white soldiers. General Lee's revolutionary ideas had not been embraced, but the results of limited integration still had a revolutionary impact.

This survey had not even been conducted at the time I made my report to McCloy on my trip to the European theater. However, I had seen enough on my own to know that even the watered-down version of Lee's integration plan had produced stunning results. The results demanded, I told McCloy, nothing less than a critical reexamination of the whole concept of complete segregation that had been the mantra of the army from the start of the war. "Many officers of long service in the Army believe that there are too many problems incident to the maintenance of large segregated combatant units to justify their future retention. They expressed the opinion that the pattern now being followed with the small units in ETO should be continued in future Army plans for the utilization of Negro combatant troops. I share this opinion."[15]

Fully aware of the army's wall of preconceived opinion, stubborn refusal to abandon obviously false concepts, and fear of getting out front of civilian society on racial issues, I suggested the army didn't have to rush into anything it was uncomfortable with. "This does not necessarily require the immediate abolition of all segregated units. It would permit the army to make use of individuals and small units on the basis of ability alone." This was a gradual approach. Later I would push for a more concerted drive to wipe out segregation, but at that time this approach offered the appeal of building on the clear success in Europe. I closed by recommending that the War Department start planning for the inclusion and utilization of black soldiers in the postwar army.[16]

Unfortunately, I was to find out that the army brass, despite the clear demonstration of the efficiency of integrated units in Europe, would dig in their heels. The battles producing what little progress that had finally been achieved in World War II would have to be fought again. The forces of the status quo weren't about to let African American heroism on the battlefield push the army down a road it didn't want to go down. And blacks fighting in Europe didn't do a damn thing to change attitudes among the most recalcitrant forces back home in America.

15

More of the Same

Bigots weren't impressed by black soldiers spilling their blood on the battlefields of Europe. An African American's life was still cheap in the American South. Shortly after I returned from my gratifying tour of the European theater, I was confronted with one of the ugliest crimes I had seen in a long time.

In April of 1945, Private Adam Green was riding a train through Arkansas, part of a group of soldiers being shipped from Camp Livingston, Louisiana, to Fort Ord, California. When the train stopped in Dumas, Arkansas, on April 23, Green stepped off to stretch his legs. The train started pulling out, and Green moved to reboard it. J. R. Wilson, the Dumas city marshal, pulled his sidearm and fatally shot Green—for no reason. The testimony from several witnesses could not have been more damning for the marshal. Green had done nothing wrong. He had uttered no threatening words to the law officer. Wilson had made no attempt to arrest the soldier, so obviously Green couldn't have been resisting arrest. When asked why he had shot Green, Wilson would testify that "he clenched his fist."

Well, I had seen a lot of atrocious murders of black men in the South during the war, but this one struck me as especially heinous. "Brutal and wholly unprovoked" were the words I used to describe it to Assistant Secretary of War John McCloy. I noted that in a case from Georgia, the U.S. Supreme Court had affirmed the right of the federal government to prosecute law enforcement officers for the murder of black soldiers.

I stated that the attorney general should bring charges against Wilson and prosecute him for the murder of Green.[1] Indeed, McCloy wrote the Department of Justice urging prosecution, but of course nothing came of it.

Enlightened white opinion increasingly registered complaints about the Jim Crow society of the South. Agnes Meyer, the wife of *Washington Post* publisher-editor Eugene Meyer, forwarded to McCloy a letter from John Hammond, the scion of a wealthy family who as a record producer and talent scout for the Columbia Broadcasting System had promoted the popularity of blues music. A private assigned to Camp Gruber in Oklahoma, Hammond got an up close and personal introduction to the mores of the South. It was natural that, given his background, Hammond found himself tagged by the camp's special services office to work on an entertainment program for the camp. He took off for the neighboring town of Muskogee in search of talent.

In Muskogee, Hammond wrote Mrs. Meyer, he had run across excellent black musicians playing at a white dance. They told him that an African American bandleader from New York whom he had known for years was playing in a black dance hall that night. "I immediately went over to see him, not only to say hello but to arrange for him to come to camp," Hammond recalled. "As soon as I arrived I was greeted with enormous enthusiasm by the band's manager and all the boys in the band."

Hammond had been there less than five minutes when four white military police showed up, arrested him, and carted him off to the guardhouse. "I was so astonished that for once I was speechless." The MPs, all from the Deep South, instructed Hammond that black areas of Muskogee were off limits to white personnel. "I was then given a long story about Muskogee's violent knife-wielding 'Niggers' and warned never to be caught there again." With that, his pass and credentials were returned, and he was let off with a warning.

The next day Hammond busied himself getting permission to return to Muskogee. He was told he had to be accompanied by an MP and check in with the police station on each visit. Hammond was disgusted. "For all the few months I was in New Orleans, a very reactionary city,

I had complete freedom of movement in the Negro section; but in Northeastern Oklahoma the army has imposed segregation that is as complete as anything one might find in Fascist countries."[2]

The sad thing was there wasn't much that could be done about it. The army wasn't about to interfere with a local commander's dictates on such issues. Still, I urged the Army Service Forces in Washington to pass along Hammond's complaints to the commanding officer of the MP detachment in northeastern Oklahoma.[3] I let Mrs. Meyer know we were following up on her letter, and she later dropped me a note of thanks.[4]

One of the perverse ironies of segregation was that helpful gestures by whites could boomerang against African Americans. An ugly incident in Georgia was instructive. Sergeant Aubrey E. Robinson Jr., stationed at Fort Gordon, Georgia, was traveling by bus from nearby Augusta to Aiken, South Carolina. Those on the bus, of course, observed the rules of the South—white people sat up front and black folks in the back of the bus. As the bus made its journey with people getting on and off, pretty soon all the seats for blacks were filled. At one point one empty seat in the white section remained. A black soldier stood in the aisle until a white soldier next to the empty seat told him to sit down. They talked until the bus reached Warrenville, South Carolina, and the driver noticed the two men sitting side by side. He ordered the black soldier to move, which he did immediately despite the indignant protests of the white GI. Worse was to come.

At Warrenville some seats in the white section came open. A black woman got on the bus. She noticed a white man sleeping in a seat toward the back of the bus and requested the driver ask the man to move forward. No, the driver snapped, and told her if she didn't like it she should get off and get a refund. As the woman stepped down from the vehicle, the bus driver balled his fist and hit her in the back of the head, staggering her. Several white soldiers grabbed him, preventing further violence against the poor woman. Robinson and several black soldiers told the bus driver not to harm the woman but did nothing more than that. They soon found themselves kicked off the bus and confronting two cars filled with county police and armed civilians. Lacking money to pay all the fines imposed in a farce of a trial, all but one of the GIs were jailed, detailed to a chain gang, and denied the right to contact their army commanders. As a result they were declared absent without leave. The one not jailed, Robinson, remained free because the soldiers pooled what little money they had for his fine. Back at the camp, enlisted men reached into their pockets for the cash to free the other men. Their officers did nothing.

Robinson, from Virginia, could scarcely believe this nightmare. "It shook to the very core my faith in a nation where such things could receive the sanction of so many people as it does here in the South. I had to call upon every ounce of training and premilitary experience to keep from becoming bitter, and to realize that I must continue to sacrifice to be a soldier so that I may fight and if necessary give my life for my country."[5] Only his belief that some Americans worked to cure this cancer on the nation sustained Robinson, later a federal judge, in his duty as a soldier.

"This is another excuse for impressing upon post commanders the necessity of establishing an understanding with civilian peace officers in surrounding communities," Roy Wilkins of the NAACP wrote me. "Of course the men should have been released to the military police, but the least that could have been done was to allow them to communicate with their post."[6] Part of my burden as civilian aide was speaking up on the army's behalf, even in the worst situations, and finding at least some modicum or shred of rationalization for military behavior, but this time I replied to Wilkins that "I find myself in a strange position of agreeing with you without any reservations whatsoever."[7]

The truth was that the War Department still refused to interfere with local custom in the South—and wasn't ashamed about saying so on the record. In early 1945, my aide Louis Lautier complained about white military police in Florida abusing black soldiers traveling in the state. Colonel Harrison A. Gerhardt, serving as executive to McCloy, responded to Lautier with a note of irritation about my persistence in complaining about mistreatment of black soldiers on buses and trains in the South. "As you know, Mr. Gibson and I have been over this ground many times before and the question of equal facilities under the segregation laws of the State of Florida is not a question that the War Department can take to the Supreme Court in the case of individuals traveling on southern carriers." Furthermore, he said, War Department policy required military police to assist in enforcing state and local laws.[8]

That's the kind of thing that made it hard to get out of bed in the morning to face the job. Being the African American advocate in the War Department required nimble instincts. One moment you were on the defense, struggling to overcome some antediluvian directive or to push back against Jim Crow tradition. The next moment found you on the offense, pushing the envelope to modify army policy to overcome the military's ingrained tendency to opt for segregation on every occasion.

One thing that had to be constantly countered was the army intelligence service's regular reports on race relations that never failed to blame black soldiers for any trouble. The military brass liked to knock black newspapers for exaggerating racial tensions for political purposes. Well, army intelligence was just as guilty in trying to paint black soldiers and civilians as seething with sedition and fomenting discontent and violence. In addition, of course, no accusation of rape of a white woman by an African American went unrecorded.

Typical was the June 5, 1945, report alleging "group violence . . . continues to reflect lack of restraint of Negro soldiers." It cited trouble at Drew Field, Florida, where 350 black soldiers returning from a hike rioted in a service club because "two white attendants could not serve them fast enough." In Memphis, Tennessee, five black soldiers and one white GI "were rowdy, used profanity and molested white women" at a railroad station. In Chicago, a white gang shot and killed a black youth and wounded two others near a mail-order company "because of alleged incidents in which Negroes molested Italian girl employees." Reflecting the growing tensions between the United States and the Soviet Union, an intelligence report recorded eight instances of communist activity aimed at African Americans.[9]

The July 25, 1945, intelligence report alleged the rape and murder of a seventeen-year-old white girl in Eufaula, Alabama, and the rape of a five-year-old white girl in Greenville, Florida, both attributed to African Americans. More positively, this document took note of army efforts to improve race relations, such as Camp Lee, Virginia, opening recreational facilities to both races, Camp Butner, North Carolina, inaugurating Thursday night dances for black patients at its hospital, and Harlington Army Air Field, Texas, promoting athletic contests between white and black soldiers.[10]

In April 1945 there occurred a disturbance serious enough to warrant the attention of the Advisory Committee on Negro Troop Policies. Sadly it showed how little progress we had made in some quarters. The commander at Freeman Field, Indiana, decided to return to a policy of segregation by race at the officers' club. Several African American officers—one of them being Coleman Young, a future mayor of Detroit—refused an order to patronize a black officers' club. They were brought up on charges before a court-martial. After a spirited defense led by future U.S. Supreme Court Justice Thurgood Marshall, all of them were acquitted.

The initial reaction of the Army Air Forces to Freeman Field reinstituting racial segregation was to back the commander's decision. Outraged, nearly all of the four hundred black soldiers stationed at Freeman Field turned out at a demonstration at the club. Emotions ran high, and there was some sort of physical confrontation between black officers and a military policeman. More than one hundred African Americans were arrested, but all were released except for three officers. Given the strict protocol on discipline, the committee had no choice but to recommend trial of the three as quickly as possible. I dryly observed that they had been arrested, but no charges had been filed against them. McCloy rose to the occasion. He got on the record as seeing the post commander's decision and the Army Air Forces' support of it as "a step backward." The advisory committee, acting at McCloy's direction, decreed that the post commander had no right to contradict army policy prohibiting segregation by race. The committee ordered up a rewrite of the army policy to make that clear. The only dissent came from the panel's member from the Army Air Forces.[11] Policy, of course, continued to allow for segregation through assigning post exchanges, theaters, and other recreational facilities by military units, which were still rigidly segregated.

Given the meager prospects for advancing the cause of black soldiers, that small adjustment in policy had to go down as something of a victory. Naturally, there were things you could do nothing about. Like the bigotry of a powerful politician. On June 29, 1945, Senator James O. Eastland of Mississippi took the floor of the Senate to denounce the army's use of black soldiers as an abysmal failure and to charge that black GIs were guilty of—what else?—raping large numbers of white women. James M. Hinton, president of the South Carolina Conference of the NAACP, wrote Secretary of War Stimson demanding an apology from Eastland.[12] I certainly sympathized, but this was the era of southern dominance of the U.S. Senate, and nothing was going to come of that protest.

With black soldiers finally getting into combat in Europe and the South Pacific, I devoted increasing time to making sure they got proper care. By 1945 all but two of the hospitals in the United States treated both white and black patients. That came not out of any grand gesture of moral rectitude, but the simple fiscal facts of life demonstrated that it was economically wasteful to set up parallel hospitals for the races.

War inflicted psychological as well as physical wounds on men. I became alarmed when I discovered that army policy in effect prohibited the assignment of black psychologists and psychiatrists to hospitals serving both races. Given the special social and cultural conditions of the day, I felt it imperative that black psychologists and psychiatrists be available to treat the rising number of African American patients with mental disorders. I urged McCloy to get this policy changed.[13] And it was. It was a natural follow-up to previous army policy changes that had hospitals care for soldiers of both races and opened up service in all hospitals to black nurses.

Medicine and health care can have a way of busting stereotypes. The integration of hospitals threw blacks and whites together in ways never dreamed of before—white patients benefited from treatment from African American physicians. A case in point was reported to me by my old friend Colonel M. O. Bousfield at Fort Huachuca, Arizona. He cited the example of a doctor named Harold W. Thatcher, a lieutenant colonel on the staff of the fort's hospital and another friend from my

Chicago days. As valuable as he was to the medical care of the hospital, Bousfield wrote, "his ability to engender appreciation for the Negro officer among the white military and civilian population has been far greater."[14]

Bousfield provided several dramatic examples. "Happy" Chandler, the baseball pioneer then a U.S. senator from Kentucky, had two sons attending a military school in Arizona. One of them came down with a skin disease, and the school's principal, aware of Thatcher's reputation as a first-rate physician, brought the boy to the fort for Thatcher to treat his condition. Chandler and his wife visited Fort Huachuca and were very grateful that the doctor cured the boy's condition. Grover Land, a former baseball coach with the Chicago Cubs who had been working as a civilian at Fort Huachuca, had his wife treated by Thatcher. Colonel Hardy sought out Thatcher for advice on treating his arthritis and glaucoma.[15] At the start of the war, the surgeon general's office and the War Department had harbored doubts that black doctors would be of much use. Thatcher exemplified how wrong they had been, and his record of achievement was far from unique.

Another small victory for integration was scored regarding rest and recreation facilities called redistribution centers. They were aimed at providing a break for soldiers who had served overseas for some specified time or in combat zones. Of course the army brass planned for segregated centers in a few places and only white centers in most locations. I objected right from the start when discussions on this issue began in 1944. The first thing, I said, was to keep these facilities out of the South. In the North, I didn't see any particular need for a separate center for black soldiers. To establish separate operations for the races in places like New York and Chicago "might invite difficulty," I observed with diplomatic understatement. In addition, the idea of only placing white centers in big cities was abhorrent and was sure to bring down charges of discrimination against the army.[16]

Unfortunately, the McCloy Committee went along with the army's thinking at its July 19, 1944, meeting and recommended to Secretary of War Henry Stimson that "separate facilities be established to which will be sent colored returnees with their wives. These establishments to be comparable in physical quality and facilities, to the extent practicable, of those for white personnel."[17] New York and Chicago would be the first locations. In a bit of egregious condescension, the committee was told, "There is no equal among Negro hotels to the Hotel Teresa in Harlem and the Hotel Pershing in Chicago is probably the second best."[18]

I wasn't at that meeting, and no one had sought my views even though I was the point man on African American issues in the War Department. I protested to Assistant Secretary McCloy. With the 1944 political season under way, I noted the army's policy would excite protests among blacks over segregation and the disparity of the facilities for the races. Black troops returning from overseas duty would be forced to fill two centers, one of them relatively small, while white soldiers enjoyed access to forty-nine centers. "I am genuinely alarmed that irreparable harm may result."[19]

Selling the sorry concept of separate centers to black communities in New York and Chicago fell like a death sentence on me. My predictions proved prescient when African Americans at a meeting on the issue in New York exploded in anger. They vowed to the army brass attending to oppose the program in every way possible. Reporting to McCloy, I said, "I had to volunteer my advice here because it was not requested, though I cannot but observe that my warnings have been fully borne out by subsequent events. Notwithstanding my opinion about the proposal, I did everything possible to assist in a full and fair presentation of the matter to Negroes in Chicago and New York, exposing myself to personal criticism in the process."[20] Such was my lot in those days.

I recall the issue coming to a head in a clash before the McCloy Committee between myself and General Brehon Somervell. He proudly announced that Chicago would be one of the lead areas for establishing redistribution centers because of its central location. The historic and elegant Congress Hotel at Congress Parkway and Michigan Avenue alongside the city's famous Loop business district was to be set up for white troops. Black troops would be relegated to the Pershing Hotel at Sixty-fourth Street and Cottage Grove Avenue on the city's South Side. Now, I had represented the Pershing Hotel as a lawyer, but I had to acknowledge that it was a second-class hotel compared to the Congress.

I vehemently opposed the idea of separate facilities. Somervell bristled and snapped, "Let the coons go to the desert for all I care." He turned and walked out, leaving the committee members in shocked surprise. In the end, the African American soldiers went to the Congress Hotel, and I had won another small victory.

Other battles ended more inconclusively. Legislation was proposed in the Congress in 1945 to prevent restaurants at railroad stations from discriminating against black soldiers. Most train stations in the South of course had only one restaurant, reserved for whites, and just to get a meal meant long treks by foot for black GIs. The army's Legislative and Liaison Division objected in writing that the bill promoted the mixing of the races. Outraged, I argued that the army would be more concerned with the treatment of its men, their ability to get a decent meal, and less worried about the "sociological questions incidental to uniformity of treatment regardless of race or color," as the division had put it in its turgid prose.[21] Major Davidson Sommers, an assistant in the War Department, took my objections to heart and told the legislative division that the proposal before Congress would only require for interstate commerce a policy parallel to regulations for army installations.[22] Ignorant of the policies of the army it was supposed to represent on legislative issues, the division asserted that the legislation would prohibit segregation, causing social friction in the South. Sommers responded that the bill did not require "more than equal facilities, which may or may not be designated for segregated use."[23] I had gotten the army to stand up for the idea that black soldiers ought to have a place to eat at train stations in the South as they traveled home or between postings. Unfortunately, this much needed piece of legislation died in Congress.

By then the war was over in Europe and near an end in the Pacific. I had been with the War Department for more than four and a half years. A few gains had been made. Officer training installations, hospitals, and redistribution centers had been integrated. Most satisfying of all had to be the glorious record of the heroics of black soldiers fighting in platoons integrated into white companies in Europe. Still, these gains had been achieved against massive resistance. The emotional toll on me aches to this day, but I resolved to soldier on.

The isolationist impulse in American politics suffered a fatal wound in the war. Even as the battle against fascism raged across the globe, policymakers grew aware that Western democracy would face a terrible challenge from the Soviet Union, and in a world laid waste by war, only the United States could confront the threat of communist expansion. The savagery and staggering casualties of World War II proved America could no longer disband its armies and retreat behind two oceans. Once hostilities ended, the United States would be required to maintain a military force like nothing before in its history. I saw opportunity. No efficient military power with global reach and quick mobilization was possible without participation of America's black citizens. Here was an opening to strike at segregation, and I was determined to seize it.

16

A Presidential Order

The Allied armies storming onto the Normandy beaches on D-day emblazoned in history the turning point in the war on the western front. June 6, 1944, is as good a milestone as any to date the beginning of the end for Adolf Hitler and the Nazi nightmare he had unleashed on the world. The sacrifice in human life in a hurricane of machine-gun and artillery fire, so vividly re-created for a later generation by movie maker Steven Spielberg in *Saving Private Ryan,* portended a day when the guns would fall silent. Never doubting for a moment that desperate fighting and moments of crisis still confronted our hopes for a conclusion to the carnage, I nevertheless realized also that mid-1944 was not a moment too soon to start planning for the postwar environment and the promise and hazards it would afford African Americans.

Several factors impelled my thinking. First was the often meager successes won for black soldiers during the war. We had underestimated the inertia and strength of resistance to change from the army's command structure. The piecemeal, reactive, planning-on-the-fly, contingency-based, policy-driven-by-events approach to tackling the supreme obstacle to black advancement had proved woefully inadequate. Only a coordinated, well thought out, comprehensive, long-range plan to attack segregation had any hope of succeeding. Furthermore, the postwar years were fraught with the possibility not only of progress but of regression as well. I remembered the wave of repression, rioting, and murder that so wounded black communities in the years after World War I when America too often embraced reactionary politics. Indeed, the post–World War II years did bring some difficult times for black Americans, although nowhere near the scale of the crisis in the wake of the Great War.

More positively, I also knew that African Americans were better prepared to face whatever came. Like all wars, this one had proved to be a transforming event to millions of lives. The insatiable hunger of the industrial war machine had quickened the pace of the Great Migration and drawn ever increasing numbers of black families from the suffocating Jim Crow society and tenant-farming economy of the South to the industrial jobs, freer social environment, and invigorating intellectual climate of the North and Midwest. The Fair Employment Practices Committee, created by executive order by President Roosevelt, had been effective in ensuring that black workers got a share of the jobs in defense industries. Civil rights organizations found their voices listened to more and more as the swelling black communities of America's bustling metropolises amassed political clout. For all the hardships and setbacks I had seen in the army, service in a uniform had set African Americans on a journey down a road from which there was no turning back. Black men, three-quarters of them from the South, who had volunteered or been drafted into the greatest military machine the world had ever seen, acquired education and job skills previously denied them and traveled to regions where segregation was not king and, even better, to countries where skin color was not stigmatized as representing some second-class rank of humanity. In short, black Americans had seen a better future and weren't about to settle for anything less.

In fact, thirteen editors and publishers of black newspapers had met with President Roosevelt in the winter of 1944 to discuss the postwar aspirations of African Americans. It was, as the *Chicago Defender* noted, "the first time in this country's history that a president had formally received representatives of the Negro press as an organized group" speaking on behalf of black America.[1] The session was off the record, so the *Defender* couldn't report what had happened during the thirty-five-minute session. The group did issue a statement expressing the commitment of African Americans to the war effort but also vowing to work to end segregation and the second-class citizenship it imposed on America's black citizens.

All this and more filled my mind in July of 1944 as I put down on paper my thoughts about the postwar world for Assistant Secretary of War John McCloy. With American troops on the verge of breaking out of the Normandy bridgehead, I delineated what I saw as the important themes: the proper demobilization of black troops, preparing them for the new and lingering old realities of the American economy and society; the inclusion of African Americans in the postwar army; and the imperative of ridding the army of segregation. These were issues I would return to time and again as I felt a growing urgency that the country do both what was right by its black citizens and what was best for the efficiency of the kind of army necessary as the nation confronted an uncertain world and a new challenge from the aggressive brand of communism espoused by the Soviet Union. In that first memo, I described "some sketchy ideas," but they proved to be the foundation for all the memos, talks, and debates that were to come.[2]

First of all, most black soldiers didn't want to be discharged into the South. Perhaps nothing more than this reflected the change of attitudes among black men that had been wrought by their service in the army. Besides giving African Americans education they would never have received in civilian life, the army had "also disciplined them, given them a respect for leadership and then sent them in large numbers to stations throughout the world where they have had their ideas of race changed by attitudes of other people who have not regarded racial matters in the same light as white Americans." It must not be forgotten, I reminded McCloy, that black troops had been embittered by their experience in training at posts in the South. And even at this late date and after so many outrages against African Americans wearing the uniform of their country, Congress had yet to pass long-pending legislation to protect African American soldiers from physical attack in the South.

The new attitudes of these troops had to be considered as the army prepared to reintroduce them into civilian society—and that didn't mean resorting to superficial measures such as the speeches made by Tuskegee Institute president Robert R. Moton in France urging black soldiers to be "good boys." Besides hearing admonitions to "positive direction" in their thinking, black GIs must be assured of "some semblance of fair treatment" by having the War Department make sure government agencies worked to safeguard their rights as veterans. If it took an executive order to get black civilians hired in war industries during the time of crisis, obviously some type of government action would be necessary after the war "when patriotism presumably will not be at its present high peak and unemployment lists will have increased."

However, black soldiers weren't the only ones in need of some conditioning for their reentry into American society. White Americans should be "prepared in some measure for the shock attendant on the realization of the changed attitudes of Negro soldiers." The movie *The Negro Soldier* was a start on this.

Then I turned to the question of involving African Americans in the postwar army and recounted recent history. Three years after the army's "grudging realization" that it had to include African Americans in its forces, the military brass in early 1944 had been doing no more than just talking about committing them to combat. "It seems to me crystal-clear that the Army must begin planning now, not only for the inclusion of Negroes in the post-war Army but for their intelligent utilization." Political pressure would be exerted to that end. "The issue then is not *whether* Negroes can be made into good soldiers but rather *how*." Many problems confronted by the army during World War II resulted because blacks had been excluded from the peacetime military of the 1920s and 1930s. Acknowledging that many issues must be answered in transforming the army, I wrote:

> None among these will be tougher than that of segregation. They will not get any easier to solve, however, with the passage of time. Much has been said about the performance of Negro troops in combat determining their future utilization. This is important but I submit that unless conditions change radically in this country, the fact that Negroes can exert pressures of various sorts is of even greater importance. The necessity of a workable plan is self-evident in the event of a post-war Selective Service System.[3]

I closed by urging McCloy to begin "a realistic staff study" of the issues of demobilization of black soldiers and their inclusion in the post-war army. McCloy agreed, telling the Advisory Committee on Negro Troop Policies that "it is highly desirable that some thought and study be given to the racial problems which will arise in the post-war period as they affect our future Army."[4] A month later he issued another statement to the committee, often employing the same language, saying the committee should recommend the War Department immediately begin studying changes needed to effect the efficient participation of black troops in the army after the war.[5]

Word that such a study was under way inspired me to share some further thoughts with McCloy. The fall 1944 political season was at hand, and the army's treatment of black soldiers was emerging as a major issue among African American voters. That had, "rightly or wrongly, transformed the Army into sort of a whipping boy" for both the Democratic and Republican Parties. The army "has the choice of initiating some intelligent and constructive steps itself or of being forced again by pressures from outside sources."[6]

Looking back on this memo six decades later, I can't help but notice how the pressures of the job were affecting me and how I made no attempt to hide that from McCloy. "Though I know it is not necessary, I want to assure you that I have no political interests one way or the other. If I had a major interest at the moment it would be to get out of my present position as rapidly as possible, having just about reached the limit of my ability to serve as a 'middle-man,' absorbing gripes and complaints in person by mail and telephone all day and most of the night."[7] And this was written months before the firestorm of criticism engulfed me over my comments about the Ninety-second Division's performance in Italy!

"My concern," I continued, "is that the War Department adopt a decent and fair overall policy in order that the devastating effect of our tortuous experiences during the last few years be avoided in the future. I believe few officers in the army realize the effect on the spirits of Negro soldiers and civilians alike of the experiences during the last four years, while the many statements of policy were developed on a hit-and-run, trial-and-error basis."[8]

These issues were being pressed by the African American newspapers. I was constantly in communication with the editors of these papers, gauging community opinion, sharing information about what the army was doing regarding black troops, offering my appraisal of current conditions, and seeking feedback from the editors. For example, early in 1945, I wrote the editor of New York's *Amsterdam News,* "The period immediately ahead of us is most important for Negroes in the Army. There will either be compulsory military training or a similar program that will necessitate the inclusion of large numbers of Negroes in the armed forces. In 1940, we started out 20 years late insofar as Army planning was concerned. We should all join to see that this experience is not repeated."[9]

The newspapermen would keep me abreast of their communications with others in the government. For instance, John H. Sengstacke, publisher of the *Chicago Defender* and president of the Negro Newspaper Publishers Association, carbon-copied me a letter he had mailed to President Roosevelt complaining about the army's history of segregation and urging integration of blacks into all branches of the peacetime military.[10]

After Germany surrendered, I renewed my efforts to get some special preparation for black soldiers due to be discharged back into civilian life. One idea was for the army to make a film exploring the special problems African Americans would face finding work. Such motion pictures about reentering civilian life that existed were general in nature with no insights to the particular issues black veterans would confront. Surveys indicated a surprising number of African Americans intended to seek agriculture and small business loans. They were sure to encounter more difficulties and different ones than white veterans. Black veterans likely would need more help in capitalizing on the education and skills they had learned in the army. In addition, many of them would be migrating from the South; they, and the country, would benefit from them getting the best information on where to go for employment opportunities.[11] Repeating virtually the same language I had used, McCloy urged the Army Pictorial Service to make such a film.[12] Regrettably, no instructional motion picture was made.

Meanwhile, the army's study for the postwar plan was progressing, and what I had seen of it alarmed me. A study outline, dated May 23, 1945, framed the issues in a biased manner and asked leading questions that couldn't possibly elicit worthwhile information on segregation. They seemed predestined to portray African American soldiers in the worst light. The experience of black GIs would be viewed in isolation. No attempt was envisioned to compare white troops operating in the same areas under similar conditions. The planners appeared to be unquestioningly accepting the premises of the past—that history and tradition required separation of the races, that racial characteristics meant black soldiers couldn't adapt to modern combat, and that African American officers failed because of lack of character and mistrust of their leadership from the men they commanded. None of that reflected the material changes experienced in the last four years.[13]

The only productive way to develop postwar policy had to focus on the performance of black troops—with full consideration of all they experienced in this country and overseas—and on the army's performance in developing policies to include and utilize African American soldiers. The May 23 document in no way attempted to "scientifically determine and weigh prejudices and pre-existing opinions" the army imposed on black soldiers. In fact it "expressly forbids the use of scientific research studies" of the attitudes of enlisted men and officers and the attitudes of white and black soldiers toward each other. "Mere injunctions of objectivity do not work in the racial field where more often than not decisions are made on a basis of emotion, prejudice or pre-existing opinion." Any just consideration of the army's role in the way black soldiers turned out had to examine its testing procedures, personnel practices, and preconceived notions about African Americans.[14]

> Segregation . . . is the basic problem before the War Department. Experiences during this war in Army hospitals and Officer Candidate Schools and with the integrated Negro platoons in Europe certainly raise questions about the continuance of this policy which should be inquired into. . . . Every possible precaution must be utilized to

> avoid the error common to all previous studies of this problem, namely, that of ascribing failures of Negroes to racial characteristics without considering the possibilities that such failings as occur may be due to lack of educational, social and economic advantages which would affect other personnel in the same way under similar conditions, or the possibility that these failures may be due to defects in Army policy.[15]

The navy was well ahead of the army on race issues, having instituted some partial integration in its ranks, I noted. The army study should take a long-range view. Civilian attitudes were in flux, so the military should be flexible.

As my concerns indicated, the army brass was going to have to be dragged kicking and screaming into the modern world. Nothing that would happen over the next few years would change that assessment. Men of vision and fairness like McCloy and Robert Patterson, who succeeded Henry Stimson as secretary of war on September 27, 1945, would keep the pressure up for the army to do the right thing.

The army demonstrated the agility of a gymnast in presenting an enlightened acknowledgment of the clear evidence at one moment and then falling back the next moment on any excuse to continue the status quo. Consider some observations from General Joseph T. McNarney, who earlier in the year had insisted that the men of the Ninety-second Division had melted away under fire before the Gothic Line. In the summer of 1945 he described as sound the concept of mixed organizations going into combat. "I am convinced that had it been possible to put this proposal in a test in combat elements in an active theater of operations, there would have been no measurable loss of combat efficiency, and we would have been able to demonstrate that the colored soldier individually can be made into a good combat man, whereas we have in general failed to accomplish this using colored troops collectively in segregated units."[16]

Then came the qualifiers. "Impartial treatment" meant few black officers in mixed units "since it must be accepted that in competition with white soldiers of average ability few negroes will rise to command responsibility." Segregated units must be maintained to offset "the inevitable reaction of the radical elements against this certain result." The failure of segregated units could be traced to their poor black officers. "I doubt, however, that we can blame this entirely upon inherent racial characteristics." He *doubts* that racial characteristics are *entirely* at fault! "The lack of initiative, the unwillingness to accept responsibility, and the defensive attitude of negroes in general must be attributed in large part to the history of the race since its emancipation." There wasn't even a suggestion that army policies had the slightest impact. Still McNarney had to acknowledge that it was imperative upon the army to "provide for a proper proportion of negro personnel" and to develop command ability among them.[17]

That was a point beyond denial. In August 1945, General George Marshall, the army's chief of staff, told McCloy, "I agree that the practicability of integrating Negro elements into white units should be followed up."[18] Yes, but how?

That autumn Marshall, acting on instructions of Secretary of War Patterson, impaneled a board headed by Lieutenant General Alvan C. Gillem Jr. to prepare policy on the use of black soldiers in the postwar army. Less than a month after the four-member board's first meeting on October 1, 1945, it had reached some preliminary conclusions, and in six weeks it had finished its work.

I got a look at the interim report and identified problems that would ultimately plague the board's final recommendations. The fundamental weakness was the absence of an "unequivocal statement on the issue of segregation which is the basic issue confronting the War Department. To the contrary, the word itself is not mentioned anywhere."[19] And in an observation that would prove unhappily all too prescient, I wrote, "the statements and recommendations are ambiguous and susceptible to misinterpretation." Its language appeared to reverse the rigid segregation that had existed in promotions, assignment and billeting of black officers, but a closer reading suggested otherwise. In fact, a senior officer who read this section confirmed my fears by asserting "that no substantial change in present practices was required." To him, the Gillem recommendations did no more than open some new job opportunities to African American officers.

Provisions that seemed to build on the success of the mixed units in combat in Europe actually turned out to be insulting. They were, I observed, "consistent with the present pattern of the army that has been so violently criticized, namely that of relegating substantially all Negro troops to laboring units." Noting that history proved the "absolute necessity of clear, plain and forthright statements" in implementing policy goals, I urged that the Gillem Board's final report "be so clear that there could be no doubt in anyone's mind as to just what Army policy is."[20]

I wish I could say that the Gillem Board's completed report answered my fears. It did identify many of the problems of the past, but its recommendations, while often sounding fine and noble, tended to be vague and left the army plenty of wiggle room to avoid outright integration. Elimination of "any special consideration based on race" was the objective. While not abandoning segregated billeting, the board pushed the concept of black and white soldiers working together, sought to deny reenlistment of blacks with the lowest Army General Classification Test scores, and required the same standards for officer promotions. However, it adhered to the concept of quotas, which turned out to be difficult for the army in the postwar years as points earned in combat enabled whites to obtain earlier discharge and as many black soldiers opted for continued military service over returning to the uncertainties of civilian life. While integration of individuals was the goal, the Gillem Board, for the time being, favored integration by small units as had proved so effective in Europe.[21]

McCloy and I reviewed the Gillem report, discussed it, and wrote separate memos on it to Judge Patterson. Echoing my complaints about the interim report, McCloy found "a conscious avoidance of the word 'segregation' " and for that reason said the recommendations did "not speak with the complete clarity that is necessary." The War Department's experience demonstrated that policies could not be enforced when they are open to "any possibility of misconstruction." The Gillem report implied but did not state that black officers could command white men nor did it explicitly call for "unsegregated units." Furthermore, McCloy found the board's continued support of a quota inconsistent with a philosophy of making the most efficient use of available manpower. Of course, McCloy prefaced his criticisms with praise of the work of the Gillem Board, calling it "a real service" that constituted "a great advance" and read as "objective and constructive and, unlike many earlier papers, realistically states the problem in terms of making the most efficient use of available manpower."[22]

I seconded those observations in my analysis for Patterson. The board's recommendations were vague and cautious to the point of proving to be timid. Like McCloy, I, of course, had to sound optimistic. "The report is heartening evidence that in the future the Army will not attempt to utilize Negro manpower on the basis of the same temporizing day-to-day approach that has been followed in the past."[23] But the devil is in the details, and that's where the work of the Gillem Board came up short. The Gillem report declared that segregation didn't work and established a goal of integration. The problem was that it was largely silent on what should happen in between. That was a loophole the army could drive a battalion of tanks through and subsequently did.

First up, what was missing was a statement explicitly asserting that segregation didn't work and establishing specific intermediate measures aimed at accomplishing the objective of integration. Without such a clear declaration, those charged with executing the Gillem goals "will be in a hopeless predicament because they would be assigned the task of implementing a vague policy." A clear and explicit policy statement was required. "It should state unequivocally that the present Army policies requiring segregation are no longer binding. It should state clearly that the eventual goal is the elimination of segregation. It should state that any intermediate steps to be taken immediately should be defined so clearly as to permit no misconstruction."[24]

Of course, none of that happened. Within months I was complaining about interpretations of the Gillem report that suggested it supported "the fictional separate but equal plan" for officers' clubs and recreational facilities and concluded equal rights for black officers were consistent with segregation. "Many of the conjectures resulted from the ambiguous and vague character of several of the recommendations and some of the language used in the body of the report." Still sounding hopeful, I noted that the ultimate goal was the complete elimination of segregation.[25]

Black newspaper publishers heard some fine words about noble goals from Howard C. Petersen, the assistant secretary of war who would be largely responsible for trying to implement the Gillem goals. Yet he was cautious about the potential of the recommendations to produce change. Petersen acknowledged the fears about the Gillem report, noting that "a strong policy weakly enforced will be of little value to the Army." Still, he asserted that the Gillem recommendations constituted "a firm foundation for further progress" and defended the board for not laying down a "rigid formula to govern all states of future development" because such rigidity had proven ineffective. He acknowledged that while segregation by unit was not required under Gillem policy, "it is anticipated that for some time most Negroes will be used in Negro units."[26] To the army generals, that sounded like an invitation to stymie the ultimate goal and they readily accepted that invitation.

By the autumn of 1945, I had had enough. Enough of the obstacles the army threw up at every turn to frustrate the aspirations of black soldiers. Enough of the persistent racism of the officer corps. Enough of the preconceived determination that African American soldiers would fail in combat. Enough of the incredible balancing act I was performing—behind the scenes waging war against all that, while on the surface endeavoring to put the best face on War Department dictates and policies. All the while I was being damned in the black press as a traitor to my race. I had chosen to work within the system for the advancement of African American dreams of simple justice. I had gone into it knowing it would be a thankless task, but I guess the reality turned out to be crushing in a way I never envisioned. I wanted out of the War Department and told McCloy so.

December 1945 marked five years in the War Department, and I decided that would be the time to leave. Even with the war over, African Americans needed a representative in the hierarchy of the department, and I urged that the office of civilian aide be retained. That office "could not only assist in the evaluation of Army experiences with Negroes during the war just concluded," I told McCloy, "but could also keep those charged with the responsibility for the development of policies and plans advised of changes in civilian attitudes generally, and particularly those changes in the educational and economic levels of Negroes that could affect Army plans." Never again could African Americans sit idly by while military attitudes and policies about black troops were frozen in time, as happened with the "rigid stratification" that took hold after 1918 and prevailed with the opening of hostilities in World War II.[27]

I had a candidate to succeed me: Lieutenant Colonel Marcus Ray. Field experience would be invaluable, and Ray had achieved an outstanding record in the 600th Field Artillery Battalion of the Ninety-second Division. Artillery units, it should be recalled, were among the few Ninety-second organizations earning praise in Italy. In addition, Chief of Staff George Marshall knew Ray, an important asset for his candidacy. I also suggested creation of a War Department board to "evaluate the performance of Negro troops under existing policies, consider and recommend such policy changes of both a short and long term nature as may be necessary to effect the most efficient utilization of Negroes in the Army."[28]

McCloy and Patterson both accepted my recommendations, and Ray became my successor.

Patterson responded to my letter of resignation: "I assure you that I regret to see you leave. You have served your country in a critical time with marked ability and with wholehearted devotion. On behalf of the War Department I express our deep appreciation for what you have achieved. I hope that we can count on your assistance as problems come up in the future. With your background of experience, your advice will be of particular value."[29]

As my days in government service wound down, I wrote some of the editors and publishers of black newspapers explaining my decision. "On December 1, I shall cease being a bureaucrat." That was the opening line of my letter. "I am doing so principally because I believe the nature of the job here has materially changed." My endeavors had been directed toward "getting a decent basic policy," which meant "a constant attack on the firmly entrenched system of segregation." Now that the war was over and the country was planning to maintain a standing army, universal military training emerged as the mantra of the day, and I knew African Americans would never support that concept so long as segregation ruled the army. So, segregation's days were numbered. The best person to make sure that a new policy not based on segregation was working would be someone with "a thorough and comprehensive knowledge of the way the Army operates in the field." I closed by observing that the gains made during the last five years had been achieved in large part by black newspapers "persistently and intelligently forcing the attention of the Army to the problem of the utilization of Negro soldiers."[30]

December rolled around and I was free of the War Department. I returned to Chicago to resume my law practice, setting up shop in the Supreme Liberty Life Building on the South Side with my brother Harry and CPA Theodore Jones, who had spent the last two years laboring on the Fair Employment Practices Committee created by President Roosevelt to ensure black participation in war-industry employment.

However, my government service was not at an end. Several times I was brought back to Washington to do consulting work for the secretary of war. The Gillem Board's recommendations continued to top the agenda. I again expressed my reservations, saying the board's recommendations would improve the army only if they were effectively carried out.

As the new Defense Department, formed to gather all the military services under the direction of one cabinet secretary, grappled with the question of what to do about black aspirations to serve equally whenever called to the country's service, I found myself called on to provide guidance. Another assignment had me serving on the Advisory Commission on Universal Training. In 1948, I was summoned by Defense Secretary Forrestal to take part in the National Defense Conference on Negro Affairs.

The postwar service brought me in contact with a couple of impressive men: President Truman, whom I met for the first time, and Philleo Nash, whom I had gotten to know well during the war years.

I met Truman when he appointed me to the universal training commission. Like all men, he was a captive of his times and his upbringing.

Social integration was too much for him, and his famous penchant for salty language encompassed terms today rightly seen as awful slurs. Still, he had a basic sense of right and wrong, and he saw segregation as wrong. I have a copy of a letter he wrote to someone he had known in Kansas City, Missouri, who had complained about the president's civil rights activism. It's worthwhile quoting that letter at length:

> The main difficulty with the South is that they are living 80 years behind the times and the sooner they come out of it the better it will be for the country and themselves. I am not asking for social equality, because no such thing exists, but I am asking for equality of opportunity for all human beings and, as long as I stay here, I am going to continue that fight. When the mob gangs can take four people out and shoot them in the back, and everybody in the country is acquainted with who did the shooting and nothing is done about it, that country is in a pretty bad fix from a law enforcement standpoint.
>
> When a mayor and city marshal can take a negro sergeant off a bus in South Carolina, beat him up and put out one of his eyes, and nothing is done about it by the state authorities, something is radically wrong with the system.
>
> On the Louisiana and Arkansas railway, when coal burning locomotives were used, the negro firemen were the thing because it was a backbreaking job and a dirty one. As soon as they turned to oil as a fuel, it became customary for people to take shots at the negro firemen and a number were murdered because it was thought that this was now a white-collar job and should go to a white man. I can't approve of such goings on and I shall never approve of it, as long as I am here, as I told you before. I am going to try to remedy it and if that ends up in my failure to be reelected, that failure will be in a good cause.[31]

That's the President Truman I knew. He told me that he couldn't sleep until all citizens were free. "Until everybody can go to school with freedom of choice, until everybody can vote, until Jim Crow is gone, nobody is really free." That marked a sharp contrast with President Roosevelt. I never met Roosevelt, but an infamous story circulated in the black community about him. Roosevelt once told an African American, "I understand your people because of my conversations with the mess boy who brings me hot coffee every morning." It's hard to imagine a more condescending remark. Roosevelt did many things that benefited black Americans, but they stemmed more from political expediency than from a deep commitment to the civil rights of African Americans. The latter came from Eleanor Roosevelt, his conscience on these issues.

The Advisory Commission on Universal Training occasionally met with President Truman. I vividly remember one session in the Oval Office when the president called Sam Rosenman, Roosevelt's speechwriter, Anna Rosenberg, and me up to his desk. "My namesake" is how Truman would sometimes refer to me. That day, he had a stunning revelation. "I've been mulling over this issue of segregation," he said. "I'm going to take the bull by the horns. I'm going to help your people." He repeated the story about the black sergeant beaten so horribly that he was blinded in one eye. "This shit has to stop." He voiced his opinion that black Americans should have equal access to the important institutions of society like schools. Then he told us he planned to issue an executive order eliminating segregation from the armed services. He knew it wouldn't be popular. "My wife kept me from sleeping last night. She doesn't agree with my views on race."

That order was to come months later. The issue confronting the nation at the moment turned on matters of national defense. Right after the war, memories of our inadequate prewar peacetime military force—inadequate though in keeping with a long-held national aversion to standing armies—inspired many in government to believe that the nation needed to impose universal military training on its young men to be prepared for the eventualities of the world, most notably the threat posed by the Soviet Union. President Truman called the commission into session on December 20, 1946. We met on sixteen different occasions, sitting for a total of twenty-nine days. Our sessions occurred on Fridays and Saturdays. Our meetings invited testimony from army officers as well as authorities on military preparedness. More than two hundred witnesses testified.

Our work gained us access to army intelligence, giving me an insight into just how poorly spy agencies operate. On several occasions we met in a room at the Princeton Inn in Washington to review classified documents. The fact that we were not granted the liberty to go to the washroom would suggest that these papers revealed highly sensitive information crucial to national security. But no. This, the intelligence files on German politics, covered Nazi activities from 1930 to 1939! This, the intelligence officers insisted, was the most recent material they had. Looking back six decades from a time when America is learning how its intelligence agencies failed to anticipate the September 11, 2001, attacks, you can only conclude that the more things change, the more they stay the same.

The commission devoted several sessions to the issue of race and the military. I asserted that African Americans would never participate in a universal training program that was segregated. Supported by Rosenman and Rosenberg, later an assistant secretary of defense, I argued strenuously against segregation, laying out chapter and verse on its deleterious effect on military efficiency and its injustice to black men who wanted nothing more than the chance to serve and defend their country. The commission's final report rejected segregation. Notably, however, that objection was not specifically included in the report's summary, the only part reprinted in full in the nation's newspaper of record, the *New York Times.* The summary had only a general reference, saying that "we recommend that every young man upon reaching the age of eighteen or upon completing or leaving high school, whichever is later, to undergo a period of training that would fit him for service to the nation in any future emergency."[32]

The report itself tackled racism more directly. "Want, ill health, ignorance, race prejudice, and slothful citizenship are enemies of America as truly as were Hitler and Mussolini and Tojo," it asserted.[33] Noting how vital the National Guard was to military preparedness, the report said, "[T]he Commission considers harmful the policies of the States that exclude Negroes from their National Guard units. The civilian components should be expanded to include all segments of our population without segregation or discrimination. Total defense requires the participation of all citizens in our defense forces."[34]

Furthermore, any program for universal military training "must provide equality of privilege and opportunity for all those upon whom this obligation rests," we wrote.

> Neither in the training itself, nor in the organization of any phase of this program, should there be discrimination for or against any person or group because of his race, class, national origin, or religion. Segregation or special privilege in any form should have no place in the program. To permit them would nullify the important living lesson in citizenship which such training can give. Nothing could be more tragic for the future attitude of our people, and for the unity of our nation, than a program in which our Federal Government forced our young manhood to live for a period of time in an atmosphere which emphasized or bred class or racial differences.[35]

I testified about universal training before the House Armed Services Committee on June 19, 1947. Segregation per se did not come up. However, in my opening statement, I made an oblique reference to it, asserting that defense of the nation is a universal responsibility. "It is an obligation that ought to be imposed on all of us. It is not a privilege for the few, but a responsibility and an obligation." During questioning about my experience as civilian aide, I noted that during the war illiteracy among recruits hindered the army but that experience had demonstrated adult education systems were beneficial. Expanding literacy could only augment any universal training program.[36]

The satisfaction I felt in getting the principles of inclusion enunciated in the commission's final report crashed on the rocks of reality when the army subsequently kept African Americans out of its experimental universal military training unit at Fort Knox, Kentucky, in 1947.[37] This angered me, and I was much more specific and pointed when I testified to the Senate Armed Services Committee the following year. "[A]ll physically qualified youth must be trained," I asserted. "This means that Negroes, comprising as they do roughly 10 percent of the available manpower potential, must be trained and must be used. Not to do so would make a mockery of the whole program that is designed to prepare our country for all-out warfare. Now, this use must not be hedged about by quota restrictions and certainly not by segregation."[38]

"The war-time experiences of the Army in utilizing Negro personnel reflect the absolute impossibility of measuring a man's value by the color of his skin," I argued, reflecting on my experiences with the War

Department. My tour of Europe provided me with the chance to see mixed and integrated units in battle, and "I had occasion to compare the efficiency of troops properly used with the inefficiency of Negro troops improperly used. The Army has come out of that experience with many convictions that were strongly held prior to the war now completely and thoroughly shaken." I noted the navy had moved toward integration, which must be incorporated into universal military training. "Men must be trained for the future in accordance with individual aptitudes, abilities and skills. Bombs in any future war will not come marked for white or for colored." I observed that African American opinion on universal military training mirrored the views of the nation as a whole, with 66.7 percent of blacks surveyed by the Gallup poll favoring it.[39]

In the back of my mind loomed the many injustices inflicted on black men in uniform during the war, including the inequities of the judicial system for African Americans, especially in the South. Federal courts should be open to black GIs charged with crimes outside military posts, I told the committee. Severity of punishment varied from region to region of the country, defying any rational explanation. Federal law should be enacted to prevent assaults on military personnel.

The bitter experience of the war, combined with what seemed to be the harsh realities of the opening of the cold war, made me a convert to the idea of universal military training. As it turned out, the nation wasn't ready for the idea of military training for all young men, and the Truman administration directed its energies toward reinstating the draft.

During the course of the commission's deliberations, I got to know Defense Secretary James Forrestal. As secretary of the navy, he had been responsible for initiatives introducing integration into the navy. Still, he was not a radical reformer, believing that persuasion and education could bring about evolutionary change in the several branches of the military. Recalling the good work done by the McCloy Committee, I urged Forrestal to form a similar interservice committee to demonstrate to the black community his commitment to changing the racial policies of the armed services. The various policies among the branches of the military had been publicized in the black press and by African

American politicians and civic leaders, provoking opposition to the concepts of universal military training and the selective service. In fact, a Committee against Jim Crow in Military Service and Training was established by A. Philip Randolph of the Brotherhood of Sleeping Car Porters, and Grant Reynolds, an erratic black chaplain during the war whom I tried to help out when he frequently landed in trouble but who constantly denounced me as not being extreme enough in prodding the army toward more enlightened racial policies.

My idea of a continuing panel like the McCloy Committee never went anywhere. But Lester Granger, Forrestal's classmate at Dartmouth and head of the National Urban League, proposed the Defense Department create a biracial "critics group" to address the issues of employment of black servicemen in the armed forces.[40] In the end Forrestal invited only African Americans, fifteen of us, to gather at the Pentagon on April 26, 1948. Called the National Defense Conference on Negro Affairs, the one-day session served the usual function of providing a forum for a substantial discussion of racial problems in the armed services.

That session was followed by the hearings before the Senate Armed Services Committee on selective service legislation. Randolph stunned the senators by suggesting that even in a time of national emergency black Americans should rise in civil disobedience against the draft so long as the army adhered to segregation. "The Government now has time to change its policy on segregation and discrimination and if the Government does not change its policy on segregation and discrimination in the interests of the very democracy it is fighting for, I would advocate that Negroes take no part in the Army," Randolph declared. Senator Wayne Morse of Oregon suggested that what Randolph was proposing would be treason if the country was at war. Randolph responded, "I would anticipate Nationwide terrorism against Negroes who refused to participate in the armed forces, but I believe that that is the price we have to pay for democracy that we want."[41]

During my service on the universal military training commission, I had expressed my own fears of a black refusal to participate in universal training if segregation continued, but appearing before the Senate committee, I represented the spirit of patriotism I had seen among black soldiers in World War II. I didn't name Randolph but condemned his views. "I can express my shock and dismay at a report that appeared last week in the *Chicago Sun-Times* to the effect that a spokesman presumably for Negroes told the president that Negroes would not bear arms in the defense of this country unless segregation in the armed forces was discontinued and unless legislative safeguards against these practices were included in any universal training legislation." I told the committee I was confident that African Americans would not shirk their duty. "Patriotism is not the subject of cynical bargaining. Negroes have participated in the military history of this country to the fullest extent allowed in the past. They certainly will do so in the future. To express sentiments to the contrary is unfair to the millions of loyal citizens who know only this country and who do not look to any foreign ideology to correct the plaguing domestic evils that concern us."[42]

Though supportive of Randolph and his ideas about civil disobedience, the black press for once didn't jump on me. However, Representative Adam Clayton Powell of New York did, denouncing me as a "rubber stamp Uncle Tom." That was foolish and ignored the political atmosphere of those years. America had spent its treasure in blood and matériel to defeat one form of totalitarianism, fascism, and now was confronted with an even stronger, expansionist version in the Soviet Union. African Americans rejecting the call of their country would be denounced as traitors. That was the last thing we needed if we hoped to build on whatever gains we had made in World War II.

In the meantime, behind the scenes away from this sound and fury on Capitol Hill, President Truman was forging ahead with his plans for an executive order to banish segregation from the military. The assignment to write the order fell to Philleo Nash, a presidential specialist on minority issues who had served during the war years in the Office of War Information and had been an advocate for expanded participation of African Americans in civilian and military life.

By then, I had known Nash for years. His advocacy on black issues and the insular world of Washington in those days threw us together. In fact, Nash and his wife, Edith, lived across the street from Isabelle and me. Our daughter, Karen, and his two daughters were roughly the same age. We socialized from the start. My memories of those early days in Washington are dim on some points, but I certainly remember Nash introducing me to the French 75 on our first Christmas in the nation's capital. Named for a French artillery piece, the French 75 was a concoction of brandy, champagne, and gin. It was deadly and guaranteed to afflict you with a headache the next morning.

Philleo proved himself to be a good friend and a forthright advocate for racial justice. I think it was he who recommended me to serve on the President's Advisory Commission on Universal Training. He and I and our wives joined forces with other progressive-thinking people in Washington to found the Georgetown Day School, the first integrated school in Washington. Karen and Nash's daughters attended this school.

I wasn't surprised when he called me in the spring of 1948 seeking my thoughts on a presidential executive order to integrate the armed forces. The advice I gave him wasn't radical, and he agreed with my view that the goal could best be achieved through a step-by-step approach advancing the cause of integration in each of the services. Executive Order 9981 was signed by President Truman on July 26, 1948. It declared the "policy of the President that there shall be equality of treatment and opportunity for all persons in the armed services without regard to race, color, religion or national origin." It created the President's Committee on Equality of Treatment and Opportunity in the Armed Services to determine the changes in rules, procedures, and practices necessary to achieve the order's goals.

It was a historic document, a major victory on the road to racial justice, but it had one flaw: At Forrestal's urging, the executive order set no deadlines for achieving Truman's goals, instead stating they should "be put into effect as rapidly as possible . . . without impairing efficiency or morale."[43] Thus, there was another loophole the army could drive a battalion of tanks through.

The top generals—George C. Marshall, Dwight Eisenhower, and Omar Bradley—reflected the southern bias of the command structure and defended the status quo. Again, the old excuse that the army couldn't be subjected to social experiments was trotted out. Integration couldn't come to the army "until it had been achieved by the American people," asserted Bradley. "To have desegregated the Army overnight as Truman wished would have caused utter chaos, not only within the Army ranks but also within the Deep South communities where our bases were located."[44] In fact it would take two presidential commissions and a new war to finally effect an end to segregation. In 1950, the army finally abandoned the quota for participation of black soldiers, and the urgent demands for an efficient fighting machine imposed by the shocks of the Korean War at long last knocked down the walls of segregation, marking the start of the military emerging as the most color-blind institution in American society.

By then, my work with the military was a memory. Building on a friendship that had ripened during the war, I had embarked on a new career as a professional boxing promoter.

17

Joe Louis, War, and Boxing

Joe Louis leaped right into the war effort. Within a month of the Pearl Harbor attack, he was boxing to raise money for the Navy Relief Fund. The next day, January 10, 1942, he volunteered for the army. And on March 27, he put on his gloves to aid the Army Relief Fund.

His boxing stardom had made Joe a national hero, and he never gave a moment's thought to not serving his country should it find itself at war. Nearly a year and a half before Pearl Harbor, he told the *Pittsburgh Courier,* "I'd fight my best fight against any foreign foe who'd try to attack America—and I'm ready any day my country needs me!"[1] Joe could have earned a deferment of his 1-A draft status because he was the sole support for his wife and mother. Julian Black, his manager, and I discussed his status, and Julian decided Joe would volunteer. Since I knew Joe loved to ride horses, I suggested to the War Department that he be assigned to the horse cavalry at Fort Riley, Kansas. Boxing promoter Mike Jacobs came up with the idea of a boxing match to help out the charity for the families of navy men killed in action.

At this time, the navy had a worse record for blacks than the army. Mess boy was the only duty open to African American sailors. However, Joe brushed aside a few suggestions that he bring up discrimination before the fight. Joe's patriotic gesture earned lots of praise in white newspapers. In truth, it was more than a gesture. Joe would be putting his heavyweight title on the line, facing off against a powerful puncher, Buddy Baer. As it happened, Joe had no trouble with Baer, knocking him out in the first round. Two and a half months later, Joe knocked out Abe Simon in six rounds for the Army Relief Fund.

These two fights would add to Joe's financial problems by marking the start of his tax troubles, although he had no idea of that at the time. Even though the champ turned over everything he earned, except for training costs, to the two military funds, the money technically went through his hands. This put Joe on the hook for taxes on more than ninety thousand dollars that had legally—but not actually—passed through him on the way to charity. That would haunt him in battles with the tax man after the war. In addition, he had gone into the army in debt to Jacobs. The boxing impresario loaned money to fighters all the time, and he kept it up for Joe throughout World War II.

Jacobs hatched the idea for another fight, initially suggesting Bob Pastor but later settling on a rematch for Joe against Billy Conn, who in 1941 had given Louis a tough test before being knocked out in the thirteenth round. Jacobs proposed to underwrite all costs, with 10 percent of gross receipts going to army relief and the fighters also chipping in a portion of their take. "There is great public interest in this bout. It would greatly help Joe Louis pay his outstanding obligations for taxes for the year 1941. The Army Relief would gain a substantial sum of money."[2] Unsaid was that it would afford the opportunity for Louis and Conn, also living on borrowed money, to pay their debts to Jacobs.

The Louis-Conn bout never came off. I saw problems right from the start and advised Julian Black not to make any kind of statement until the fight was approved.[3] Still, word got out. Most accounts assert that Secretary of War Henry Stimson nixed the bout because he didn't feel that the two fighters should be able to make money to pay off financial obligations when the rest of the men serving in the army and navy had no such opportunity. The truth is more complicated and nefarious than that.

I believed the relief fund should be the big winner from any Louis exhibition fight, so I proposed to Undersecretary of War Robert Patterson that tickets for the first twenty rows be reserved for the charity. Well, Jacobs didn't like that one bit. As a partner in a ticket-selling operation in New York, Jacobs stood to reap big bucks scalping tickets. In fact, he had made himself rich from selling tickets, not from putting on boxing matches. The fight didn't come off, and Jacobs retaliated through the New York press, blaming me for killing the bout. I was demanding money from him, Jacobs alleged in his wild and false charges. Bill Hastie rose to my defense. "Numerous stories have appeared in the press during the last week to the effect that Truman K. Gibson Jr. of my office had made commitments concerning financial arrangements for the proposed Louis-Conn fight," Hastie told the Associated Negro Press. "These allegations are untrue."[4]

In the meantime, Joe had been assigned to the army's entertainment division. I came up with the idea of the champ forming a boxing troupe to put on bouts at army posts across the country and overseas. Joe and the army eagerly grabbed onto the notion. Sugar Ray Robinson, Archie Moore, Sandy Saddler, Jackie Wilson, and Louis's sparring partner George Nicholson were among the fighters who signed up for the boxing company. They maintained a torrid schedule. For example, between November 12, 1943, and January 17, 1944, nearly four dozen boxing matches were scheduled at posts in California, Arizona, Texas, Oklahoma, Missouri, Arkansas, Louisiana, Mississippi, Alabama, Georgia, Florida, South Carolina, and North Carolina.[5] Joe had traveled twenty thousand miles across the country when the War Department decided to ship him overseas to entertain the troops.[6] During 1944, the troupe fought exhibition bouts at posts in England, Italy, northern Africa, and the Aleutian Islands. By one estimate, nearly two million soldiers enjoyed these matches.[7]

Wherever he traveled, Joe was generous with money, Mike Jacobs's money that is. He spent freely on steak dinners at posts across the country. By the end of the war, Joe was in the hole to Jacobs for two hundred fifty thousand dollars. That would only add to his problems with the Internal Revenue Service after the war.

When word broke that Joe would be traveling with his boxing company, I got an unusual request. In a "Dear Mr. T.G." letter, Lieutenant Mildred Osby volunteered her service as "competent secretarial assistance on this morale-lifting world tour."[8]

I responded: "I will have to drop you a well-cushioned 'NO' on your proposal to accompany Sergeant Joe Louis around the world. Male officers for several good and cogent reasons have been selected to go with him. I am afraid that even your resistance, built up over years of battling life on your own, would be melted away by the Sergeant's charm with the ladies."[9]

The Brown Bomber enjoyed star status. The knockout of Max Schmeling transformed this black athlete from the cotton fields of Alabama and the auto assembly lines of Detroit into a transcending symbol of everything that was great about America. He was just what the doctor ordered for patriotic fervor at the outbreak of war. Press photographers and newsreel cameramen turned out when Joe reported for duty at Camp Upton, Long Island. A full-page photo in the *New York Daily News* pictured Joe saluting the flag. Former *Daily News* sports columnist Paul Gallico, writing in the *Reader's Digest,* observed, "I write of him now, not especially as a hero—every unsung youth who has shouldered a gun has made a similar sacrifice—but as a simple, good American."[10] Film of Joe knocking out Schmeling and doing his military training figured prominently in Frank Capra's *The Negro Soldier.*

In 1943, Joe had a part in the propaganda film *This Is the Army,* starring a future president, Ronald Reagan. The movie included stereotypes, such as white performers in blackface, that would make us cringe today. Still, overcoming all that for millions of Americans were the images of Joe delivering a patriotic speech and punching a speed bag.[11] Louis biographer Chris Mead believes Joe's high profile as an American hero helped white Americans begin to face the contradictions of racism and segregation.

Our friendship matured during the war years. Joe's rise to the top of the boxing world earned him a privileged berth in the complex, contradictory America of the 1930s. Being sent to an all-black unit at Fort Riley reintroduced him to the realities of ordinary African Americans. As I indicated earlier, he became a keen observer of racial issues and called me almost daily. In his autobiography, Joe credits me with getting Jackie Robinson and more than a dozen other African Americans into officer candidate school.[12] That's not what happened. The army, for simple reasons of efficiency, already had ruled against segregated schools. That bit of forward thinking stood out in contrast to the backwardness of most army practices. The ugly incidents already written about weren't the only ones where Joe rose up to challenge the racial barriers of the day.

The black newspapers splashed across their pages in early 1944 stories about an insulting incident for Joe and Ray Robinson. *PM,* the famous left-wing newspaper of the day, headlined its account of this incident on its front page in early April. Louis and Robinson had gone to a bus depot at Camp Sibert, Alabama, to phone for a taxi. While waiting for the cab, they took a seat on a bench in the waiting room, there being no one else around. A couple of military police showed up and asked the boxers, as I reported at the time, "if they did not know where they belonged." The MPs ordered them to a black waiting room, which had no telephone. Joe said they weren't moving, which got the two of them arrested. Appearing before the provost marshal, Joe said he was a soldier like any American soldier, and "I don't want to be pushed to the back because I'm a Negro." The provost marshal blustered some, and Joe demanded the right to call Washington. Well, this martinet knew he was on the losing end and let Joe and Robinson go.[13] Word got out, and the army got another black eye in the press.

When Joe was overseas, he took his complaints to that descendant of the Old South, General John "Court House" Lee. In Salisbury, England, Louis found himself in a segregated movie theater—segregated not because of local custom but because of imported attitudes from the American South. The theater manager recognized the champ and apologized. Lee ended the practice. On another occasion, Joe learned that a couple of American generals, trying no doubt to protect the sanctity of white British womanhood, had declared several English towns off limits to black GIs. Lee had those generals busted and sent home.

Those incidents illustrated the power and reach of the Louis mystique. As I said, the War Department was ever ready to capitalize on it for propaganda purposes. I was with Joe when he went out to California to do his part in *This Is the Army.* That marked my one and only meeting with the future president, Ronald Reagan. For reasons that I never understood, Captain Reagan asserted that the latest technology in sound recording, the phonograph disc, was unbreakable. Then, against all logic for anyone who ever owned one of those 78-rpm records, Reagan took one out, tapped it, and, of course, it shattered. We had a good laugh over that.

By then, Joe had begun a torrid relationship with the talented, sultry beauty Lena Horne. It had been going on for some time. She tended to be clingy and possessive. One day after they had spent some time together, Joe said he was taking off. She said, "No, you're not," and blocked the door. Joe charged ahead, brushing by her and inadvertently throwing her for a severe fall. She suffered a broken leg. Joe didn't intend to hurt her, but he had. That was the end of that romance.

Joe had contributed an inestimable value to the war effort, but he had never actually been in a battle. Now, when the war ended, the first men mustered out of the service were those who had accumulated a lot of points for serving in combat. Joe ached to get out. He was getting older, had a lot of debts, and needed to get back in the ring. I got Assistant Secretary of War John McCloy to vouch for the champ and urge an early release. In addition, others and I lobbied for Joe to get the Legion of Merit. (The Legion of Merit was the highest noncombat medal awarded to military personnel. The civilian equivalent was the Presidential Medal of Merit, which I was awarded.) The officer in charge of the Louis troupe's tour, Captain Fred Maly, detailed the reasons Joe deserved the honor. "Louis's exhibitions in the various theaters visited shattered existing attendance records, over and beyond any combination of two and three visits from cinema, theater, radio, and sports personalities previously used under the entertainment policy invoked by the War Department," Maly wrote.[14] The champ had endangered his professional boxing career by injuring his fist in exhibition bouts. Dying soldiers had experienced a "lift" from Joe's visits. Maly continued, "There is no question but that thousands of white soldiers drew a fairer and better evaluation of the negro soldier upon seeing and talking with Louis." His two defenses of his title for charity had raised a quarter of a million dollars for military relief. I added my voice in recommending that Joe get the Legion of Merit. Time was running out for him to get back into his career of professional boxing, a young man's business.

Word came back to me that Joe would get the Legion of Merit on October 1, 1945, making him eligible for immediate discharge, although

I couldn't tell him that at the time. Joe called me, asking me to meet him at Mike Jacobs's office in New York to talk about his discharge. Once there, Joe asked me to drive with him to Camp Shanks to see Mercer Ellington, son of the legendary musician Duke Ellington. This trip began with a surprise. Joe, who always had a driver, slid into the car behind the driver's wheel, and off we went. Midway during the journey, Joe pulled the car over on a country road.

"I've got something to tell you," he said.

Facetiously, I said, "It looks like you're propositioning me."

"Jacobs says there's ten thousand dollars for you when I get my discharge," Joe confided.

"Meet me in Mike's office at nine o'clock tomorrow," I replied, and we said not another word about his suggestion. However, I was angry about the insinuation that I was open to some sort of bribe.

They were waiting for me when I showed up that morning.

"Joe," I announced, "as of an hour ago, you're discharged from the service, so tell Jacobs to take his ten thousand and shove it."

Joe was back in boxing. And as it would turn out, I was about to be launched into a new career as a boxing promoter.

18

Boxing Promoter

Truman Gibson, boxing promoter.

That's a line of work I never dreamed I'd find myself in. In truth, I kind of fell into it. After finishing up my work with the Advisory Commission on Universal Training in June 1947, I concentrated on a career in the law. I didn't have the slightest idea that I would find myself working with Joe Louis.

In fact, Joe and I had been estranged for months. I've recounted the happy meeting in which I told the champ he was out of the army. However, shortly after that meeting, Joe and I parted in acrimony. Overjoyed at being free of the military, Joe started talking about the future and asked me to be his manager. Flattered beyond words, I thanked him but told Joe his best bet was to resume his boxing career with Julian Black, the manager who had guided Joe's career to the pinnacle of success in the prewar years. We placed a call to Chicago, and Julian immediately boarded the Twentieth-Century Limited train for New York.

The reunion of the three of us collapsed in dismal failure. The trouble was rooted in Joe's marital problems. Careless of his family when he was on the road and feckless in chasing other women, Joe could best be described as unintentionally callous in his treatment of his wife, Marva. She finally had had enough and sued for divorce on grounds of desertion in 1945. Still, it was an amicable divorce, and Joe wanted Marva taken care of financially. Julian Black, as the champ's confidante and adviser, was a partner in the agreement in which Joe wanted to pay Marva fifty thousand dollars. That called for Joe to pay her the fifty thousand dollars through Julian. However, when the time came to cement the deal in Chicago, Julian was nowhere to be found. He had taken off to Kenosha, Wisconsin, and refused to answer his phone. Joe felt betrayed. His rage at Black spilled over on me. Venting his spleen at me, Joe declared he'd never have anything to do with Truman Gibson again. I would eventually get a reprieve, but Black was never forgiven.

Joe signed on a new manager: Buffalo, New York, real estate investor, horseplayer, and numbers operator Marshall Miles. He had the kind of money required to be Joe's manager. Joe destroyed money, and he had always depended on someone else—Mike Jacobs during the war and now Miles—as a source of ready cash. I found Miles to be a witty man. After a fight in New York, Miles, Joe, and I went to dinner with some New Yorkers. As the dinner neared an end, Miles leaned over to me and asked, "Did you ever see the Broadway shuffle?"

"What are you talking about?" I responded.

"Watch, when the check comes, all these bastards will take off for the phone or the toilet."

Sure enough, the check arrived, and those fellows immediately found reason to be someplace else.

"Now you've seen the Broadway shuffle!" laughed Miles.

Though none of us was aware of it at the time, Joe was sinking into a hell of financial obligations to the tax man. It should be remembered that we're talking about the days before computers. Years could pass before IRS audits caught up with past mistakes. Joe's errors slowly accumulated. There were the charity matches for the Navy and Army Relief Funds in the early years of the war that never got put down to charity. Joe never saw a dime from those bouts, but the money legally passed through Joe's hands and got counted as regular income, meaning a tax liability on thousands of dollars the champ had never pocketed. His new financial arrangement to support Marva unfortunately left him with the tax liability for the payments, although he wouldn't become aware of it for years. Joe fought Billy Conn again in 1946 in hope of clearing up his finances; it only made things worse. Joe had to pay Mike Jacobs back for the two hundred fifty thousand dollars the fighter had lavished in steak dinners on GIs during the war years. The Jacobs debt was to be wiped out with the Conn fight proceeds. Jacobs had dispensed cash to Joe in dribs and drabs and never worried because he knew he would get it back since he handled the money for all the fights; Joe never got a cent from Jacobs, only a financial statement. In addition, under the new divorce arrangement to share his earnings with Marva, Joe got the tax liability while she got the money.

Joe's taxes had been prepared by Nate Ellenbogen, Jacobs's accountant. All the errors and unintended consequences caused by the incompetence of Ellenbogen would eventually crash down on Joe. The IRS would assess Joe taxes for the charity fights, the support payments to Marva, and the Jacobs money spent during the war. Joe was in a hell of a mess, but in those early postwar years he remained blissfully ignorant of it. I had helped him out in years past, and in 1947 he reached out to me. Joe called my office asking me to have my associate, accountant Ted Jones, call him. I did nothing. Then Joe called me. The tax man was after him for earnings from his ownership of the Rhumboogie nightclub in Chicago. I suggested he declare his investment as a loan. The ice had been broken, and we were back together. Jones and I took over supervision of Joe's finances, although we, too, at the time didn't realize the magnitude of his tax problems for the simple reason the IRS hadn't yet assessed his obligations. The first thing we did was to move everything away from Ellenbogen.

Joe spent most of the immediate postwar years jabbing in exhibition boxing bouts. There was the long-awaited matchup in 1946 between Joe and Billy Conn, but the young boxer who had nearly defeated the champion five years earlier had lost his fire, and the fight disappointed the fans even though Joe won with an eighth-round knockout. On December 5, 1947, he faced off with another aging fighter, Jersey Joe Walcott, at Madison Square Garden in New York. No longer the great jabber and devastating puncher he once was, Joe managed only to eke out a decision over Walcott and heard a chorus of boos from the crowd, who thought the challenger had won. Truth was Joe had lost that fight. Six months later, on June 24, 1948, the two boxers squared off again in Yankee Stadium. So boring was their dancing around the ring that the referee admonished them in the tenth round to do battle. In the next round, Joe reached down within himself to find what he needed to knock Walcott out.[1]

Working for the champ again, I negotiated a deal for production of a movie of the fight, which under tax law enabled Joe to deduct fight expenses and reap a big tax savings from the money earned in the showing of the film.

In the meantime, I had helped Joe get into the beer business. Joe had been approached by Louis Greenberg and Johnny Roberts, owners of a Chicago brewery that produced Canadian Ace beer, a popular beverage on the city's South Side, and marketed it on a hit WGES radio program in Chicago hosted by disc jockey Al "the Old Swing Master" Benson, the star of the airwaves whose musical shows had for years been attracting young white audiences as well as legions of African American listeners. Although familiar with Canadian Ace, I didn't know Greenberg or Roberts until I was introduced to them by Joe. They proposed Joe get into the beer business with a distributorship in Detroit. Ray Robinson and Freddy Guinyard, Joe's longtime friend, joined the enterprise, and I organized their corporation with the name RGL, taking the initials of their last names. Success blessed their entrepreneurship and they prospered. In fact, RGL had done so well that Greenberg proposed expanding to the New York market. That proved to be overreaching. Greenberg, it turned out, had mob ties. It was bad enough that he had served as treasurer for a brewery run by the notorious gangster Al Capone; even worse was Greenberg's mug staring out from a picture of the Capone outfit that had been published in *Life* magazine. Joe's days in the beer business came crashing to a close.

After the second Walcott fight, I tried to negotiate a retirement package for Joe with the Twentieth-Century Sporting Club, the boxing promotion enterprise run by Mike Jacobs, who was now aging and was no longer the dynamic force who had dominated the sport in the prewar years. While we haggled with Jacobs's moneyman, Sol Strauss, another intriguing if strange opportunity arose. By then I had organized Joe's financial interests as Joe Louis Enterprises, Inc. It distributed the films of the two Louis-Walcott fights.

In 1948, I took a call from George DeWitt, the publisher of the *Herald American,* the Hearst empire's evening newspaper in Chicago. The Hearst organization had been involved in boxing for years, with proceeds during the Depression going to the Hearst Milk Fund, said to provide milk for needy kids but really set up to funnel cash to the Hearst family for their uses and to selected writers with the Hearst newspapers. Three of these writers, the only one remembered today being short-story writer Damon Runyon, had been involved in the genesis of Jacobs's Twentieth-Century Sporting Club.

Inviting us down to his office, DeWitt announced that he had someone in his outer office he wanted to introduce to Joe and me. Harry Voiler was his name. Voiler had a shady past. Once the road manager for the world-famous motion picture sexpot Mae West, Voiler had served time in the Michigan penitentiary for stealing her jewelry. DeWitt was interested in trying to rehabilitate Voiler, a sublieutenant in the Capone gang, as a reward for his service to the Hearst corporation during a recent Chicago newspaper strike. That violent conflict with labor saw trucks owned by every newspaper but the *Herald American* overturned and damaged. Now Voiler, trying to take advantage of the goodwill he had earned protecting Hearst delivery trucks, said he wanted to get into the boxing game. He had concluded that he needed Joe's reputation to make a success of it.

After some lengthy negotiations, Voiler offered to pay Joe $250,000 up front; Joe would control 52 percent ownership of the corporation. One Hearst executive after another vouched for Voiler, although none of them would provide him financing. Where would he get the money? Voiler said he would mortgage a hotel he owned in Miami Beach to come up with the quarter of a million dollars for Joe.

Joe and I felt confident enough to lay the groundwork for our new enterprise before we had a signed deal. Madison Square Garden in New York reigned as the boxing capital of America. However, Mike Jacobs controlled fights in the Garden, and I knew we had to look elsewhere for a base for our assault on his dominance of boxing. Big, bold, brawny, bustling Chicago, my hometown, had to be the natural selection. I began lengthy negotiations to obtain a lease on the International

Amphitheater in Chicago's famous old stockyards district, the locale that poet Carl Sandburg immortalized as "hog butcher to the world." Besides Jacobs's Twentieth-Century Sporting Club, the other force to be reckoned with in professional fighting was the National Boxing Association, run at that time by Abe J. Greene, editor of a newspaper in Patterson, New Jersey. I dropped in on him and got his approval for a series of boxing matches necessary to get our enterprise going. He agreed to the idea that these matches would crown Joe's successor as world heavyweight champion.

Then it was off to Miami Beach to close the deal with Voiler. We met at the Mary Elizabeth Hotel, without doubt the best Jim Crow hotel in Miami. That hotel evokes memories of the isolation of the place and of the popular drink of the day, the Moscow mule, created by the mixing of ginger beer and vodka. Joe's manager, Marshall Miles, downed so many Moscow mules that the only way to describe him was blind drunk. He staggered over to the bar, putting the moves on a very pretty woman there and slipping her the key to his room.

"Well, darling," the lovely lady replied, "I have the key—I'm your wife, remember!"

The meeting with Voiler didn't turn out to be amusing in any way. He issued a stunning pronouncement: His wife wouldn't let him take a banknote out on the hotel, so he had to abandon the project.

"That's the end of a beautiful dream," I lamented.

But it wasn't. Joe had come to Miami at the conclusion of an exhibition tour, and with him was his publicity man, Harry Mendel.

"There's a crazy young Irishman in Coral Gables who might like the idea of a promotional venture with Louis," Mendel volunteered.

By then it was three o'clock in the morning, but Mendel picked up the telephone and called James D. Norris at his Coral Gables residence. Well, Norris liked to have a drink, and he was none the worse for wear in the middle of that night. Still, he was stone-cold sober a few hours later when we arrived at his luxurious home, complete with four-poster beds and stables for his horses and just steps away from a golf course. Ever the avid golfer, Joe took to banging golf balls across the course.

Jim Norris listened as we laid out our proposal. In part because of the demands of the war on America's young men, boxing had fallen on hard times. Joe Louis remained its only star, and he wanted to retire. Our plan called for a series of elimination bouts to determine who would succeed Joe as the heavyweight champion of the world. I already had lined up for the elimination series the five top-rated contenders, including Walcott and Ezzard Charles, by signing them to contracts. Our proposal was irresistible for anyone with the vision to see that boxing, far from dead, actually afforded the potential to captivate audiences bigger than the go-go days of the 1930s.

Norris was definitely intrigued but said he wanted to talk to Arthur Wirtz in Chicago. Between the two of them, Norris and Wirtz boasted the riches of princes. They controlled stadiums in Chicago, St. Louis, and other cities and owned the Detroit Red Wings and Chicago Blackhawks professional hockey franchises. They owned liquor distributorships, and Norris was a partner in the New York Stock Exchange firm of Norris and Kenley.

Norris asked Mendel and me to go to Chicago the next day to meet with Wirtz. So we boarded an airliner in Miami and headed north. Now, in those days before jetliners soared above most weather, air travel remained a sometimes dicey proposition. Sure enough, bad weather forced our plane down in Cincinnati, and Mendel and I caught a bus for the rest of the trip to Chicago.

After that long, difficult journey, I was tired, dirty, and not in the best of spirits when we met with Wirtz at the Chicago Stadium. Described by one of the Chicago newspapers as a man "with a Midas touch,"[2] Wirtz had accumulated huge real estate holdings in the Windy City, including the Chicago Stadium and the Bismarck Hotel, and discovered that big money could be made in ice shows. After I got to know him, I found Wirtz to be the shrewdest and wisest businessman I had ever met. On that first day, he listened to our proposal and then declared he had to meet with Norris.

"We can't pursue this any further," I said, my temper boiling over. "As Joe says, we're tired of the old rinky-dink runaround! Let's go."

Joe and I headed for the door.

"Hold on," said Wirtz, rising to his full imposing height to tower over us. He said that Norris would be in town the next day and we should get together then. We agreed.

In a bid to impress Joe, Wirtz had us meet in the Stadium Club in a room named for the famous ice-skater and Olympic medal winner Sonja Henie. "She's the star of the Hollywood Ice Revue and makes a lot of money," Wirtz allowed, referring to one of his many businesses.

"If I set up a corporation with you, I would like a piece of your Sonja Henie corporation," Joe said.

"Impossible," replied Wirtz. "We will give you the two hundred fifty thousand dollars that you were promised tax free."

Joe turned on his heels and said, "Let's go, Truman."

"No," shouted Wirtz. "What do you want?"

"That will cost you a hundred thousand more," Joe snapped.

Wirtz and Norris agreed, also stipulating that Joe would be paid twenty thousand dollars a year, and the deal was struck. They wondered how long it would take to sign contracts with the necessary contenders for the elimination series. "We've got them," Joe boasted.

Thus was born the International Boxing Club in March 1949.

Joe retired as reigning heavyweight champion on March 1, 1949, paving the way for the elimination series to crown a new champion. The National Boxing Association approved a Charles-Walcott fight to determine the new titleholder. Charles beat Walcott on June 22, 1949, to emerge as the new world titleholder.

Jacobs's Twentieth-Century Sporting Club was doomed. As I negotiated the details with Wirtz and Norris, Joe met Jacobs on a beach in Florida and told him of his plans to start up a new boxing enterprise. In the end we bought Jacobs out.

The New York sportswriters were dismissive when we announced our new venture. It was true that I didn't know a lot about boxing and was a newcomer to boxing promotion, but that made me agile. Robbing Madison Square Garden of the spotlight, I settled on the Chicago White Sox ballpark as the site for the Charles-Walcott fight for the heavyweight championship. The folks at Madison Square Garden knew they had been outmaneuvered. Ned Irish, managing director of the Garden, called me to propose establishing the International Boxing Club of New York with Norris and me heading the corporation. That saved the Garden, preserving the immensely popular Gillette Friday night fights on the NBC network for that arena. Every American of a certain age can remember the words of the commercial for the sponsor, Gillette razor blades: "Look Sharp, Be Sharp!"

Television sets were popping up in homes across the land. Commercial-driven televised bouts promised riches beyond the rewards possible from ticket sales in even the biggest arenas. I realized the future lay in television and pushed boxing onto the small screen. Gay Talese of the *New York Times* described me as "a profound advocate of television's marriage to boxing." He wrote, "When television first entered the scene . . . Gibson saw the futility of a battle and advised boxing to 'join' television."[3]

These were the pioneering days of TV, and New York reigned as the center of that newly emerging media empire. We had a lease on the Chicago Stadium, but that arena was left out of the lucrative TV market because of New York's dominance of the medium. Lester Malitz of the New York advertising agency of Warwick and Legler began pestering Wirtz with the novel idea of televising from Chicago. Wirtz dismissed the idea as silly, saying that the technology of the day required transmission from east to west. Malitz was nothing if not persistent. Securing access to a cable running out of Chicago to Ohio and on to New York, Malitz conjured up the idea of the Wednesday night fights, sponsored by Pabst Blue Ribbon beer, moving to originate them in Chicago. History was made in 1949 with the first television transmission from the Midwest to the East Coast.

Soon Wednesday night fights on the CBS network were emanating from Los Angeles, San Francisco, and Miami as well as Chicago. New York's lock on television had been shattered. Further diversification in sports broadcasting came when I took advantage of my War Department contacts to talk to Bob Kintner. He had worked with the public relations bureau of the War Department during the war, but now he was president of the American Broadcasting Company, and soon ABC was telecasting fights on Saturday night, and later on Monday night.

Another innovation came on June 15, 1951, when we telecast the first closed-circuit boxing match into theaters, with Joe Louis back in the ring to knock out Lee Savold in the sixth round.

The International Boxing Club maintained offices in Chicago and New York. I was the IBC secretary, and Norris was president. Wirtz until the final stages of the IBC held no office, satisfied to wield his influence through Norris since he, Wirtz, was the dominant personality in that relationship. Wirtz lurked in the background, maneuvering to make sure Jim's attention was focused on him, and Norris did his bidding. Working with Tommy King, Ben Bentley, and Issy Kline in Chicago, I concentrated on the Wednesday night fights. Staffing the New York office at Madison Square Garden was managing director Harry Markson, who liaisoned with NBC. Matchmaker duties there fell to Al Weill and Billy Brown. I did some matchmaking of my own, always with an eye to scheduling matchups and fighters likely to produce exciting bouts and generate plenty of fan interest, as reflected in the Nielsen ratings. Weill came in for some criticism for playing on racial and nationalist antagonisms in making matches.

The contracts with the networks called for the International Boxing Club to be paid forty thousand dollars a week for the bouts, of which 60 percent went to the fighters. Championship matches garnered extra money to be shared between the fighters. Contestants in the weekly nonchampionship matches earned seven thousand each. Promoters of fights not held in the Garden or Chicago Stadium received five thousand.

Long-term success in boxing required the development of young fighters. In Chicago Issy Kline took over the Midwest Athletic Club and scheduled budding fighters to square off at the Rainbow Arena. We scouted out local promoters in a number of cities, the most notable being Cal and Eilen Eaton in Los Angeles and Chris and Angelo Dundee, who would achieve fame managing Muhammad Ali in later years, in Miami. They could earn ten thousand dollars for getting one of their protégés in a match in Chicago or New York. These local gymnasiums afforded a way off the mean streets of big cities for young men. Not every kid who popped through the door of a place like the Midwest Athletic Club with a dream of being the next Joe Louis made it in boxing, but enough did—for the simple reason that the International Boxing Club needed a plentiful supply of fighters.

With a set amount of time booked on network TV, the show had to go on even in the event of knockouts, which of course were much desired to arouse fan enthusiasm. Therefore, a main event pitted two fighters against each other, with two more boxers waiting in the wings should one of the participants in the main event knock the other one out. That meant we had to have four fighters ready on fight nights fifty-one weeks of the year. We took only Christmas week off. The greatest boxers of the era—Robinson, Ezzard Charles, Ike Williams, Archie Moore, Johnny Bratton, Rocky Graziano, and Carmen Basilio—faced off in International Boxing Club contests.

Boxing, which had seemed in the doldrums at the end of the war, had roared back, and its popularity soared to new heights. Boxing and TV complemented each other and grew together. Here was a place where race didn't seem to matter, or at least not so much as in society in general. The boxing excellence of a Sugar Ray Robinson impressed white audiences looking for live sports action. Boxing seemed just the right fit for the small TV screen and primitive imaging technology of the day. Sugar Ray excelled as a showman on TV, and I quickly seized upon the goal of putting on a good show as the surest avenue to success on this new medium. The Wednesday and Friday night fights consistently scored third and fourth in the Nielsen ratings in those early years of the International Boxing Club. TV promoted consolidation and bigness, and Wirtz and Norris owned or had controlling interest in the big stadiums in New York, Chicago, Detroit, and St. Louis, so the IBC solidified its hold over professional boxing as smaller boxing clubs without TV access faded. Later this development would be the basis of the government's antitrust attacks on the IBC.

We were ever watchful for exotic ideas to pump more excitement into our fights. Cuba defined exotic in the pre-Castro days, so in 1958 we put together a fight in Havana pitting Joe Brown against Cuban Orlando Echevarria. To ensure maximum press coverage, I arranged a junket to fly in newspapermen from New York and Chicago to the sunny island in the Caribbean. Ever mindful of the tourist dollar, Cuban authorities seized upon our boxing match to put on a sports week extravaganza. A new arena was dedicated for the first televised event outside the United States. A five-hundred-mile auto race along the Malecon Road on the island nation's oceanfront attracted such world-renowned drivers as Phil Hill, Porfirio Rubirosa, and Aly Khan. Unfortunately, the race came to a bad end. Two Cuban drivers lost control of their cars on the first lap; the autos careened off the road and smashed into a crowd, killing thirteen people. The deaths, though, failed to dampen the festivities, and the fight on February 26 scored as a big success with "Old Bones" Brown knocking out the Cuban fighter in the first round.

The greatest fighter that we ever had under contract, greater even than Joe Louis, was Sugar Ray Robinson, and he was involved in one of the most stunning upsets ever. We scheduled a bout between Robinson and Randy Turpin for London in 1951. It marked my first visit to England since the war. This being the days before jetliners darted around the globe, Isabelle insisted we enjoy the luxury of an oceanic liner, and we, along with our daughter, Karen, then twelve years old, set sail on the *Queen Mary.* The time required for a transoceanic trip seemed wasted to me, and I didn't like this mode of travel. The trip over to England wasn't improved by the constant sermons I got from a fellow passenger, the famous preacher Preston Bradley.

Still, Isabelle didn't like to fly, so we also came home by ocean liner, the *City of Paris.* The second day out we sat down for a meal when I spotted a surprising selection on the menu. "This is in your honor," I announced. That first item on the menu was chitterlings, or as they were commonly called in the South, chitlins. Americans might be surprised to hear such a delicacy on a French menu, but in France they have a knack for using all possible parts of the hog. I had eaten chitlins in the South, but my wife never had and wasn't about to start that day.

Britain was a sports-crazed country, with sports gambling going full tilt fifty-two weeks a year. At the top of the heap in sports and gambling towered British promoter Jack Solomons. I'd never met him before this trip. He turned out to be an incredible host. Hanging out with him immersed us in the glamorous nightlife and sports world of London, a city that was finally then emerging from the privations of World War II. Solomons's office sat on Great Windmill Street, just steps down the road from the oldest continuous burlesque show in the world. Pretty tame by today's standards, the girls there set the pulses of young men pumping in high gear in those more innocent days.

Among Solomons's many sporting ventures happened to be a dog track outside London. He invited Isabelle and me and some others out to dinner and a night of dog racing. Isabelle placed some wagers, relying on such nonsense as astrology to make her picks, and she won five times. Not putting any faith in the stars and convinced that the races were fixed, she profusely thanked Solomons. The races were not rigged; she was just incredibly lucky that night.

As the days passed, excitement built about the fight. In the end, Sugar Ray, the greatest fighter I ever saw, would lose—because of a rainstorm.

Solomons and I drove out to visit the Robinson training camp at Windsor. We watched him work out for a while. Then he took to punching the speed bag. At one point, Ray missed the bag completely. That caused Solomons to raise his eyebrows and, as I subsequently learned, to bet against Robinson in the match against Turpin.

In one facet at least, sports then were no different than today. Big-caliber athletes attracted good-looking women. I spotted two comely lasses, one a redhead and the other a blond, hanging around the Robinson camp at Windsor. "That's one for Robinson and one for you," I remarked to his manager, Harold "Killer" Johnson. Oh no, Johnson said. It turned out that Robinson shared in a superstition that a lot of boxers held dear in those days—that sexual intercourse before a sporting contest could drain an athlete of the energy he needed to prevail.

When the big night arrived on July 10, Robinson flopped—big-time. He managed to connect on only six punches in fifteen rounds and was soundly beaten by Turpin. To say it was an incredible upset is an understatement! What happened? I asked Killer Johnson. Well, Robinson's wife had visited him two weeks before the fight. A sudden rainstorm confined them indoors and, voilà, they spent the night together. Robinson fell victim to the self-fulfilling prophecy of his superstition. A few months later, on September 12, Robinson took on Turpin in a return bout in the Polo Grounds in New York, and Sugar Ray hammered the poor fellow to win in eleven rounds.

After the London fight, however, came one of those seemingly minor encounters that would have haunting reverberations in later days. Solomons had a custom after big fights of taking the top fifteen British sportswriters to the Carlton Hotel at Cannes on the Riviera. Isabelle and I were invited along. On our second night there we found ourselves dining with Solomons at a table in an outdoor dining area. Next to us was a boisterous table to which I didn't pay much attention at first. However, as the night wore on, someone kept pushing up against my chair. I turned around and to my surprise found myself facing one of the girls, the blond, I had seen at Robinson's training camp. She was only about nineteen years old, but she was immersed in the decadent life of the Riviera that so contrasted with the middle-class complacency and conformity of America in the 1950s. She spoke with a French accent, and I later learned her home was Paris. She leaned forward and confided, "I have some live ones here."

Indeed, she was seated at a glamorous table. Around it were such notables as the Duke and Duchess of Windsor, Rita Hayworth and her husband at the time, Aly Khan, and Judy Garland. The dime store heiress Woolworth Donohue was there as well, planting a kiss on movie actor Sonny Tufts. They had had plenty to drink. The high spirits of the evening, their insouciance with the conventions of society, and their comfort with their own fabulous wealth erupted with the men at the table stripping the women of all their jewels and throwing thousands of dollars of gems into the ocean. The next morning, predictably, regret set in, and hotel staff were dispatched to wade into the sea in search of the precious stones so carelessly tossed away the night before. For us mere mortals, it meant we couldn't plunge into the waters for a swim while this search-and-recovery operation was under way.

A few months later I was back in New York, walking one evening from the Roosevelt Hotel to my office at Madison Square Garden. A car lurched to a stop right at Sixth Avenue. Inside was a laughing Sammy Davis Jr. As I was crossing the street, I bumped into a woman who was weeping. Imagine my surprise when I realized this was the same blond girl I had encountered at Robinson's training camp at Windsor and at the Carlton Hotel on the Riviera. Trying to comfort her, I asked if she had tried to call Robinson. She only said she had just arrived from California on her way back to Paris. I took her to a bar Robinson owned. Gathered around were a crowd of merrymakers including Robinson and Lena Horne. They welcomed the girl. As all seemed okay, I resumed my journey to the Garden. A couple of hours later the phone rang. It was Sugar Ray, who stunned me with the news that shortly after I left the bar, the unfortunate girl had left and subsequently committed suicide by jumping into the East River.

I've often thought of her, so young, so full of life, so beautiful, so vibrant, but obviously so wounded in some way I didn't know that she felt she had to take her life. What had gone so horribly wrong in her life? Of course, I never found out.

After the London fight, Isabelle, Karen, and I traveled to the Continent for a little rest and relaxation. We couldn't get away from our London associates, and in truth we didn't try very hard. In Paris, Killer Johnson took us to a nightclub called Freddy's. Owned by Marlene Dietrich, the club was a lesbian hangout. Well, Johnson, who had earned his nickname "Killer" from his days with the Harlem Globetrotters, fancied himself as quite the ladies' man. He was out to show the yokels, that would be Isabelle and me, how women dancing with women should be handled. He stepped onto the dance floor, grabbed a beautiful young woman, and started to strut his stuff. He had hardly taken two steps when another woman tapped him on the shoulder. The lady he had commandeered on the dance floor announced that she had not asked him to dance. The two women locked their arms about each other and spun out onto the dance floor, gyrating to the music and leaving Killer Johnson, man about town, with his arms empty. We yokels had a good laugh.

Isabelle, Karen, and I also were invited out to brunch by the famous photographer Gordon Parks, who we had known in Chicago and whose wife was friendly with Isabelle. Promising to afford us a peek at a segment of Parisian life that midwesterners weren't likely to encounter, Gordon took us to an elegant Russian restaurant, deemed by him to be one of the finest in the City of Lights. He was accompanied by a Middle European countess. Hot borscht, chicken Kiev, and assorted vegetables were served.

Sitting on the table was a carafe containing a colorless liquid I took to be water. The borscht, chicken Kiev, and exciting surroundings stimulated my thirst, and I started throwing back glasses of the stuff.

"Do you know what you're doing?" asked Gordon.

"Yes," I replied in all innocence.

"No you don't, you fool," he laughed. "What you've been drinking is not water but vodka!"

Too much vodka, my daughter reminded me years later, made for a bad mix with chicken Kiev and strawberries with sour cream. I lost a day in Paris and acquired a lifelong aversion to vodka.

Isabelle, Karen, and I completed our European tour, taking in the sights, and then headed home. Things were going pretty well for me. Business skills and legal expertise had gotten me into the International Boxing Club. I'd never taken a swing at anyone in my life, but slowly the brutal charms of pugilism worked their magic on me. When not traveling to arrange bouts or strike deals to reap the rewards off the burgeoning television cornucopia spawned by the public's thirst to see men slugging it out, I managed to find time to watch a few fights.

None was ever greater than the February 14, 1951, matchup at the Chicago Stadium between Sugar Ray Robinson and Jake LaMotta, the Bronx Bull immortalized by Robert De Niro in the movie *Raging Bull.* Robinson reigned as the greatest fighter of the day. LaMotta strutted as the tough guy brawler who could take as good as he could give. This would be the sixth and final matchup between them in their long rivalry. LaMotta insisted on being paid seventy-five thousand dollars. That was big money back then. In truth, his star power as a big draw earned him that on top of his normal percentage from the fight, ten thousand dollars.

Simply put, it was the greatest fight I ever saw, a bruising battle of titans refusing to give quarter and expecting none. However, midway through the contest Robinson grabbed control and was building up points as the rounds progressed. At one point, Ray dropped his hands, ducked, and dodged as LaMotta wore himself out furiously throwing punches at Ray. Hammering the Bronx Bull into the ropes in the thirteenth round, Ray administered a brutal beating on Jake, but LaMotta would not fall. The referee stepped in. Ray had pummeled the world middleweight crown away from LaMotta. The crowd went wild.

Robinson looms in my memory as one of the most difficult men I ever had to deal with. Beset by his own devils, spawned out of the hell that defined his upbringing in an America where black lives were worthless, Ray could quickly turn from hail-fellow-well-met to a scheming, conniving, mistrustful foe. The demons from his background made him a tortured soul but also made him something of an actor. In 1943, a black soldier was found wandering around the New York port, claiming he didn't know who he was. As it happened, a writer for one of the Hearst newspapers recognized the man as Ray Robinson. An army officer, Colonel Robert Munson, had a physician examine Robinson. By a quirk of fate, that physician turned out to be the nephew of Mike Jacobs. The examination determined Ray had a ruptured eardrum. Ray was discharged, and all hell broke loose in the War Department. To smooth things over, Ray agreed to five fights for the Hearst Milk Fund. Ray had a way of being guilty of doing wrong things that turned out well in the end.

Another example came in 1952 when we scheduled a fight between Ray Robinson and Rocky Graziano. Ray had a sharp, scheming manager by the name of Joe Glazer. Boxing wasn't Glazer's only game. He had all the black musicians under contract, including the top ones such as Cab Calloway, Louis Armstrong, and Duke Ellington. Glazer announced that he and Robinson would take ancillary rights for the fight.

"What do you mean?" I asked.

"Television and motion pictures," he said.

Standing in the room with us was Joe Louis. I turned to him and said, "Joe, every shoemaker should stick to his own last." I turned back to Glazer to say, "If we were dealing with Duke Ellington or Armstrong, I would defer to you. I would defer to you on running whorehouses because you've run all the whorehouses for Capone from the Loop to Gary, Indiana."

Ray jumped up out of his seat, but Joe warned him off. "Sit down, or I'm going to drop you out of the window."

Now Ray suffered from a sometimes crushing fear of heights. That phobia manifested itself in strange ways. For example, Ray wouldn't fly, and he would never ride in elevators if he could avoid it. I remember him climbing thirteen flights of stairs to avoid riding in an elevator to get to a State of Illinois Boxing Commission hearing.

Bouncing back from Joe's threat, Ray shouted, "You aren't going to have a fight unless I get twenty-five thousand dollars for training expenses by nine o'clock tonight!"

I got on the phone to Jim Norris at his Park Avenue apartment, and he produced the cash for Ray. More difficulty followed. Just four days before the bout, Robinson fell into a conversation with Archie Moore. Their discussion of a complicated IRS issue provoked Ray to demand a hundred thousand dollars from the International Boxing Club or he wouldn't fight. Ray said the government had placed an "anticipatory lien" on the proceeds from Archie Moore's last fight. I'd never heard of any such thing, but clearly Ray feared he wouldn't get his money.

I knew Ray too well to just fork over a bundle of cash that big. "We're in a quandary," I said. "Once you get that kind of money, if you have a sprained eyebrow, you'll pull out of the fight."

I came up with a solution: I told Ray's manager, Killer Johnson, that I'd put the money in a safety deposit box at City National Bank and turn over the key to the senior vice president. Once Ray stepped into the ring, the vice president would give Killer the key. So it went, with Sugar Ray knocking out Graziano in the third round.

As tough as he was in the ring, Ray obviously was no less tough outside of it when it came to finances. Negotiations with Robinson usually took three months, I once told a newspaper reporter. "He has a very sophisticated and stubborn knowledge of financial agreements. He reads every line in his contracts and insists on changes that even his lawyers don't catch." The toughest part came down to the terms over motion picture and television rights. I always negotiated with Ray face-to-face, never over the telephone. "I want to see if he has a roguish twinkle in his eye or whether he's really mad about something."[4] So difficult could dealing with Robinson be that toward the end of the International Boxing Club years, when the organization faced a lot of legal problems, I quipped, "I safely can say if I can handle Robinson, most of my other problems won't look like mountains."[5]

Sometimes I found myself helping Ray out of financial jams. Once, the IRS placed a lien on the purse on a fight in Chicago because Ray hadn't paid eighty-one thousand dollars in taxes. I established a payment plan for him to clear up his debt to the government. However, the biggest thing I ever did for Ray—and, as it turned out, for generations of professional athletes—was to attack IRS regulations forcing boxers to be credited for the entire purse after a fight. Big payout meant big tax bills. I got Robinson to agree to having his winning purse from one fight at Madison Square Garden paid out over five years. That posed risks to Ray. The IRS might disallow the entire contract, but we prevented that in court finally in 1965.[6] Robinson won, and professional baseball, football, and basketball players today reap the benefits because they can sign lucrative contracts extending their paychecks over years. They all owe a debt to Ray.

What a great job I had—rubbing shoulders with some of the era's great sports stars, negotiating TV deals for scores of fights a year with the networks, matching talented fighters to ensure exciting contests to cement boxing as a memorable chapter in what's often called television's golden age, traveling at least a hundred thousand miles a year at a time when air travel remained something of an exotic luxury to make deals for fights, and, yes, enjoying a bit of spotlight myself as a player in big-time sports. For years I was the International Boxing Club's secretary until succeeding Jim Norris as president after his resignation in 1958. Behind that story, however, loomed the one issue that plagued professional boxing throughout the 1950s and consequently caused me plenty of headaches—questions about mob influence.

19

Mob Allegations

Allegations of mob influence stuck to the International Boxing Club all the years of its existence and afterward. It was more a matter of appearances than substance. For Jim Norris and Art Wirtz, boxing provided a veneer of legitimacy to ventures actually tainted by organized crime—horse racing and casino gambling. But organized crime never fixed a single fight while I ran the International Boxing Club.

Norris and Wirtz, titans of finance and business, ruled over a complex empire encompassing the legitimate and the illegitimate. They had invested in stadiums in Chicago, New York, St. Louis, and other cities and owned the Detroit Red Wings and Chicago Blackhawks professional hockey franchises. They owned lucrative cash-generating liquor distributorships, including Judge and Dolph in Chicago, Edison Liquors in Milwaukee, Erhlichman Liquors in San Francisco, and companies servicing Nevada and Texas. Another cash cow was the Hollywood Ice Revue headlining Sonja Henie that Wirtz controlled. His partner in a Sixth Avenue ice palace in New York was John D. Rockefeller. Cash businesses were made to order for money laundering. In addition, Norris was an avid horseman, baseball enthusiast, and partner in the New York Stock Exchange firm of Norris and Kenley.

When Joe Louis and I dived into the boxing business with Norris and Wirtz, I of course had heard of the rumors of mob ties. However, my close examination of the deal they offered and the way the International

Boxing Club operated persuaded me no organized crime taint would be attached to our boxing promotion business.

While aware of the rumors, I got my first jolt of reality about Norris and the mob after returning from the 1951 Robinson-Turpin fight in London to find trouble knocking at the door of professional boxing.

In Detroit, our base of operations was the Olympia Auditorium. Two hoodlums, affiliated with the Teamsters Union, decided to move into the building as boxing matchmakers. The union had a contract with Olympia to move chairs around the arena to set up the ice rink for the Detroit Red Wing games. These two hoodlums clearly were trying to muscle their way into the boxing business to establish mob influence in the sport.

In New York at the time, I got a call from the manager of the Detroit building announcing that Teamsters pickets were marching around in front of the facility. Why, he didn't know. I immediately hired an attorney to secure a restraining order against the picketing. The next couple of weeks I scheduled bouts featuring local talent, Chuck Davey and Chuck Speiser, both Michigan State graduates and, in Davey's case, a hit with TV audiences. Troubled by the events in Detroit, I flew in to try to find out what was going on. While at the offices of the Michigan State Athletic Commission, I was approached by two men who said they were responsible for the picketing.

"You think you're goddamn smart," said one of them. "You had the help of an attorney; you got an injunction." Then the conversation turned threatening. "You better not schedule any events in Detroit."

The next day found me back in Chicago. I was worried about the threat. Then out of the blue, a man who had been a regular patron of our fights showed up at my office.

"You have problems in Detroit," he declared.

"No," I said, because I intended to order a halt to fighting at Olympia Auditorium.

"That's not necessary. I'm Paul Dorfman. Let's go to Detroit tomorrow and we'll settle this."

I had no idea who Paul Dorfman was. Later I learned he was a confidant of Teamsters boss Jimmy Hoffa. In any event, Dorfman and I did go to Detroit, where we met with two Teamsters officials in my office.

"Jimmy don't want this crap," Dorfman barked at the two men. "Stop this while you're still alive."

That marked the end of our Detroit Teamster problem. These two guys made no further attempt to control matchmaking in Detroit. Norris, however much he profited from gambling on horses and later from casinos in the Bahamas, had put out the word that boxing was off limits to organized crime. No one was going to interfere with the International Boxing Club.

The realization of how big the stakes were in the Detroit gambit came to me later. At the time, I asked Dorfman what exactly was the nature of the problem we had in Detroit.

"Nothing, I'll let you know later" was his cryptic reply.

Later came in 1957 when Hoffa stood trial in Washington on attempted bribery charges for trying to place a spy inside a congressional committee investigating union corruption. Dorfman telephoned to declare, "Payoff time!" He wanted Joe Louis to take the stand as a character witness for Hoffa. Nothing doing, I replied. However, I did agree that Joe could travel to Washington to sit in the courtroom as a friend of Hoffa. The Teamsters boss already was ably represented by the well-regarded attorney Edward Bennett Williams, but I suggested that he add to his defense team a woman who would become Joe's third wife, Martha Jefferson, a noted criminal attorney in Los Angeles. With all that legal eagle firepower and Joe sitting in the courtroom as a silent witness supporting Hoffa and at one point throwing an arm around him, the labor chieftain soon won acquittal. This turned out to have consequences for me.

Hoffa already had earned the enmity of Robert Kennedy. The youthful scion of the Boston Irish nouveau riche Joseph Kennedy spent part of the 1950s serving as counsel to the Kefauver Committee. The panel, headed by Tennessee Democratic senator Estes Kefauver, was looking into mob influence in American life. Racketeering in labor emerged as a major focus of investigation. Exulting in his acquittal, Hoffa brashly told reporters that Robert Kennedy had threatened to jump off the top of the Washington Monument if Hoffa were not convicted. Practically rubbing his hands in glee, Hoffa declared he wouldn't miss that leap if it occurred.

Less humorous was the visitor from the racketeering committee who showed up afterward at my office at the Chicago Stadium. He demanded that I sign an affidavit asserting that Joe Louis had been paid fifty thousand dollars to show up at Hoffa's trial. Nothing doing, I replied. I would prepare an affidavit to the effect that Joe was grateful for Hoffa's efforts to resolve the picketing in Detroit but that I had paid for Joe's transportation to Washington and his hotel expenses there for the trial. Frustrated, the Kennedy agent left. Unfortunately, but unbeknownst to me at the time, I had landed myself a spot alongside Hoffa on the Kennedy enemies list, and retribution would come later.

A dramatic indication of Norris's clout with the mob came while I was in pre-Castro Cuba for the Joe Brown fight in 1958.

Havana reigned as a gambling mecca in those days. George Raft, a Hollywood actor of mediocre talent who had made a name for himself starring in gangster films, strutted about town as the front man for the big casinos. He threw a party for us, and the booze flowed freely. I fell into a conversation with a man whom I knew to be a high-ranking gangster from New York. This guy, introduced to me as Tommy Brown but actually named Tommy Lucchese, asked me about Jim Norris. I allowed that I was a partner with Norris. This mobster pointed to a scar on his nose between his eyes and said he got it when Norris smashed a beer bottle across his face. This story alarmed me. This hood, I had been told, was the number three man in the New York underworld—and Norris had roughed him up with impunity. The implication couldn't have been clearer—Norris had plenty of clout where it counted.

"Where's your bullshit boss?" he asked me.

"He's drinking gin fizzes with Ernest Hemingway," I said. Indeed, Jim was in Cuba at the time, matching the famous writer drink for drink.

"Well, give him my regards," the mobster said. "And tell him I carry the scar from a beer bottle he inflicted on me. It's lucky I didn't lose the sight of one eye."

That gave me something to think about. Still, whatever skeletons hung around in Jim's background, I knew Norris had not let gangsters intrude into boxing.

The allegations on mob influence stuck to boxing like Velcro. How could it be otherwise with Norris hobnobbing with gangsters? Norris and Wirtz owned the Cameo restaurant on Walton Street, just steps away from Chicago's magnificent Michigan Avenue. There Jim's constant companions were underworld figures "Golf Bag" Sam Hunt and Ralph Pierce. Hunt, an enforcer for the Capone mob, earned the sobriquet "Golf Bag" for his penchant for hauling around a submachine gun in a golf bag. Hunt was put on trial in 1942 for gunning down a man after a traffic accident in Chicago. Three of the city's South Side policy kings tried to bribe a witness to the crime to change his story.[1] Norris and Wirtz also owned the Bismarck Hotel in Chicago's Loop. The hotel's Green Room was a favorite watering hole of the city's politicians and, hence, a magnet for gangsters with wads of cash to influence city policy.

Toward the end of the 1950s, all the charges, accusations, and allegations combined with assertions that the International Boxing Club constituted an illegal monopoly over the fight game came together to wreck the IBC and wreak havoc in my life.

Did the gangsters want to muscle their way into the popular renaissance boxing experienced thanks to television? Of course. I've already talked about the brush with a couple of shady characters in Detroit. As I indicated, however, Norris had the clout to keep would-be fight fixers out of the ring. That's because he and Wirtz were in bed with the mobsters in horse racing and, later, in casinos in the Bahamas. That's where the big money was, not in fixing boxing fights. The money in boxing came from television contracts and proceeds from the stadiums hosting the bouts. Still, the troublesome characters who pursued profits from illegal gambling on boxing, who tried to illegally control boxers or make matches, and who clustered around fighters, gymnasiums, and big-time bouts cast a cloud over the sport that we couldn't shake. Mob influence in boxing was a pimple compared to its impact in horse racing.

Norris had his own stable of thoroughbreds at his Spring Hill Farm in Kentucky and quarter horses at his Florida home. I remember his running a thoroughbred horse, Nell K., in competition for the Kentucky

Derby. Nell K. had won the Prioress Stakes in New York in 1949 but came up short after being lamed in a Derby prep. Another Norris horse, Jamie K., finished second and third, respectively, in the Preakness and the Belmont Stakes in 1953. That was on the up-and-up, but what do you say about the time Norris and British promoter Jack Solomons entered a horse in a Canadian race? Norris had called me asking that I meet in Toronto for the running of the Queen's Plate race. I was not, and am not, a racing fan. However, Norris said I'd be interested because he and Solomons had entered a horse from England. Norris liked to bet on the ponies and consistently wagered big bucks. He liked to be in the action on the track and off the track. He would gamble six thousand dollars a day, every day. I knew this because when he was out of the country, his bookie in Washington, D.C., known to me only by the name Kingy, would keep me abreast of the outcome of Norris's bets. Despite the tremendous odds against her, Norris's horse won the Queen's Plate and then disappeared from the face of the earth. It was never again raced; it showed up at no track nowhere. Norris pocketed his winnings and that was that.

The ownership of banks in Florida and Illinois and of liquor businesses in Chicago, Milwaukee, and San Francisco afforded Norris and Wirtz the cash to be powerful men in the legitimate and not-so-legitimate worlds. During a conversation with Herbert Muhammad, Muhammad Ali's manager, and me, Wirtz once boasted that he supplied the booze for two out of every four drinks poured in Las Vegas.

When the Cuban revolution and deteriorating relations with the United States doomed gambling in Havana, Wirtz and Norris shifted their sights to the Bahamas. The saga of a ten-million-dollar yacht named *Blackhawk* emerged as the most visible sign of their involvement. Wirtz took possession of this luxury vessel after it was built in Holland and sailed it to Gibraltar. There he left, but the crew sailed on to drop anchor in the waters off Lucaya Beach, the Bahamas, the location of a big casino. This yacht boasted sophisticated electronic communications equipment at a time when this island still relied on a rickety, often uncertain telephone system. The *Blackhawk* turned into a floating communications center for the casino, its radio being used to contact banks in Miami Beach to clear credit for the high rollers at the roulette tables and other games. However, that wasn't the sole function of the *Blackhawk;* it also served as the electronic nerve center for the world's biggest bookie operation.

Raking in the winnings from Caribbean gambling was just the start. In order for Norris, Wirtz, and the mobsters to collect on their winnings, the money had to travel back to the United States. Norris and Wirtz owned banks in Florida and the First Bank of Elmhurst in Illinois, which served as conduits for funneling the proceeds from gambling back into the states. The transfers were facilitated by Keith Gonsalves of Barclay's Bank in the Bahamas. "Lucrative" is a poor word to describe the profits from casino gambling. For example, Max Courtney and his associates running the Lucaya Beach Hotel Monte Carlo Room in the Bahamas collected annual salaries of $102,200 plus free housing plus bonuses of $490,511. For the actual owners of these gambling emporiums, the weekly take came to two million dollars.

Later I got an idea of just how profitable a casino free of government oversight could be when I visited Cairo, Egypt, in 1980 with Bill Butters in an unsuccessful attempt to put on a Muhammad Ali fight there. Butters was friendly with the manager of the casino in the Cairo Hilton. By comparison with the big, glitzy gambling halls of Las Vegas, the Cairo casino was a modest two-room affair. The manager told us that because he was free of government oversight, meaning he controlled the backroom counting, his dinky little operation outgrossed the big neon light casinos of Las Vegas.

Norris's mob links came up in unexpected ways. Norris was close to the infamous gangland figure Albert Anastasia, the chief executioner for Murder, Inc., who would himself be gunned down while sitting in a barber's chair at New York's Park Sheraton Hotel in 1957. In the days before parimutuel betting, Anastasia made book on the New York racetracks, and that's how Norris got to know him. I got quite a surprise one day when Norris asked me to go along with him "to see a guy" at St. Clair Hospital near Madison Square Garden. That sick guy turned out to be Anastasia, recovering from a heart attack. In one of the small-world encounters, a woman sitting at Anastasia's bedside was his cousin Josephine De Feo. Isabelle and I had met her on the beach at Martha's Vineyard. Josephine, who ran a business producing clerical garb for the Roman Catholic Church, and Isabelle became warm friends and often traveled together overseas, including journeys to Africa and the West Indies.

More surprising than the hospital meeting with Anastasia, and infinitely more troubling, was an attempt by Norris to get me to help Anastasia defeat a government drive to deport him. Anastasia's case was being heard by my old associate from the War Department, Bill Hastie, now a justice in the Second Circuit of the U.S. Court of Appeals. Over lunch one day, Norris broached the issue with me. "Are you still friendly with your old boss at the War Department, Judge Hastie?" he asked.

"Yes, we're close friends," I replied. "We're having lunch in a few days."

"If you will speak up for Anastasia—"

"No!" I immediately interrupted. "If you're implying that I should interfere with a case in the court of appeals, you are out of your mind."

A week later, I had lunch with Hastie. We talked about a book for which I had written the foreword, *Views from the Back of the Bus during World War II and Beyond* by Chicago author Dempsey Travis. The book recounted a riot between white military police and black soldiers at Indiantown Gap, Pennsylvania, one of the many unhappy disturbances we had confronted together during our time at the War Department. As the discussion progressed, Hastie added, "Incidentally, I have finished my decision involving Anastasia, who was a sergeant stationed at the time at Indiantown Gap." Anastasia should be treated, Hastie said, like any other soldier who had illegally entered the country and served in the armed forces.

I didn't let on to Norris that I knew the Anastasia case had been resolved. When it became public a few weeks later, a mobster by the name of Frank Carbo approached me to say friends of Anastasia would like to give Bill Hastie a house in the Virgin Islands, where he had served as governor.

"No," I immediately replied. "And if you ever say anything like this again, you're likely to find yourself being whisked off to jail."

"What do you want?" Carbo asked.

"Nothing, and never again repeat any offer like this at any time!" I shot back.

The name most frequently mentioned when racketeering is alleged in boxing is indeed that of Frank Carbo. There's no doubt he was a bad guy, and he had been lurking around boxing for a long time. He and another underworld figure named Frank "Blinky" Palermo fixed a fight between LaMotta and Blackjack Billy Fox in 1946. But the idea of Carbo influencing boxing when the International Boxing Club ran the game is the equivalent of a second lieutenant telling President Bush how to run the war in Iraq.

It wasn't for lack of trying on Carbo's part. Once he tried to muscle in on the International Boxing Club's lock on the Wednesday night fights. Carbo put together a company with wildly popular entertainer Frank Sinatra as the front man to grab sponsorship of twenty-eight dates of the popular Wednesday night bouts. The company actually was in the grips of Carbo and the notorious Chicago crime boss Sam Giancana. The sports director for ABC came to me to say it had to lay off our summer promotions because it had a deal with Sinatra. I was stunned, mostly by the naïveté of ABC.

"If you think you're getting too much criticism about the mob and the IBC, wait until you see what happens when word gets out about this Sinatra-fronted deal," I said.

The deal evaporated overnight. Sinatra, whom I had gotten to know a bit through my business dealings in Hollywood, never spoke to me again.

Carbo, like Anastasia, was just one shady guy in the constellation of mob-connected men around Norris and Wirtz. Norris did business with the unsavory trio of Max Courtney, who had introduced Norris to Anastasia; Frank Ritter, sometimes known as Red Reed; and Charles Brudner, aka Charlie Brud—operators of the nation's largest bookie network. They were the front operators for New York's Cotton Club, the famous Harlem attraction actually owned by gangster Dutch Schultz. Black performers such as Duke Ellington, Cab Calloway, and Louis Armstrong headlined at the Cotton Club, but no African American was permitted to cross the threshold as a customer. I knew these guys, too, and I upbraided them about the club banning black patrons. "It's not our call," they responded.

On another occasion, I listened intently as Courtney reminisced about his days as a Prohibition era bootlegger for the Schultz outfit, running booze from Canada to New York. His Canadian supplier was Edgar Bronfman; the American end of the operation was run by Joseph Kennedy.

Norris's dealing with Courtney and his partners brought him into contact with Meyer Lansky, the brains behind the syndicate who reigned from Florida as czar for offshore gambling, meaning casinos in prerevolutionary Havana and then the Bahamas. Courtney and company emerged as the front men for a casino on Paradise Island in the Bahamas in the 1960s.

Now, with a cast of hoods like that hanging around, hobnobbing with Norris, showing up at big fights, running bookies, and occasionally turning up in newspaper headlines, it's no wonder boxing got the attention of anyone looking into organized crime. Subpoenas went out in 1957 from a grand jury in New York investigating Carbo. Norris suffered a heart attack, a little too convenient in timing some would say. But he never recovered from the ordeal. He resigned April 18, 1957, as president of the International Boxing Club. "My doctors advised me last fall following a severe heart attack to restrict my activities by resigning as head of this Company," he wrote in his letter of resignation. "Mr. Truman Gibson was elected Executive Vice President of the Company last Fall and has been very helpful in relieving me of many of my executive duties, and I am sure that he and the organization can effectively carry on."[2]

The speculation immediately fell on me as his successor. "The evidence points to Gibson's taking over the leadership of IBC, either officially or behind the retiring Norris," wrote *The Ring* magazine.[3] "As a lawyer, with well known craft and acumen, Gibson is better equipped than Norris for coping with boxing's problems, which have become largely legalistic." The magazine described me as "matchmaker behind matchmakers, trouble shooter par excellence, manager of the two weekly television shows, an expert, a man familiar with the Washington climate." Furthermore, "Gibson may look and sound, at times, like a church deacon. But he is no babe in the woods. He is crafty, he knows the angles. One thing he would give to the IBC, which it now lacks, is service 24 hours a day, seven days a week. . . . Since boxing has become a business requiring close application, Gibson's contributions would be of vast importance."[4] The job of president fell to me with much fanfare.

Also falling on me was the burden of Carbo. *The Ring* article said "Norris has suffered from reputed association with Carbo." It describes as "doubtless" the truth of Norris's denial that Carbo never dictated a match. But, *The Ring* asserted, "the man in the street believes that Norris has favored Carbo and his fighters. This is one of the reasons for Jim's gradual move out of the boxing limelight."[5]

Of course, I immediately found myself besieged with questions from the press about Carbo. My answer was the same. "I have never associated with Frankie Carbo and won't start now," I told the *New York Herald Tribune.* "Like the question, 'When did you stop beating your wife?' I was asked when would I stop associating with Carbo."[6] To United Press, I said, "I never did associate with Carbo, so I don't have to stop."[7] To questions from Gene Ward of the *New York Daily Mirror,* I responded, "One of the first questions asked of me as the new president was whether or not I would stop associating with Frankie Carbo. I have never associated with Carbo, so I don't have to stop."[8] I also told Ward I would fight any baseless libelous charges connecting me to organized crime. Norris "was too prone to let these things go by," I said. No matter how many times Norris had met with Carbo, I had not been involved in those sessions.

Carbo's name kept coming up, but the truth was he carried nowhere near the stature of a Lansky or Frank Costello, to name another one of the notorious gangsters of the postwar years. Carbo was no more than a messenger boy who operated at the fringes of mob activities and boxing. Oh, he tried to make out he was a player, boasting to managers of fighters that he could make matches. If a fighter later got a match with the International Boxing Club, Carbo would brag he pulled it off. If no match came, he'd huff and puff that his influence had cost the fighter the bout. However big he may have been in horse racing or casinos, Carbo was no more than a pimple on a gnat's ass when it came to boxing.

Like a pimple, Carbo was ugly and hard to hide. Bobby Kennedy's Justice Department, seeking retribution, I'm convinced, for my refusal to lie about Jimmy Hoffa, tried to hang Carbo around my neck in a

California trial in 1961. The pitiful best the prosecutors could do was assert that I had had telephone conversations with Carbo. Big deal, I thought. However, after the first judge died, the second judge reviewed the transcript and found me guilty of conspiracy on flimsy evidence. I was put on five years' probation. Carbo, Frank "Blinky" Palermo, and I had been accused of trying to take over the management of welterweight champion Don Jordan, a mediocre fighter. I hardly knew the fighter or his managers.

Guilt by association combined with the enmity of Bobby Kennedy is the best description of what happened to me. Given Carbo's ties to Norris and his well-cultivated relationship with boxing promoters and managers, I couldn't escape running across this fellow from time to time. I had to pay for that regardless of the truth of my innocence.

Still, with all the allegations, accusations, and testimony against Carbo, no one ever successfully tagged boxing through the International Boxing Club as being crooked. As I told an Atlanta reporter in 1959, "Not a single TV fight that we've put on has ever been contested as being crooked. If we had been putting on fixed fights, we would have been out of business long ago."[9] After all, the Vegas gambling kingpins would have taken a suspicious fight off the morning line in a heartbeat, and word of that getting out would have killed our Nielsen ratings, jeopardizing our profitable contracts with the television networks. A fixed fight, however much it might have reaped in one night, would have been bad business, costing us much more over the long run.

In the end, allegations of corruption didn't bring down the International Boxing Club. The deathblow was struck January 12, 1959, when the U.S. Supreme Court, abandoning precedent that sports wasn't ruled by antitrust law, declared the International Boxing Club to be an illegal monopoly. The IBC, the Court declared, "had exercised a stranglehold on the [boxing] industry for a long period . . . and still dominated the staging of championship bouts and completely controlled the filming and broadcasting of those contests."[10] The Court's opinion linked the ownership of the big stadiums by Norris and Wirtz with IBC's agreements with boxers with our TV contracts to assert the IBC constituted an illegal monopoly.

Still, even after the Court ruling brought the dissolving of the International Boxing Club, my confrontations over boxing had another chapter to go. The allegations of mob influence, worry over lack of national regulation of the popular sport, and the Court ruling about monopoly had caught the eye of Washington. It was a sensational topic, just the kind of thing politicians like to seize upon to make their own headlines. Senator Kefauver of Tennessee had emerged as one of the nation's best-known politicians in the 1950s, having run unsuccessfully for the Democratic presidential nomination twice and having served as the vice presidential candidate on the ticket in Adlai Stevenson's unsuccessful attempt to unseat President Eisenhower in 1956. Much of his reputation arose from his investigations into organized crime's influence in American life. In 1960, his Subcommittee on Antitrust and Monopoly of the Senate Judiciary Committee turned its focus on boxing and—who else?—Frank Carbo. By then, Carbo already had been convicted and sentenced to two years on a gambling misdemeanor charge in New York and was banned from boxing. A misdemeanor charge was the best the prosecutors so far could nail Carbo with after twelve years of investigations.

I spent two days, December 5 and 6, in the hot seat. The subcommittee's assistant counsel took me through a long list of boxing managers and promoters, asking if they were controlled by Carbo. While virtually all of them were associated with or were friends of Carbo, I could testify that only a couple were to my knowledge controlled by him. I acknowledged it could be difficult to distinguish between the two. "The line between the control and friendship is very difficult, because in the very nature of this business the actions were not always on a businesslike basis or not on an open-and-above-board basis, so that it is very difficult to separate the line between the friendship and the control which calls for certain conclusions."[11] Carbo had been building friendships long before the International Boxing Club was founded in 1949 and continued to do so after.

Time and again, I told the panel Carbo had not been allowed to influence International Boxing Club decisions and contests. "When efforts were made to apply pressure as a result of the friendship, we would not go in."[12] I testified, "Nobody has ever told us, 'Pay a fighter *x* number of dollars,' on a cheap or bargain price."[13] I came back to that point over and over. "The only times, as I testified, the Carbo influence became an issue, we stopped, we discontinued our activity with the individuals."[14]

Carbo and others like him remained a fact of life in professional boxing, and we couldn't just ignore them. Boxing, I reminded the subcommittee, "does not exactly attract Sunday school teachers or people who go to Sunday school."[15] Still, we never cooperated with the more unseemly elements, although we did have to "live with them." They could cause trouble, interfere in a bout by having a fighter feign sudden illness, or foment a strike by sports arena labor.

However, there never arose even a hint of a fixed fight. A thrown fight would have been death to TV ratings.[16] This reigned as paramount with us. Television ruled us. A hundred fights a year required us to come up with four hundred fighters. We didn't care whether managers or promoters cozied up to Carbo or warred with him. "We wanted to provide a continuity of our weekly televised series so that while there were many managers who were not friendly with or influenced by Carbo, there were several, in fact many, who were friendly to Carbo, so that . . . we did not want to give the impression that we didn't want to deal with all managers so long as we got fights that weren't fixed."[17]

While Carbo maintained a close relationship with Norris, he had no claim of friendship with me, and our relationship could not even be characterized as pleasant. "Mr. Carbo and I understand each other very well. I think I represented an antagonistic element to him,"[18] I told the Kefauver subcommittee.

Once when I had denied fights to a promoter close to the mobster, Carbo called someone who was defending me "a nigger lover." Hearing about that, I confronted Carbo, telling him, "So long as I was in the International Boxing Club, he was not going to tell me where to put fights."[19]

Naturally the panel expressed interest in the profits from boxing. International Boxing Club gross revenues ran five million dollars to seven million dollars, but after production costs, payments to the fighters, arena charges, and other expenses, profits amounted to two hundred fifty thousand dollars to three hundred thousand dollars.

"What kind of salaries," Senator Kefauver asked me, "do you fellows draw?"

"Wholly inadequate, Senator," I responded, evoking an outburst of laughter in the hearing room.[20]

Sitting through this grilling for two days emboldened me to finally cut to the chase. "It is interesting, in connection with the hearings so far, there has been no charge of fixed fights. . . . I would be greatly surprised if any evidence is adduced at any of your hearings that would seem to indicate even a fixed fight, because the [television] sponsors have looked carefully, and we certainly have looked carefully, and we try to police and regulate ourselves."[21] A little later, I added, "We knew if there were fixed fights, we would be out of business, so that we try to protect ourselves in every way against the possibility of a fixed fight. But you only need one or two and you have no more boxing."[22]

My testimony closed with Senator Kefauver describing me as "forthright and factual and cooperative."[23]

My glory days as the nation's top boxing promoter were over. They hadn't made me, or Joe Louis for that matter, rich. Norris and Wirtz funneled profits to their stadium holdings, bypassing the International Boxing Club. I was paid less than ten thousand dollars a year, the deal I struck with Wirtz in 1949 setting my pay at seventy-two hundred. My relationship with Wirtz ended on a bitter note with his making the incredible claim that I somehow owed him six thousand dollars. "You measure everything in terms of money," I wrote him on March 6, 1962. "What measure do you put on a man's life?" I never heard from him again.

Still, looking back on those years, I take a lot of satisfaction in one thing that wasn't talked about much. I brought it up in an Atlanta newspaper interview as the International Boxing Club began to fade from the sports scene: The IBC, through its promotion of black athletes and interracial bouts, "has brought before the American public examples of racial harmony that would perhaps not have been witnessed by the mass of people otherwise." I'll leave it to others to assess the impact of African American excellence in the ring during the 1950s—exemplified by Sugar Ray Robinson, the greatest fighter I ever saw—on changes in attitudes among white Americans and on the successes of the civil rights movement in the 1950s and 1960s. But, I think, no one should minimize it.

20

Remembrances

The struggle for racial justice during World War II has dominated these pages, with my career in boxing taking a secondary role. That leaves out a lot from a life spanning more than nine decades. Faces and places dance out of my memory as I contemplate friends who helped me at crucial times in my life. I wouldn't want to leave this memoir without recalling a few vignettes.

While most of the last several decades have been devoted to the practice of law, my work in sports and visits to Hollywood inspired some dabbling in the world of music, unfortunately with more misses than hits. I once had the honor of representing the great star Sarah Vaughan. I thought I might have an in with Atlantic Records. That's because there was something of a family connection, albeit a tenuous one. Isabelle's first cousin and University of Michigan roommate was Carol Carson Williston. She was married to Tom Williston, a Washington, D.C., physician and an avid jazz fan. They had a music room on the third floor of their home, and Tom numbered among his friends all the important popular musicians. Also among his friends were Nesuhi and Ahmet Ertegun, sons of the ambassador of Turkey. The two brothers had formed Atlantic Records. I made a pitch for Sarah to Nesuhi Ertegun, but, alas, he graciously declined to sign her to a contract. Sarah had no trouble achieving wide fame and renown.

I was more directly involved with a record company owned by Johnny Nash and Danny Simms with a studio in Kingston, Jamaica.

That location proved fruitful in that Nash had a hit record, "I Can See Clearly Now," using background music from a group led by the great Bob Marley. Marley's death, however, killed off the record label with which I was associated. Simms called to tell me that the master recordings of Marley's humming and singing had been sold to Universal Records for two million dollars. I reminded him that I was an associate and a partner. I was crushed when he replied, "Yes, you *were* a partner." Another miss.

Even though it turned out to be a bust for me, this musical venture marked just one of several occasions when I benefited from the unfailing friendship and cooperation of Rex Nettleford, a Rhodes scholar at Oxford University whom I met in Belize when he was dean of the University of the West Indies, based in Jamaica. A man of many talents, Rex founded and served as lead dancer of the Royal Jamaican Dance Troupe and wrote books about Jamaica and Norman Manley, the island's best-known prime minister. Also a gracious host, Rex introduced me to the Jamaican delicacies of roast goat and pepper pot soup.

Rex and I shared several memorable moments. Once he visited me in Chicago, and we traveled together to New York. Behind his Oxford accent and dress lurked a man passionate about jazz. So I took him to Basin Street East. As it happened at the bar we encountered Count Basie and New York congressman Adam Clayton Powell, resplendent in a white panama hat and white suit. A short while later Duke Ellington came in and sat at the bar with Dizzy Gillespie and Kiko Morgan, the wife of jazz trumpeter Lee Morgan. We were treated to Basie's incomparable sounds and Dizzy's unforgettable voice. Ellington wasn't performing that night, but he joined in the spirited conversation that lasted until six o'clock in the morning. At one point during the conversation, Dizzy turned to me and, in the presence of those famous musicians, asked, "Truman, who's the greatest piano player in the world?" He was a little taken back when I replied, "Earl Hines!" Rex and I agreed that this chance meeting would be remembered as among the highlights of our lives.

Another astounding experience we shared, one that was beyond my understanding, came during a visit to Jamaica in 1963. Rex had taken me to the Kingston airport. We found the airport and the area around it crowded to overflowing with Rastafarians. They numbered twenty-four thousand and were on hand to welcome the man they worshiped as a god, Haile Selassie, the Lion of Judah and emperor of Ethiopia. The weather was awful; thick dark clouds scudded overhead and a steady rain fell. Then, just as the emperor's plane approached for a landing, the rain abruptly stopped, the clouds parted, and a bright sun cast golden light over Kingston. I can't explain it; I only recount what I witnessed.

I also got involved in some legal work while in Jamaica. It stemmed from my association with Hank Schwab in a talent agency named Hollywood by the Stars. Among the personalities we represented were actor Broderick Crawford, best remembered for his role in the movie *All the King's Men,* and Patrice Wymore, wife of the star of swashbuckling movies and womanizer Errol Flynn. When Flynn died in the arms of a sixteen-year-old girl in British Columbia, his estate became snarled in a complex tax dispute. Patrice was named a coexecutor of Flynn's will along with a New York law firm. The estate included $2 million in cash, $5 million in British housing bonds, and five thousand acres of land in Jamaica as well as a garish house in the Port Antonio area of the island. The law firm paid bills of more than $1.2 million to doctors who had supplied heroin to Flynn. The attorneys themselves claimed legal fees of $400,000. Then entered the bane of all beneficiaries—the IRS. The death tax claimed a huge portion of Flynn's estate.

But the IRS bureaucrats ran afoul of the law. Advisers to Patrice, an American citizen, got her to resign as coexecutor and instituted legal proceedings based on the unassailable fact that Flynn, who was born in Tasmania, was a British citizen and that the bulk of his estate was in England and Jamaica, then a British colony. The case lasted six years, but in the end the assets were rescued from the grasps of the American tax man, and the lawyers had to make good on the money squandered on themselves and the doctors. The last I heard, Patrice was raising cattle in the Port Antonio area.

After the war, although the boxing career had me on the road a lot, Isabelle and I settled down in Chicago. We enrolled our daughter, Karen, in the Francis Parker School, one of the city's best private schools, located on Chicago's North Side. Isabelle and I got to be friendly with the president of the Parker board of trustees, David Wallerstein, and his wife, Carolyn. David, president of the Balaban and Katz theater corporation, which operated the best-known movie palaces in Chicago, engineered my election to the board. Also on the board then was Marshall Field III, scion of the family that owned the famous department store in Chicago's Loop as well as the *Chicago Sun-Times.*

As it happened, David also was a friend of Jackie Robinson, the black baseball player whom I had helped out when his temper got him into trouble in the army during World War II. Jackie by then had achieved star status as a player for the Brooklyn Dodgers. Once when the Dodgers were in town to face the Chicago Cubs, David invited Jackie to a dinner party. During the course of conversation around the table, I said to Jackie, "I know you, and I know your temper. How have you endured the slights in the big leagues?"

"Well, you know me, and you know my army situation," he replied. When he joined the major leagues, Jackie said, he made clear to baseball commissioner Branch Rickey that he would not suffer physical attack. "I told Mr. Rickey that if a pitcher hits me intentionally with a fastball, his ass belongs to me. And if a second baseman strikes me intentionally, his ass belongs to me."

Apparently the warning was passed down the line. "When we went to St. Louis and faced the gashouse gang, the pitcher Burley Grimes threw a fastball that hit me," Jackie recalled. "I lay my bat down and started toward the pitcher. He said, 'God, Jackie, I didn't mean that!' So the word got down the league. They called me names, but I expected those. But nobody hit me intentionally."

While we are on sports, I'll recount one more story from my boxing days. I've already related my meeting Tommy Tucker, who managed the Los Angeles bar the Playroom, and my association with Killer Johnson, the manager for Sugar Ray Robinson and owner of the bar the Archway in Chicago. They liked to play jokes on each other. Once Tucker and Johnson, while visiting San Francisco for a Sugar Ray Robinson fight, stopped by the Blue Moon Bar. The bar was tended by a beautiful

Eurasian girl, and Johnson, who fancied himself the ladies' man, made his move. He asked her if she would be interested in going to see the Robinson fight. Sure, she said. Tucker was present when she said she had to go but would call the bar later to find out where she could procure the tickets. Shortly afterward, Tucker wandered away to find a phone and called the bar asking for Killer Johnson. Feigning what he thought to be an Asiatic accent, Tucker said, "Mr. Johnson, my daughter no go. She with Mr. Tucker." Johnson's hopes of conquest were crushed.

Some months later, Tucker, who had an interest in boxing and held a manager's license, was in Chicago on some business before the Illinois Boxing Commission. After meeting with the commission, he went to the Archway. One of the bar's waitresses was an expert dancer whose specialty was a dance called the Madison. She also was beautiful. As he pulled down one drink after another of his favorite champagne, Veuve Clicquot, Tucker asked the lovely young woman to accompany him to the Bismarck Hotel in the Loop, where he was staying. She did. Once there, they embraced, and then suddenly the girl broke away, saying "Toodle-doo, good-bye." Tucker was incensed and spit out, "People get killed for doing things like this." The girl, alarmed, replied, "Mr. Johnson told me to act like this!" Killer had had his revenge for San Francisco.

Back in the postwar days when race ruled the conventions of society, the West Indies were a natural vacation destination for African Americans seeking relief. I recall running into the future U.S. Supreme Court justice Thurgood Marshall at a Chicago NAACP meeting in 1955. He announced that he would be going to the Virgin Islands at the end of the week. I told him I planned to be in St. Thomas the next day. Marshall, whom I knew from the Depression when he was general counsel to the NAACP, reminded me that I had promised him a fishing trip and that the coincidence of our being in the Virgin Islands at the same time afforded an opportunity for me to make good on my promise. What's more, Thurgood said, Adam Clayton Powell and Daniel "Chappie" James, a pilot who flew 160 combat missions over Korea and Vietnam and who would become the first black four-star general in the air force, would be there as well. What he didn't tell me at the time was that this trip also was his honeymoon with his second wife! I never heard what his bride thought of the idea of him taking off with the rest of us for a day of fishing during their marriage celebratory trip.

I chartered a fishing boat, but it was clear that Thurgood was in charge of our expedition. He announced that for every fish caught, each of us would have a drink. Well, we sailed into a school of tuna and caught twenty of the big fish. Adam, Chappie, and I partook of only a moderate amount of alcohol. Not so the writer and photographer assigned by *Ebony* magazine to record Thurgood's honeymoon. They took Thurgood's charge seriously and downed a lethal portion of his favorite drink, Wild Turkey, ruining their stomachs for all time.

After returning to the island, we enjoyed a memorable evening of conversation and debate, with Thurgood holding forth forcefully, Chappie offering his thoughts, and Powell's eloquence outshining us all. Eventually, Chappie had to get back to his base in Massachusetts. But he provided the exclamation point for the day. He took off in his plane, turned on the afterburners to build up speed, and roared through the sky over our hotel, shaking the building.

For our family, Martha's Vineyard in Massachusetts became a favorite vacation spot. Isabelle and I first visited Oak Bluffs in 1946, staying as paying guests with friends of Etta Moten Barnett, the star of the Broadway production of *Porgy and Bess.* I'll never forget sitting down for the first time on the bed in that house. My weight hitting the bed caused it to emit a vegetablelike odor. I soon learned the mattress was stuffed with corn shucks.

For the next eight years, we vacationed at Oak Bluffs, renting a house built by Joseph Kennedy for the Hollywood actress Gloria Swanson. Needless to say, corn-shuck mattresses had no place among furnishings in a Kennedy home. A wine vault was located in the basement but unfortunately no bottles of wine. The house was situated along a jetty. My daughter, Karen, and her two friends, Sandra Forney and Julie Morris, all teenagers, had the time of their lives swimming at that jetty, rushing to don bathing suits whenever the local ferry passed by.

Surrounded by many friends, we found our stays at Oak Bluffs to be idyllic. Still, the serpent racism reared its ugly head on occasion. Edward Brooke, in those days attorney general for Massachusetts and later elected to the United States Senate, threw a party that came to an unfortunate end. (Brooke, by the way, had served with the Ninety-second Division, working with an intelligence unit in Italy. There he had become fluent in Italian by way of pillow talk and met his wife.) As the party's festivities encouraged high spirits, one of his guests, whose name escapes me now, announced that he wanted to play golf. Eddie and several of his guests trooped over to the local golf course. Well, that facility prohibited play by African Americans, so the group soon found themselves at the village jail. In more recent years President Clinton and his good friend Vernon Jordan, among the nation's most prominent African American lawyers, played the course regularly.

Still, the passage of time didn't wipe away all the vestiges of racism. A few years ago, I visited Martha's Vineyard as the guest of my nephew, Dr. Edward Gibson, and his charming wife, Nanette, who had rented a summerhouse. Eddie took me to the pool shared by several rental houses. A number of people were splashing around in it. I noticed some black kids had shown up. I entered the pool, swam a lap, and looked up to see that the four black kids and I were the only ones still in the pool. At a party that night, I struck up a conversation with a group that included a commodore of the local yacht club. Reflecting on my experience at the pool, I made myself unpopular with that group by commenting, "It's the same game with different players."

Old ways and attitudes die hard. Sometimes their echoes pop up in the most unexpected places. A few years ago I read some remarks made by Colin Powell. The gist was that Powell believed President Truman's condemnations of segregation were politically motivated. I wrote Powell disputing that. I told him Truman spoke from his heart. I sent the general copies of Truman memos bemoaning violence against black soldiers in the South. Powell replied, thanking me for my letter but asserting that he still thought politics were behind Truman's views.

Here we have America's most famous black general echoing the animus of the army for Truman, an animosity that sprang from the president's order to desegregate the military. That's a bit of irony that can surprise even a man who's endured more than nine decades on this earth.

Notes

Preface

1. Morris J. MacGregor Jr., *Integration of the Armed Forces, 1940–1965* (Washington, D.C.: Center of Military History, U.S. Army, 1981), 41.

Chapter 1: The Way We Were

1. MacGregor, *Integration of the Armed Forces,* 23.
2. Ibid., 20–21.
3. A wealth of information about the 364th is found in *A Historical Analysis of the 364th Infantry in World War II* (Washington, D.C.: U.S. Army, 1999). The account of the 364th here is drawn from this document.
4. Frank Capra, *The Name above the Title: An Autobiography* (New York: MacMillan, 1971), 339.
5. Ibid.
6. Gibson memorandum to the deputy chief of staff, "Subject: Inspector General's Memorandum Regarding the 364th Infantry Regiment," June 15, 1943, Papers of Truman K. Gibson, Manuscript Division, Library of Congress (hereafter cited as Gibson Papers).

Chapter 2: Atlanta, Columbus, and W. E. B. DuBois

1. Truman Gibson, *The Lord Is My Shepherd* (Chicago: Childrens Press, 1970).
2. Papers in author's personal possession.
3. Carole Merritt, *The Herndons: An Atlanta Family* (Athens: University of Georgia Press, 2002), 161–63.

4. Philip Dray, *At the Hands of Persons Unknown: The Lynching of Black America* (New York: Random House, 2002), 16.

5. Walter White, *A Man Called White: The Autobiography of Walter White* (New York: Viking Press, 1948), 9.

6. Gary M. Pomerantz, *Where Peachtree Meets Sweet Auburn: The Saga of Two Families and the Making of Atlanta* (New York: Lisa Drew Book/Scribner, 1996), 72–77.

7. Merritt, *The Herndons,* 190.

8. Gibson, *The Lord Is My Shepherd,* 50–51.

9. David M. Kennedy, *Freedom from Fear: The American People in Depression and War, 1929–1945* (New York: Oxford University Press, 1999), 31.

Chapter 3: Black Metropolis

1. Gibson, *The Lord Is My Shepherd,* 51.

2. St. Clair Drake and Horace R. Cayton, *Black Metropolis: A Study of Negro Life in a Northern City* (New York: Harcourt, Brace and Company, 1945).

3. Harold F. Gosnell, *Negro Politicians: The Rise of Negro Politics in Chicago* (Chicago: University of Chicago Press, 1935), chaps. 1 and 4.

4. Ibid., 125.

5. Drake and Cayton, *Black Metropolis,* 481–84.

6. Ibid., 474.

7. Ibid., 488–90.

8. Gosnell, *Negro Politicians,* 14.

Chapter 4: *A Raisin in the Sun*

1. Lorraine Hansberry, *A Raisin in the Sun: A Drama in Three Acts* (New York: Random House, 1959).

2. Drake and Cayton, *Black Metropolis,* 179.

3. As quoted in the original Cook County Circuit Court decree in *Anna M. Lee et al. v. Paul A. Hansberry,* 37 C 6804. (The original complaint had Hansberry's first name wrong.) Quoted from electronic transcription by Wendy Plotkin, University of Illinois at Chicago.

4. Complaint with Cook County Circuit Court, *Lee v. Hansberry,* 37 C 6804.

5. *Hansberry v. Lee,* 311 U.S. 32 (November 12, 1940).

Chapter 5: The Black World's Fair

1. "Truman K. Gibson's Dynamic Influence Felt in Direction," *Chicago Defender,* May 9, 1940.

2. "One Man's Dream Comes True," *Pittsburgh Courier,* June 13, 1940.

3. American Negro Exposition brochure, Gibson Papers.

4. "Negroes Display Achievements in First World Fair," *Chicago Tribune,* July 5, 1940.

5. *Illinois and Chicago Invite You to American Negro Exposition,* Gibson Papers; "Both Houses Pass Measure Giving $75,000 for Big Chicago Exposition," *Pittsburgh Courier,* June 1, 1940.

6. Ibid.

7. "Exposition to Be Held behind Wall of Notorious Confederate Prison," *Pittsburgh Courier,* July 6, 1940.

8. Ibid.

9. Program for Exhibition of the Art of the American Negro (1851 to 1940), Gibson Papers.

10. Ibid.

11. Ibid.

12. "Around the Galleries," *Chicago Defender,* undated newspaper clipping, Gibson Papers.

13. "Director of Ill. World Fair Exhibits Supervising Work for Chi Exposition," *Pittsburgh Courier,* June 15, 1940.

14. Ibid.

15. "Negro Exhibit Coming to Life in Oil, Colors," undated newspaper clipping, Gibson Papers.

16. "Three Buildings of Chicago Coliseum Will Be Utilized," *Pittsburgh Courier,* June 22, 1940.

17. "Director of Ill. World Fair Exhibits."

18. Arnold Rampersad, *The Life of Langston Hughes,* vol. 1, *I, Too, Sing America (1902–41)* (New York: Oxford University Press, 1986), 386.

19. "Critics Are Lavish in Praise of Exposition's Chimes of Normandy," *Pittsburgh Courier,* July 27, 1940.

20. " 'Nude' Ranch Opens Friday," *Chicago Defender,* August 17, 1940.

21. "Contest to Name U.S. Negro Queen," undated newspaper clipping, Gibson Papers.

22. "Miriam Ali, Defender Beauty Queen Leaves Sunday for New York City," *Chicago Defender,* August 31, 1940.

23. "Award Prizes for Exposition Poster Design," undated newspaper clipping, Gibson Papers.

24. "Director of Ill. World Fair Exhibits."

25. "Negro Exhibit Coming to Life in Oil, Colors."

26. Ibid.

27. "Negro Artists Prepare for Coliseum Show," *Chicago Herald American,* June 30, 1940.

28. "Negroes Display Achievements in First World Fair."

29. "Blackman to Direct Expo Show," undated newspaper clipping, Gibson Papers.

30. Rampersad, *The Life of Langston Hughes,* 386.

31. "Huge Nightclub Gives Up Ghost after Two Weeks," *Pittsburgh Courier,* August 3, 1940.

32. "Duke Accepts Post as Musical Consultant for Chicago Exposition," *Pittsburgh Courier,* June 22, 1940.

33. Writers' Program of the Work Projects Administration in the State of Illinois, *Cavalcade of the American Negro* (Chicago: Diamond Jubilee Exposition Authority, 1940).

34. Rampersad, *The Life of Langston Hughes,* 386–87.

Chapter 6: Joe Louis: Chicago

1. Ronald K. Fried, *Corner Men: The Great Boxing Trainers* (New York: Four Walls Eight Windows, 1991), 126.
2. Ibid., 116.
3. Ibid., 137–38.
4. Ibid., 138.
5. Ibid., 142.
6. Chris Mead, *Champion: Joe Louis, Black Hero in White America* (New York: Charles Scribner's Sons, 1985), 94–97.
7. Ibid., 140.
8. Ibid., 139–52.

Chapter 7: On to the War Department

1. Ulysses Lee, *The Employment of Negro Troops* (Washington, D.C.: Office of the Chief of Military History, U.S. Army, 1966), 74–75.
2. Kenneth Robert Janken, *White: The Biography of Walter White, Mr. NAACP* (New York: New Press, 2003), 253.
3. Lee, *The Employment of Negro Troops,* 75–76.
4. William H. Hastie, oral history interview by Jerry N. Hess, January 5, 1972, Harry S. Truman Library, Independence, Mo., 14–15.
5. Memorandum from the civilian aide to the secretary of war, September 22, 1941, U.S. National Archives and Records Administration, College Park, Md., archived under Office, Assistant Secretary of War, Civilian Aide to the Secretary (hereafter cited as CASW). This is the source for the quotations that follow.
6. Lee, *The Employment of Negro Troops,* 139–40.

7. McCloy memorandum to Hastie, July 2, 1942, U.S. National Archives and Records Administration, College Park, Md., archived under Office of the Secretary of War, General Correspondence of John J. McCloy, 1941–45.

8. Thomas letter to Gibson, July 18, 1941, CASW.

9. M. R. Cox (Lt. Col. 17th F.A., public relations officer) letter to Gibson, July 12, 1941, CASW.

10. Memorandum from the civilian aide to the secretary of war to the acting director of the Bureau of Public Relations, War Department, August 6, 1942, CASW.

11. The account of the broadcast is taken from the script prepared by the Radio Branch, Bureau of Public Relations, War Department, CASW.

12. Gibson letter to Dickerson, August 20, 1941, CASW.

13. Radio script (see note 11).

14. Ibid.

Chapter 8: The War at Home

1. Report by G. Maynard Smith to Victor W. Rotnem (chief of Civil Rights Section, Department of Justice), December 15, 1942, CASW.

2. Memorandum to the secretary of war from the civilian aide to the secretary of war, November 17, 1942, U.S. National Archives and Records Administration, College Park, Md., archived under McCloy Committee (hereafter cited as MC).

3. William M. Simpson, "A Tale Untold? The Alexandria, Louisiana, Lee Street Riot," Louisiana History (spring 1994): 134–38.

4. "Should I Sacrifice to Live Half-American?" *Pittsburgh Courier,* January 31, 1942, quoted in Simpson, "A Tale Untold?" 148.

5. Mitchell letter to Major General Robert Donovan (Fort Sam Houston, Texas), February 13, 1942, CASW.

6. Memorandum to the secretary of war from the civilian aide to the secretary of war, November 17, 1942, MC.

7. Cannon letter to McCloy, June 16, 1942, MC.

8. McCloy letter to Cannon, July 28, 1942, MC.

9. Memorandum from the District of Columbia Branch of the NAACP, "Civilian Morale among Negroes in the District of Columbia," January 14, 1942, MC.

10. Gibson letter to Hastie, December 23, 1941, CASW.

11. Eleanor Roosevelt letter to Stimson, September 22, 1942, MC.

12. Eleanor Roosevelt letter to McCloy, May 27, 1943, MC.

13. Eleanor Roosevelt letter to McCloy, September 29, 1943, MC.

14. Memorandum to the secretary of war from the civilian aide to the secretary of war, November 17, 1942, MC.

15. Memorandum to the army inspector general from Brigadier General B. O. Davis, December 24, 1942, MC.

16. G. Maynard Smith report, December 15, 1942, MC. This document is the basis for the account of the murder that follows.

17. Memorandum to the secretary of war from the civilian aide to the secretary of war, November 17, 1942, MC.

Chapter 9: Negro Troop Policy

1. Patterson memorandum to McCloy, September 23, 1942, MC.

2. William H. Hastie, oral history interview by Jerry N. Hess, January 5, 1972, Harry S. Truman Library, Independence, Mo., 16.

3. Ibid., 29.

4. Ibid., 21.

5. Ibid., 16; Hastie memorandum to the secretary of war, January 5, 1943, MC.

6. Hastie memorandum to the secretary of war, January 5, 1943, MC.

7. Patterson memorandum to McCloy, September 23, 1942, MC.

8. Lee, *The Employment of Negro Troops,* 157.

9. Suggested draft of a directive to be issued by the adjutant general, "Subject: Organization with the War Department for the Development of a Consistent Policy Pertaining to Negro Military Personnel," MC.

10. J. M. Hall memorandum to McCloy, September 28, 1942, MC.

11. Davis memorandum to the Advisory Committee on Negro Troop Policies, undated, MC.

12. *Chicago Defender,* undated newspaper clipping, Gibson Papers.

13. "Three Forward Army Steps," *Washington Afro-American,* May 15, 1943.

14. Gibson memorandum to Poletti, February 9, 1943, MC.

15. Memorandum to General White, December 16, 1942, MC.

16. Memorandum to General Eisenhower, "Subject: The Colored Troop Problem," April 2, 1942, MC.

17. Memorandum to the assistant secretary of war from Major General I. H. Edwards, February 17, 1943, MC.

18. Ibid.

19. Edwards memorandum to the chief of staff, "Subject: Employment of Grade V Personnel in the Army," March 12, 1943, MC.

20. Minutes of advisory committee, April 2, 1943, MC.

21. Gibson memorandum to Major General Idwal H. Edwards (assistant chief of staff), April 1, 1943, MC.

22. American Red Cross, "Statement of Policy Regarding Negro Blood Donors," January 21, 1942, MC.

23. Memorandum to McCloy, "Subject: Digest of War Department Policy Pertaining to Negro Military Personnel," September 26, 1942, MC.

24. Gibson memorandum to Patterson, January 28, 1942, MC.

25. Letter signed by Brigadier General C. C. Hillman, August 10, 1942, MC.

26. Gibson memorandum to Lieutenant Colonel H. A. Gerhardt (executive officer, assistant secretary of war), November 12, 1943, MC.

27. Minutes, April 22, 1943, MC.

28. Gibson memorandum to McCloy, May 14, 1943, CASW.

29. Memorandum to McCloy from Brigadier General M. G. White (assistant chief of staff), June 2, 1943, CASW.

30. Minutes, June 28, 1943, MC.

31. Minutes, April 2 and June 28, 1943, MC.

32. Gibson memorandum to McCloy, March 4, 1943, MC.

33. Gibson memorandum to Poletti, March 22, 1943, MC.

34. U.S. Bureau of the Census, "Negro Newspapers and Periodicals in the United States: 1940," *Negro Statistical Bulletin,* 1940.

35. Gibson memorandum to McCloy, December 20, 1943, MC.

36. Memorandum to the adjutant general from Major General James E. Edmonds (Fort Lee), "Subject: Inflammatory Publications," December 31, 1942, MC.

37. McCloy memorandum to Hastie, July 2, 1942, MC.

38. Memorandum from Colonel Lathe B. Row, July 16, 1943, MC.

39. Committee memorandum for the chief of staff, March 16, 1943, MC.

40. J. S. Leonard memorandum to the advisory committee, "Brief Summary of News Items in the Negro Press on Military Subjects for Week of March 27–April 1," April 17, 1944, CASW.

41. Wilkins letter to Gibson, March 22, 1943, CASW.

42. Gibson letter to Wilkins, March 24, 1943, CASW.

43. Wilkins letter to Gibson, April 1, 1943, CASW.

44. Wilkins letter to Gibson, July 14, 1943, CASW.

45. Ibid.

46. Ibid.

47. Gibson letter to Wilkins, August 5, 1943, CASW.

48. Ibid.

49. Ibid.

50. Memorandum for McCloy, June 24, 1943, MC.
51. Gibson memorandum to Davis, June 30, 1943, CASW.
52. Committee minutes, June 28, 1943, MC.
53. Memorandum for McCloy, July 3, 1943, MC.
54. Memorandum from Colonel Lathe B. Row, July 16, 1943, MC.
55. Gibson memorandum to the chief, Army Exchange Service, April 30, 1943, CASW.
56. Minutes, July 2, 1943, MC.
57. Minutes, August 14, 1943, MC.
58. Gibson memorandum to McCloy, August 17, 1943, MC.
59. Memorandum to McCloy from Colonel J. S. Leonard, August 26, 1943, MC.
60. Gibson memorandum to McCloy, September 9, 1943, MC.
61. McCloy memorandum to Gibson, August 27, 1943.
62. Statement by Colonel Benjamin O. Davis Jr. at press conference, September 10, 1943, MC.
63. "Experiment Proved?" *Time,* September 20, 1943.
64. Memorandum from Major General J. K. Cannon, September 18, 1943, MC.
65. Memorandum to Cannon from Major General Edwin J. House, September 16, 1943, MC.
66. Memorandum from Major General J. K. Cannon, September 18, 1943, MC.
67. Memorandum to Cannon from Major General Edwin J. House, September 16, 1943, MC.
68. Minutes, October 13, 1943, MC.
69. Ibid.
70. Ibid.
71. Ibid.
72. Minutes, October 16, 1943, MC.
73. Ibid.
74. Lee, *The Employment of Negro Troops,* 466–67.
75. Gibson memorandum to McCloy, December 17, 1943, MC.
76. Davis memorandum to McCloy, November 10, 1943, MC.

Chapter 10: A Demand for Combat

1. Ray letter to Gibson, September 5, 1943, MC.
2. Ibid.
3. Gibson memorandum to McCloy, September 13, 1943, MC.
4. Ibid.

5. Ibid.
6. McCloy memorandum to Gibson, September 20, 1943, MC.
7. Gibson memorandum to McCloy, October 21, 1943, MC.
8. Minutes, April 26, 1944, MC.
9. Memorandum to McCloy from Lieutenant General L. J. McNair, "Subject: Lack of Filler for Negro Units," October 25, 1943, MC.
10. McCloy memorandum to Gibson, October 27, 1943, MC.
11. Gibson memorandum to McCloy, December 20, 1943, CASW.
12. House, *Congressional Record* (February 23, 1944), 2025–26. (Stimson's letter read into the record.)
13. Ibid. Fish's following quotations are also from this source.
14. Gibson memorandum to McCloy, February 23, 1944, MC.
15. *Chicago Defender,* March 11, 1944.
16. Lee, *The Employment of Negro Troops,* 477.
17. *Chicago Tribune,* February 28, 1944, quoted in Lee, 477, footnote 39.
18. Gibson memorandum to McCloy, November 3, 1943, MC.
19. Ibid.
20. Ibid.
21. Ibid.
22. Gibson memorandum to the advisory committee, February 29, 1944, MC.
23. Ibid.
24. Lee, *The Employment of Negro Troops,* 477.
25. Dawson letter, February 28, 1944, MC.
26. McCloy letter to Dawson, March 6, 1944, MC.
27. Gibson letter to Barnett, March 20, 1944, CASW.
28. Barnett letter, March 25, 1944, CASW.
29. McCloy letter to Lawrence H. Whiting (Chicago), March 4, 1944, MC.
30. *Chicago Defender,* March 11, 1944.
31. Fish letter, March 31, 1944, MC.
32. Lee, *The Employment of Negro Troops,* 480.
33. Stimson letter to Hastie, March 31, 1944, MC.
34. Ibid.
35. Letter to Barnett, May 16, 1944, CASW.

Chapter 11: *The Negro Soldier*

1. Leonard memorandum to McCloy, December 17, 1943, CASW.
2. Ibid.
3. Minutes, October 28, 1943, MC.

4. Leonard memorandum for McCloy, "Subject: Proposed Booklet of Information Concerning the Command of Negro Troops" (including draft of booklet), October 1, 1943, MC.

5. Ibid.

6. Memorandum for record, January 4, 1944, MC.

7. Pruitt letter, August 10, 1944, CASW.

8. Gibson memorandum to Colonel H. A. Gerhardt, August 30, 1944, CASW.

9. Babero letter to Gibson, February 13, 1944, CASW.

10. Gibson memorandum to Leonard, August 29, 1944, CASW.

11. Unsigned, undated memorandum, CASW.

12. Ibid.

13. Trimmingham letter to the *Pittsburgh Courier,* September 3, 1944, forwarded to Gibson, CASW.

14. Letter to President Roosevelt from Private Charles F. Wilson, May 9, 1944, CASW.

15. Army Service Forces, "Racial Situation in the United States, September 23 to October 14, 1944," October 19, 1944, CASW.

16. Memorandum to McCloy, November 2, 1944, CASW.

17. Ibid.

18. Capra, *The Name above the Title,* 339.

19. Ibid., 358.

20. Joseph McBride, *Frank Capra: The Catastrophe of Success* (New York: Simon and Schuster, 1992), 492.

21. Ibid., 492–93.

22. Capra, *The Name above the Title,* 362.

23. Langston Hughes, *Chicago Defender,* January 1944, quoted in Capra, *The Name above the Title,* 362.

24. *Pittsburgh Courier,* 1944, quoted in Capra, *The Name above the Title,* 359.

25. Gibson memorandum to McCloy, April 26, 1944, CASW.

26. Ibid.

27. Memorandum from Captain Alexander Klein Jr. (758th Light Tank Battalion), April 18, 1944, CASW.

28. McBride, *Frank Capra,* 492–94.

29. Prattis letter to T. S. Matthews (managing editor), *Time,* July 7, 1944, CASW.

30. Ibid.

Chapter 12: Buffalo Soldiers

1. Lee, *The Employment of Negro Troops,* 102.

2. Ibid., 103.

3. Army survey, February 28, 1943, CASW.
4. Joiner interview with authors, October 11, 2003.
5. Lee, *The Employment of Negro Troops,* 282.
6. Undated, unsigned memorandum, CASW.
7. Joiner interview with authors, October 11, 2003.
8. Lee, *The Employment of Negro Troops,* 284.
9. Hardy letter to Gibson, March 18, 1943, CASW.
10. Gibson memorandum to Hardy, August 8, 1942, CASW.
11. Bousfield letter to Gibson, March 31, 1943, CASW.
12. Bousfield letter to Gibson, October 4, 1943, CASW.
13. First Bousfield letter to Gibson, May 27, 1943, CASW.
14. Ibid.
15. Bousfield letter to Gibson, May 22, 1943, CASW.
16. Ibid.
17. Second Bousfield letter to Gibson, May 27, 1943, CASW.
18. Gibson memorandum to Colonel J. S. Leonard, July 3, 1943, CASW.
19. Gibson memorandum to General B. O. Davis Sr., June 3, 1943, CASW.
20. Davis memorandum to the inspector general, "Subject: Survey Relative Conditions Affecting Racial Attitudes at Fort Huachuca, Arizona," August 7, 1943, CASW.
21. Ibid.
22. Gibson memorandum to McCloy, August 23, 1943, CASW.
23. Ibid.
24. Davis memorandum to the inspector general, August 7, 1943, CASW.
25. Ibid.
26. Gibson memorandum to McCloy, August 23, 1943, CASW.
27. Gibson letter to Dan Burley, *New York Amsterdam News,* and several other newspapers, September 21, 1943, CASW.
28. Gibson letter to Hardy, September 25, 1943, CASW.
29. Hardy letter to Gibson, October 5, 1943, CASW.
30. Memorandum for the secretary of war, February 29, 1944, MC.
31. Minutes, February 29, 1944, MC.
32. McCloy memorandum to Stimson, March 2, 1944, MC.
33. McCloy memorandum to Marshall, March 13, 1944, MC.
34. Lee, *The Employment of Negro Troops,* 543.
35. Ibid., 549.
36. Ibid., 553.
37. Quoted in Lee, *The Employment of Negro Troops,* 560–61.
38. Gibson memorandum to McCloy, December 19, 1944, CASW.
39. Ibid.

40. Clark memorandum, December 14, 1944, CASW.

41. Ibid.

42. Gibson memorandum to McCloy, December 27, 1944, CASW.

43. Clark memorandum, December 14, 1944, CASW.

44. McCloy letter to Clark, February 20, 1945, CASW.

45. Gibson memorandum to McCloy, "Report of Visit to Mediterranean and European Theaters of Operation," April 23, 1945, MC.

46. "Report on Visit to 92nd Division," March 12, 1945, Gibson Papers and CASW.

47. Ibid.

48. Ibid.

49. "The Luckless 92nd," *Newsweek,* February 26, 1945.

50. *New York Times,* quoted in *Newsweek,* February 26, 1945.

51. "Army Studying More Effective Negro Training," *New York Herald Tribune,* March 15, 1945.

52. "Negroes' Courage Upheld in Inquiry," *New York Times,* March 15, 1945.

53. "Leaders Rap Gibson's Slur on 92nd Division," *Chicago Defender,* March 24, 1945.

54. "Somebody's Gotta Go!" *Chicago Defender,* March 24, 1945.

55. "Truman Gibson, War Aide, Back in U.S.," *Chicago Defender,* April 7, 1945.

56. "Defends Gibson from Defender Criticism," *Chicago Defender,* April 7, 1945.

57. Stimson letter, April 30, 1945, CASW.

58. Ray letter to Captain Warman K. Welliver, April 10, 1946, CASW.

59. Gibson letter to Lieutenant Colonel Robert Bennett, August 1, 1945, CASW.

60. Gibson letter to Colonel Edward Gourdin, August 9, 1945, CASW.

61. "McNarney Denies Slur on Negroes," *New York Times,* September 22, 1946.

Chapter 13: The Ninety-second Vindicated

1. The account that follows is based on Lee, *The Employment of Negro Troops;* Hondon B. Hargrove, *Buffalo Soldiers in Italy: Black Americans in World War II* (Jefferson, N.C.: McFarland, 1985); Colonel Paul Goodman, *A Fragment of Victory in Italy: The 92nd Infantry Division in World War II* (Nashville: Battery Press, 1993); Lido Galletto, *Dossier: Forte Bastione Nel Secondo Conflitto Mondiall;* and Vernon J. Baker with Kenneth R. Olson, *Lasting Valor* (Columbus, Miss.: Genesis Press, 1997).

2. Baker and Olson, *Lasting Valor,* 55–56,151–54.
3. Goodman, *A Fragment of Victory in Italy,* 91–92.
4. Hargrove, *Buffalo Soldiers in Italy,* 90.
5. Almond letter to Truscott, quoted in Hargrove, *Buffalo Soldiers in Italy,* 98.
6. Baker and Olson, *Lasting Valor,* 156–57.
7. Goodman, *A Fragment of Victory in Italy,* 99.
8. Gino Dinelli, quoted in Baker and Olson, *Lasting Valor,* 151.
9. Goodman, *A Fragment of Victory in Italy,* 95, 103–6.
10. Baker and Olson, *Lasting Valor,* 75.
11. Hargrove, *Buffalo Soldiers in Italy,* 130, 136, 140.
12. Goodman, *A Fragment of Victory in Italy,* 106.
13. MacGregor, *Integration of the Armed Forces,* 135.
14. War Department, Bureau of Public Relations, April 9, 1945, CASW.
15. MacGregor, *Integration of the Armed Forces,* 136–37.
16. Baker and Olson, *Lasting Valor,* 73–75.
17. Joiner interview with authors, October 11, 2003.
18. Baker and Olson, *Lasting Valor,* 75.
19. Hargrove, *Buffalo Soldiers in Italy,* 47.
20. Baker and Olson, *Lasting Valor,* 205.
21. Lee, *The Employment of Negro Troops,* 579–83.
22. Hargrove, *Buffalo Soldiers in Italy,* 192–94.
23. Joiner interview with authors, October 11, 2003.
24. Ibid.

Chapter 14: At Last!

1. Joiner interview with authors, October 11, 2003.
2. Lee, *The Employment of Negro Troops,* 688–89.
3. Ibid.
4. Smith memorandum, quoted in Lee, *The Employment of Negro Troops,* 690.
5. Lee, *The Employment of Negro Troops,* 691.
6. Gibson memorandum to McCloy, April 23, 1945, CASW.
7. Gibson memorandum to General Lee, "Report of Visit to European Theater of Operations," March 31, 1945, CASW.
8. MacGregor, *Integration of the Armed Forces,* 228.
9. Gibson memorandum to General Lee, March 31, 1945, CASW.
10. War Department, Bureau of Public Relations, March 26, 1945, CASW.
11. Gibson memorandum to General Lee, March 31, 1945, CASW.

12. Gibson statement, April 9, 1945, MC.

13. "Opinions about Negro Infantry Platoons in White Companies of Seven Divisions, Based on Survey in May to June 1945," July 3, 1945, Harry S. Truman Library, Independence, Mo.

14. Ibid.

15. Gibson memorandum to McCloy, April 23, 1945, CASW.

16. Ibid.

Chapter 15: More of the Same

1. Gibson memorandum to McCloy, June 14, 1945, CASW.

2. Hammond letter to Mrs. Meyer, January 28, 1945, CASW.

3. Gibson memorandum to Colonel Joseph S. Leonard, February 16, 1945, CASW.

4. Mrs. Meyer letter, May 29, 1945, CASW.

5. Letter from Aubrey E. Robinson, undated (early 1945), CASW.

6. Wilkins letter, January 19, 1945, CASW.

7. Gibson letter to Wilkins, February 9, 1945, CASW.

8. Gerhardt memorandum to Lautier, March 26, 1945, CASW.

9. "Racial Situation in the United States, May 12 to May 26, 1945," War Department, Army Service Forces, June 5, 1945, CASW.

10. U.S. Army Intelligence Service, "Racial Situation in the United States, June 30 to July 14, 1945," Army Service Forces, July 25, 1945, CASW.

11. McCloy memorandum for the secretary of war, June 4, 1945, MC.

12. Hinton letter to Stimson, June 30, 1945, CASW.

13. Gibson memorandum to McCloy, February 14, 1945, CASW.

14. Bousfield memorandum to the adjutant general recommending a Legion of Merit award for Dr. Thatcher, August 9, 1945, CASW.

15. Bousfield letter to Gibson, August 14, 1945, CASW.

16. Notes from telephone conversation between Gibson and Colonel Gerhardt, July 31, 1944, CASW.

17. McCloy memorandum to Stimson, MC.

18. Minutes, August 1, 1944, MC.

19. Gibson memorandum to McCloy, September 13, 1944, MC.

20. Gibson memorandum to McCloy, September 25, 1944, MC.

21. Gibson memorandum to Major Davidson Sommers, July 9, 1945, CASW.

22. Davidson memorandum for Legislative and Liaison Division, July 11, 1945, CASW.

23. Davidson memorandum to Division, July 24, 1945, CASW.

Chapter 16: A Presidential Order

1. "Publishers See FDR on Race's Post War Aims," *Chicago Defender,* February 12, 1944.

2. Gibson memorandum to McCloy, July 20, 1944, MC. The following quotes are from this memo.

3. Ibid.

4. McCloy memorandum to the Advisory Committee on Special Troop Policy, July 31,1944, MC.

5. McCloy memorandum to the Advisory Committee on Negro Troop Policy, September 1, 1944, MC.

6. Gibson memorandum to McCloy, September 5, 1944, MC.

7. Ibid.

8. Ibid.

9. Gibson letter to Dan Burley (managing editor, *New York Amsterdam News*), January 11, 1945, CASW.

10. Sengstacke letter to President Roosevelt, February 7, 1945, Harry S. Truman Library, Independence, Mo.

11. Gibson memorandum to McCloy, May 21, 1945, MC.

12. McCloy memorandum to Army Pictorial Service, undated, MC.

13. Gibson memorandum to McCloy, August 8, 1945, MC.

14. Gibson memorandum to McCloy, May 30, 1945, CASW.

15. Gibson memorandum to McCloy, August 8, 1945, MC.

16. McNarney memorandum to the chief of staff, August 13, 1945, Harry S. Truman Library, Independence, Mo.

17. Ibid.

18. Marshall memorandum to McCloy, August 25, 1945, MC.

19. Gibson memorandum to McCloy, November 13, 1945, CASW.

20. Ibid.

21. MacGregor, *Integration of the Armed Forces,* 153–57.

22. McCloy memorandum to Patterson, November 24, 1945, Gibson Papers.

23. Gibson memorandum to Patterson, November 28, 1945, Gibson Papers.

24. Ibid.

25. Truman K. Gibson Jr., "Gillem Report Aims to End Segregation in U.S. Army," *Pittsburgh Courier,* March 23, 1946.

26. "Petersen Remarks at Luncheon for Negro Newspaper Publishers Association," March 1, 1946, Harry S. Truman Library, Independence, Mo.

27. Gibson memorandum to McCloy, September 24, 1945, CASW.

28. Ibid.

29. Patterson letter to Gibson, November 14, 1945, Gibson Papers.

30. Gibson letter to Roscoe Dungee (*The Black Dispatch,* Oklahoma City, Oklahoma), November 27, 1945, CASW.

31. Truman letter to E. W. Roberts, August 18, 1948, Harry S. Truman Library, Independence, Mo.

32. "Summary of the Truman Commission's Findings on Universal Military Training," *New York Times,* June 2, 1947.

33. *A Program for National Security: Report of the President's Advisory Commission on Universal Training,* May 29, 1947, 21.

34. Ibid., 33.

35. Ibid., 42–43.

36. House Armed Services Committee, "Universal Training," 80th Cong., 1st sess., *Congressional Record* (June 19, 1947), 4215–20.

37. MacGregor, *Integration of the Armed Forces,* 303.

38. Senate Armed Services Committee, "Universal Training," 80th Cong., 2nd sess., *Congressional Record* (March 31, 1948), 644.

39. Ibid.

40. MacGregor, *Integration of the Armed Forces,* 301.

41. 80th Cong., 2nd sess., *Congressional Record,* Senate (April 12, 1948), 4313.

42. Senate Armed Services Committee, *Congressional Record* (March 31, 1948), 645.

43. MacGregor, *Integration of the Armed Forces,* 312.

44. Steve Neal, *Harry and Ike: The Partnership That Remade the Postwar World* (New York: Scribner, 2001), 103.

Chapter 17: Joe Louis, War, and Boxing

1. "I'll Be Ready When My Country Calls—Louis," *Pittsburgh Courier,* August 24, 1940.

2. Jacobs's letter to Army Emergency Relief, May 18, 1942, CASW.

3. Gibson memorandum to Major General A. D. Surles (director, Army Bureau of Public Relations), August 19, 1942, CASW.

4. "Claim Gibson 'Blameless' in Bout Debacle," undated newspaper stories, Associated Negro Press, Gibson Papers.

5. "Sergeant Joe Louis Barrow and His Group of Enlisted Men Boxers," undated document, CASW.

6. "Sgt. Joe Louis and Troupe to Go Overseas," *Pittsburgh Courier,* February 12, 1944.

7. Memorandum recommending Legion of Merit for Staff Sargent Joe Louis Barrow, for the director, Special Services Division, A.S.F., from Fred Maly, Captain, Officer-in-Charge Joe Louis Tour, October 16, 1944, CASW.

8. Osby letter to Gibson, July 22, 1943, CASW.

9. Gibson reply to Osby, August 6, 1943, CASW.

10. Paul Gallico, "Citizen Barrow," *Liberty Magazine* and condensed in *Reader's Digest* (1942), quoted in Mead, *Champion*.

11. Mead, *Champion*, 213–15, 222–29.

12. Joe Louis with Edna and Art Rust Jr., *Joe Louis: My Life* (New York: Harcourt Brace Jovanovich, 1978), 179.

13. Gibson memorandum to McCloy, March 31, 1944, MC; Mead, *Champion*, 231–32.

14. Maly memorandum to Special Services Division, October 16, 1944, CASW.

Chapter 18: Boxing Promoter

1. Mead, *Champion*, 240–52.

2. "Arthur Wirtz—Man with Midas Touch," *Chicago Daily News*, August 18, 1956.

3. Gay Talese, "I.B.C. Does It through Channels," *New York Times*, April 23, 1958.

4. "Robinson Champion Negotiator," *Chicago Daily News*, January 7, 1959.

5. "The Lowdown by Hugh Bradley," *New York Journal-American*, April 20, 1958.

6. U.S. Tax Court, *Robinson v. Commissioner*, 44 T.C. 20 (April 6, 1965).

Chapter 19: Mob Allegations

1. "Hunt Policy King as Conspirator in Slaying Trial," *Chicago Tribune*, August 16, 1942.

2. International Boxing Club statement, undated, Gibson Papers.

3. Dan Daniel, "The IBC 'In Truth and Consequences,' " *The Ring* (August 1957): 8–9.

4. Ibid.

5. Ibid.

6. "Gibson Repudiates Carbo," *New York Herald Tribune*, April 23, 1958.

7. "We're in TV Business—Gibson," undated United Press newspaper clipping, Gibson Papers.

8. Gene Ward, "IBC to Walk in Norris Footsteps, Gibson Says," *New York Daily Mirror*, undated newspaper clipping, Gibson Papers.

9. "IBC Plans $26,000 Suit against D'Amato?" *Atlanta Constitution*, January 31, 1959.

10. *International Boxing Club v. U.S.,* 358 U.S. 242 (1959).

11. U.S. Senate, Hearings before the Subcommittee on Antitrust and Monopoly of the Committee of the Judiciary, "Professional Boxing," 86th Cong., 2nd sess., *Congressional Record* (December 5–6, 1960), 284.

12. Ibid., 296.

13. Ibid., 298.

14. Ibid., 300.

15. Ibid., 420.

16. Ibid., 302–3.

17. Ibid., 332.

18. Ibid., 336.

19. Ibid.

20. Ibid., 401.

21. Ibid., 413.

22. Ibid., 417.

23. Ibid., 422.

Index